Media After Kittler

Media Philosophy

Series Editors: Eleni Ikoniadou, Senior Lecturer in Media and Communication at the London Graduate School and the School of Performance and Screen Studies, Kingston University, and Scott Wilson, Professor of Cultural Theory at the London Graduate School and the School of Performance and Screen Studies, Kingston University

The Media Philosophy Series seeks to transform thinking about media by inciting a turn towards accounting for their autonomy and 'eventness', for machine agency, and for the new modalities of thought and experience that they enable. The series showcases the 'transcontinental' work of established and emerging thinkers, whose work engages with questions about the reshuffling of subjectivity, of temporality, of perceptions and of relations vis-à-vis computation, automation, and digitalisation as the current twenty-first-century conditions of life and thought. The books in this series understand media as a vehicle for transformation, as affective, unpredictable, and nonlinear, and move past its consistent misconception as pure matter-of-fact actuality.

For Media Philosophy, it is not simply a question of bringing philosophy to bear on an area usually considered an object of sociological or historical concern, but of looking at how developments in media and technology pose profound questions for philosophy and conceptions of knowledge, being, intelligence, information, the body, aesthetics, war, death. At the same time, media and philosophy are not viewed as reducible to each other's internal concerns and constraints and thus it is never merely a matter of formulating a philosophy of the media; rather the series creates a space for the reciprocal contagion of ideas between the disciplines and the generation of new mutations from their transversals. With their affects cutting across creative processes, ethico-aesthetic experimentations and biotechnological assemblages, the unfolding media events of our age provide different points of intervention for thought, necessarily embedded as ever in the medium of its technical support, to continually reinvent itself and the world.

> *'The new automatism is worthless in itself if it is not put to the service of a powerful, obscure, condensed will to art, aspiring to deploy itself through involuntary movements which none the less do not restrict it'.*
>
> Eleni Ikoniadou and Scott Wilson

Titles in the Series

Software Theory, Federica Frabetti
Media After Kittler, edited by Eleni Ikoniadou and Scott Wilson

Media After Kittler

Edited by Eleni Ikoniadou
and Scott Wilson

ROWMAN &
LITTLEFIELD
INTERNATIONAL
London • New York

Published by Rowman & Littlefield International, Ltd.
Unit A, Whitacre Mews, 26-34 Stannary Street, London SE11 4AB
www.rowmaninternational.com

Rowman & Littlefield International, Ltd. is an affiliate of Rowman & Littlefield
4501 Forbes Boulevard, Suite 200, Lanham, Maryland 20706, USA
With additional offices in Boulder, New York, Toronto (Canada), and London (UK)
www.rowman.com

British Library Cataloguing in Publication Information Available
A catalogue record for this book is available from the British Library

ISBN: HB 978-1-7834-8121-7
ISBN: PB 978-1-7834-8122-4

Library of Congress Cataloging-in-Publication Data

Media after Kittler / edited by Eleni Ikoniadou and Scott Wilson.
pages cm.—(Media philosophy)
Includes bibliographical references and index.
ISBN 978-1-78348-121-7 (cloth : alk. paper)—ISBN 978-1-78348-122-4 (pbk. : alk. paper)—ISBN 978-1-78348-123-1 (electronic)
1. Mass media—Philosophy. 2. Communication—Philosophy. 3. Kittler, Friedrich A..—Criticism and interpretation. I. Ikoniadou, Eleni, editor.
P90.M3635 2015
302.23092—dc23

2014050040

∞™ The paper used in this publication meets the minimum requirements of American National Standard for Information Sciences Permanence of Paper for Printed Library Materials, ANSI/NISO Z39.48-1992.

Printed in the United States of America

Contents

Primer

The Media Question

Eleni Ikoniadou

The question of technology has largely been conceived in humanist terms. In Western thought, it is assumed that, though we may not yet know what technology can do, one thing is certain: the validity of man. Technophile and evolutionary (Johnson; Kelly), lamenting and dystopian (Lanier; Keen), sociopolitical (Couldry; Feenberg), phenomenological (Hansen), pessimist (Turkle), progressivist (Bostrom), futurologist (Kurzweil), or cataclysmic (Virilio); but always assuming an intact self who has the authority to ask the questions, having taken its own existence as a given. Our culture's commonplace distinction between the biological and the artificial has rubbed off on the study of media and its substrates—communication theories and cultural studies—where an anthropocentric interpretation of techno-human relations is gold standard.[1] In the Anglophone world especially, media studies is still predominantly associated with calculating its social and economic costs and benefits. Notable exceptions in media theory today—for example, Fuller and Goffey's *Evil Media*, Cramer's *Anti-Media*, Munster's *Aesthesia of Networks*, Galloway, Thacker and Wark's *Excommunications*, Mackenzie's *Wirelessness*, Goriunova's *Fun and Software*—provide us with hope of a climate change in the field. Such accounts develop philosophies of media and mediation that address the gray, abstract, conceptual, unknowable and yet material dimensions of media.

Having passed through the trends of fetishizing the analogue and the undeliverable promises of the digital hype, not quite old yet no longer new, the question of technology, digitality and, hence, the Media Question seems more relevant and urgent than ever before. The 'digital natives' (Palfrey and Gasser, 2008) are no longer a novelty, now being replaced by the very opposite demographic—those born before 1985—that is, the last generation to remember life before the Internet (Harris, 2014). Social/mobile/network media platforms are irremissible—albeit 'without a cause' (Lovink, 2011)—in spite of celebratory neologisms (Kelly, 2010), or anachronistic warnings against the Internet 'making us stupid' (Carr, 2010). And the (re)definition of humanity itself is up for grabs, fluctuating as it has between the posthuman (Hayles, 1999; Braidotti, 2013), the nonhuman (Grusin et al., 2012), the inhuman (Lyotard, 1991; Brewster et al., 2000; Sheehan, 2003), and currently either laying claims to the new epoch of the anthropocene (Crutzen and Stoermer, 2000; IUGG, 2012; Turpin, 2013; Crutzen et al., 2014), or challenging it (Haraway, 2014).

As Friedrich Kittler showed early on, his radical approach subverting Marshall McLuhan's well-known mantra, *we* are the extensions of media; our ideologies, subjectivities, psychical apparatuses, our humanity itself, are already inscribed and determined by media. No body existing outside the technological zone, no option to unplug or switch off. Our idea both of what it is to be(come) human and machine is fundamentally changing. Consciousness is machinic, the soul an alien algorithmic swarm and abstraction 'the most concrete thing we can experience' (Shaviro, 2014), as fancifully demonstrated in Spike Jonze's *Her*. Posthumanist, postdigital, postmedia, nonhumanist and nonconscious Media Age. Paradoxically, this is also a time when the very subjects that study these changes have become 'luxury disciplines', not worth investing in by neoliberal governments across the world. However, as Deleuze (1990) would say, the paradoxical and the absurd force thought to confront its limits. This time of accelerated change, temporality and futurity is an urgent time to rethink media, our relationship to it, what it is and what it can do, moving beyond both the naive optimism of modernity and the nostalgic melancholia of the postmodern.

It seems not enough to explore the history of media, or even its archaeology, pointless to differentiate between online and offline modes of being and 'we cannot afford to withdraw' or drown in a sea of Big Data (Lovink, 2014). On the one hand, our condition, as McLuhan

(1967) called it, is that of 'rearviewmirroring', only ever capable of looking at the past and offering retrospective analyses of our media technology. On the other hand, as Wolfgang Ernst warns, perhaps we are not yet ready to digest the changes of the past two decades—it's too soon and our digital culture is too close to historicize.[2] Hence, we need to make the leap from a history of technology towards a Nietzschean 'genealogy of media', not merely directing our attention to things just passed but cutting across the false division between 'interpreting' and 'transforming' the world. This is at once a Nietzschean-Deleuzian-Foucauldian sabotage, with Kittler extrapolating the constellation to its cybernetic future. After all, it is he who assures us that media leave us and history behind.

What then is the schema we need to develop for an unclassifiable media theory that doesn't merely 'march backwards in the future' (McLuhan, 1967)? If the answer to Lovink's (2014) question 'Are you ready to hand over the "new media" remains to the sociologists, museum curators, art historians, and other humanities officials?' is a resounding *no*, how then do we confront and overturn what is meant by media studies today? Such a project perhaps involves couplings between the speculative drive of media theory (the tendencies and crossovers between abstract materialism, speculative realism, new materialism, to name the obvious candidates) and the more hardwired, pragmatic, algorithmic enactments of the media (more akin to German media theory, for example), to build a toolkit with which to understand the unaccountable, unfinished and unlived technological reality that eludes conscious and intentional perception, since 'it is, after all, another nature [*eine andere Natur*]' (Benjamin, 1979: 243).[3]

Friedrich Kittler was a seminal figure in formulating a novel approach to media studies, understood here to lean more towards media philosophy—despite his widely known mission to 'expel the spirit of the humanities'.[4] After Kittler, media can no longer merely be what we use to communicate and express ourselves but emerge as autonomous, agential and capable of enabling new modalities of thought and subjectivity. This legacy of thinking media as a plurality of systems (artistic, scientific, technological) that make and unmake us within their networks, helps disturb the happy sleep of traditional media studies. It is a call for an emerging wave of theorists interested in pushing media in the direction of a 'politics of contamination'—between disciplines, entities, networks. The complexities and idiosyncrasies of such an approach to media studies (in the wider sense of both terms), is characterized by an explicit concern to look at technology, the life of objects, their relationship to our bodies and our experience of them, from a less or non-anthropocentric standpoint. As Geoffrey Winthrop-Young puts it somewhat effectively in his introduction to *Kittler and the Media*, his 'work will strike many as profoundly asocial or even ahuman' (2011: 6).

The present volume is part of a larger effort to incite a turn towards an unconventional media philosophy. The latter outlines a field interested in staging situations of relationality and encounter between humans, machines, events, and seeing what else might occur from their interweavings that escapes commonplace perspectives. Rather than assuming that media events are dependent on the perceptual capacities of the human and, thus, confined to an actual state of affairs, the requirement is to reinvent a theory that looks at what might lie at the periphery of the identifiable media sphere. This is a more diagrammatic method of doing media, focusing primarily on codes, programs, numbers and algorithms, in order to account for what is undeniably the century of computational media. And yet it is not merely reducible to 'technological determinism', at least not in the sense in which that label is used to mourn and defend the lost importance of subject and soul.[5] As Deleuze explains, 'Machines don't explain anything, you have to analyze the collective apparatuses of which machines are just one component' (1997: 175). The point, Kittler notes, is that 'we do not simply program the machines; they program us as well' (Kittler, 2001: 66). Hence our approach affirms both that it is possible to understand media to be more than the cognitive projections and experiences of a perceiving subject; and that subjectivity is entangled with the machine aesthetics that perpetually recompose it. This position can be viewed to germinate at the intersection between abstract, speculative and new materialist strands of thought. Crucially, it wants to signal an end to the period of 'anti-theory' that currently plagues the study of media (and the humanities, in general) and has larger implications, 'notably the lack of suitable critical schemes to scrutinize the present' (Braidotti, 2013: 4).

Yet to draw links with theoretical works that allow us to devise alternative strategies for dealing with and transforming the media sphere is by no means equivalent to historicizing a specific methodology. The undertaking in this case is not rushing to adopt the Kittlerian approach to media studies, that is the technological a priori, but rather to study *media* not just their content and to introduce ways of accounting for changes in our environment as these occur. Although Kittler can assist us with this venture, away both from clichés about the pros and cons of technology and from the new media spell, it is not a matter of assigning authority to any one figure but of making assemblages. Actually, it is hoped that this new wave of media studies will play a role in breaking with critical theory's legacy of veneration that assumes that all the important stories have already been told by men greater than us; finding instead other ways of forming creative and mutant alliances between theory, fiction, science, art and popular culture. In fact, not to do so would be going against Kittler's own 'exorcising' project. This is a core intention of this book—and of the Media Philosophy Series of which it is part—to create assemblages of thought that manufacture new ideas instead of merely recombining or paying homage to another epoch; but the clue is also in the title. Here, *After* superimposes the multiple orders, and, in particular, the triple direction of the book. In one sense, 'after' announces the end of the era of 'great men' and stresses the need to find a more open, nonfeudal paradigm for thinking technology/media/culture. In the most obvious sense, it marks the significance of questioning where we presently stand—'post-Kittler'—and teases out potential connectivities between a more 'diffuse', 'tangible' and 'affective' Anglophone dissection of media (Fuller and Goffey, 2012: 1–2) and a largely obscure and disconnected (untranslated) German media theory.[6] And yet in another way, *Media After Kittler* invites a critical rereading of his work in order to go somewhere else 'with' him. As Avital Ronell (2011) puts it, 'Kittler commands a huge area that connects so much thought from the eighteenth century to the twenty-first century—and we can't avoid his work'.

Though perhaps Kittler himself would reject any suggestion that there is 'media after Kittler', that is to say any media after (digital) media, this is an attempt to develop an understanding of concrete media systems, practices and techniques and of the abstract zones of mediation that affect us and are affected by us in nonconscious ways. Ultimately, the value of passing through Kittler in order to do so lies in his ability to identify the complete absence of a media ontology in Western thought. The present volume engages with this effort to bring forth what is largely overlooked and left behind in mainstream approaches to media theory and, paraphrasing Spinoza, to ponder over the idea that we do not know what media can do. More specifically, the book features two parts that, far from being mutually exclusive, work collectively but in two distinctive ways.

Part One presents a cluster of chapters that draw out how Kittler marks a limit beyond which one cannot go in media philosophy unless you tweak his method and relate it to other plateaus. These 'post-Kittler' accounts seek to take the debate beyond the impasse in heterogeneous but interrelated ways. In the opening chapter 'Secret Passages', Martin McQuillan locates Kittler historically, both theoretically and anecdotally, in relation to Derrida, deconstruction and Sam Weber, underscoring his debt to them. This chapter offers some important reflections on media and philosophy ('media is not only a philosophical concept, it is perhaps the only philosophical concept, the only thing worth thinking since the cave'). Recalling the 'conceptual persona' in Kittler's *Discourse Networks*—the figure who marks the emergence of the modern subject of nation-states and national culture—McQuillan tests how Derrida's method in *La Carte Postale* might shift the emphasis to the scene of *mediation* (in medias res) or *mediatisation* itself (i.e., writing). Mediatisation—for the author, the only condition of media—divides and destabilises the subject of media and the stability of time, place and memory upon which it depends. The *After* of the book title is understood here as *in the midst of* things, or terms, with Kittler as the in-between figure: in between media and philosophy, Derrida and Kittler, Kittler and Media. In this chapter, Kittler becomes the receiver of the Derridian postcard; that is to say, the one assigned to hold (the impossible condition of) the secrets of media. McQuillan asks what these secrets passed on to Kittler might tell us about media studies today, not in its current perception and classification as a (subordinate) university discipline, but in its becoming a field of profound engagement with the undecideable dimension of 'mediation, inscription, technology, and the abyssal prosthetic origin of thought, human and non-human life'.

There are clear affinities between this chapter and Sam Weber's take on the condition of the *untranslatable* and the *incalculable.* This chapter emphasises Kittler's effort—via Lacan, Derrida and Foucault—to exorcise the Spirit (*Geist*) out of the Humanities (*Geisteswissenschaften*); that is, to drive out the dominant but no longer relevant academic conventions institutionalising and limiting this area of thought. Against the universality of meaning, so dear to media studies, Kittler posits the technicity of media, data, circuit boards, gates, commands and algebraic functions. Weber suggests that as crucial as this Kittlerian coup d'état, was and still is, to the transformation of this field, his overreliance on the digital paradigm threatened to introduce a new 'sciences of media' dogma and 'would wind up reinstating the epistemic authority of the scholar as founder of a cult or school'. Weber notes this tension—alongside others, such as the materiality of hardware and immateriality of circuits and numbers, or the idea at the heart of computation that everything can be calculated vis-à-vis its extension of incalculability, which equally fascinated Kittler—nevertheless suggests it can be used fruitfully. Taking us through Hölderlin's introduction of technics and calculus to the medium of tragedy, in many ways relatable to Kittler's efforts to develop a media ontology immanent to the calculus, this chapter points out the value of connecting Kittler to a rereading of other texts (Hölderlin; Derrida) in thinking media theory today, and in accounting for the affectivity and incalculability of media and of thought.

Wolfgang Ernst's translated chapter 'Kittler-Time' takes on the risky but highly intriguing task of speculating on how Kittler's model of (media-)history might provide 'other possible ways of modelling emphatic time'. Stressing, from the outset, the problems with rushing to historicize Kittler's model of theorising technology, this chapter instead revisits a philosophy of history implicit in Kittler's writings. Ernst proposes to consider the media-archaeological questions that arise from engaging critically—through Kittler—with the machinations [*Machenschaften*] of media time. Yet, as he explains, Kittler shows that 'media archeology cannot be fully merged with the model of history', an oxymoron that results in an awareness of the 'different levels and various modes of time-writing'. From Foucault's film-like 'discontinuous timelessnesses' of history, to Kittler's technological a priori of discourse analysis, for Ernst it becomes clear that the movement of time no longer belongs to history but to media itself. If, as Kittler introduced, the agency of technical media replaces the Hegelian end of history, in the end, time itself 'becomes a time of discrete media'. Ernst's chapter shows how understanding Kittler as 'a radical archaeologist of the present' provides insight into the 'chronopoetics of technical media'. Looking to ways of writing (with) time, in fact, is for Ernst, the way out of a trap lurking in the Kittlerian model of (media-)history, to remain confined in historical discourse.

In 'The Humming of Machines', Mai Wegener similarly maps out the tensions and potential impasse in Kittler's method, this time by taking a detour from Lacan's and Kojève's statements on aesthetics and world of the symbolic—understood by Kittler to be a world of machines—through to the Hegelian End of History, 'in the form of absolute knowledge incarnated in fully completed discourse'. Kittler's unique interpretations of Lacan's statement 'there are only three things—jazz, dance, libido' and Hegel's figure of *absolute knowledge*, requires them to be plugged into the history of machines and the rule of formal (processing) languages. In Kittlerian terms, absolute knowledge is only ever incorporated in machines and is functional rather than meaningful. As Wegener argues, Kittler understood early on that we would not be able to switch off and invited us to follow the 'humming' of the machine to the unknown journey. However, Wegener indicates that following Kittler in his posthistorical claim that we are the subjects of media not the masters can only take us so far. Echoing Weber's remark on the risks of constructing a new doctrine in an attempt to overthrow an old one, this stimulating piece ponders the implications of positing the end of history as a vision for the future, to the point that there is nowhere else left to go but 'make a radical turn back towards history, to the Greece of beginnings.'

'Media After Media' takes a closer look at Kittler's genealogical approach to media, under which concepts and ideas change fundamentally when you tell their histories. Examining what media studies is for the Germanosphere (*media analyse*), and its difference from the Anglosphere (critical theory), pausing on Kittler's preference for code breaking, power relations and materiality, Bernhard Siegert reflects on what media studies could mean after the end of ontologically legitimised media (what are media after media?). In order to move beyond the constraints of a Kittlerian End of Media History, also noted in Wegener's article, Siegert proposes linkages between Kittler's techno-ontology and Latour's Actor-Network Theory (ANT). The chapter sketches how overlaps between the two thinkers, and the ANT focus on action as opposed to the imperative for German media theory knowledge (Foucault), enable the consideration of the term 'mediator-object'. The artificial opposition between action and being, characteristic of the difference between Anglo-Saxon and Germanic philosophies, is here replaced with a concept of an operational being, or *factish*, in Latour, which expresses 'the wisdom of the passage', 'from thing to sign, from the fabricated to the real'.

Part Two opens with Matthew Fuller's discussion of the 'blasphemous' highly sophisticated technological determinism in Kittler and beyond (for example, in McLuhan and Foucault) to point out that 'media are a constituted and constitutive form of power in themselves'. By transposing the famous opening line to *Gramophone, Film, Typewriter* to 'standards determine our situation', Fuller shows the significance for media theory of considering a return to a 'state of indeterminacy' before media become standardized. This is a moment in which media interweave experimental aesthetic apparatuses with stabilised objects; and one in which it is possible to address notions of futurity that escape the 'rearviewmirrorism' accusation against German media theory. Alongside Kittler's acknowledgement of the military roots of media systems, Fuller posits its medical genealogy via Hans Berger's discussion of the 1928 experiments in the electro-encephalogram. 'The Forbidden Pleasures of Media Determining' shows how the indeterminacy of these moments, prior to the settling of knowledge and method yet involving existing apparatuses, might be the place for inquiry into what media can do. Kittler's method allows for a media studies that is at least able to acknowledge technical matter and pay attention to the mechanisms of transcoding. Fuller's intervention lies in proposing to add to it 'a form of materialism that is able to work at high degrees of immanence and abstraction, across signification, and in the midst of computational culture'; including but not limited to accounting for databases, trading systems and even money 'as a form of media in itself'.

In 'The Computer That Couldn't Stop' Scott Wilson pushes the implications of thinking media 'with' Kittler further by developing the contention of Kittler's major work where he shows that the discourse networks of 1800 establish the conditions for the rise of the classic Freudian neuroses, obsession and hysteria, the former embodied by the 'bureaucrat-poet'. Wilson's chapter suggests that with the reformatting and homogenization of analogue technologies into digital code and convergence onto various platforms, particularly those predicated on the model of the personal computer, we see both a return and an a-subjective intensification and acceleration of obsessional neuroses across the whole field of techno-bureaucracy. Reiterating the essential distinction that the computer is not at all a model of the mind or brain, but the materialization of a particularly bureaucratic mode of thought, Wilson's chapter draws on the self-description of David Adam's obsessive-compulsive disorder as a computer with a glitch or virus in his book *The Man Who Couldn't Stop: OCD and the True Story of a Life Lost in Thought* (2014) in order to help characterize the life and psychic structure of machine assemblages in the discourse network of 2000.

Stefan Heidenreich's chapter attempts to analyse the current 'situation' and how it has been shaped by the move beyond technical media after two hundred years into a new era of digital convergence. 'The

Situation After Media' comments on German media theory's relative neglect of the Internet, as an object of study, in contrast to an intense interest in computation generally (including the promise of virtual reality) and the history of technical media. The chapter argues that the historicist move forecloses German media theory from analyzing the political stakes of the current 'situation' which is defined by the Internet and the way it facilitates 'new zones of collision'. In picking up from Kittler the basis for a political critique, Heidenreich looks at Kittler's 'No Such Agency' on the National Security Agency (NSA) and his emphasis on the power of the state. Against this, the author poses the ubiquity of globalized telecommunications and the way they have accelerated the autonomy of the finance markets, and perhaps even the power of the secret services. 'The Situation After Media' posits three 'structures' that are produced out of the various communication networks: finance markets, the functionally corporate monopolies dealing in 'big data', and the secret services. The chapter concludes with the intriguing suggestion concerning how the secret services have the potential to transcend the state and even pose a threat to it.

The second part of the book concludes with Olga Goriunova's chapter on 'The Ragged Manifold of the Subject' marking a new direction for where media theory might go. Drawing on Kittler's *Discourse Networks 1800/1900* and the media history described therein, this final chapter posits a 'Discourse Networks 2000' in relation to digital databases and the rise of the curator-function (particularly in its machinic form as algorithm) as the major figure for cultural production in the twenty-first century. Goriunova takes up the concept of the 'generic' (aesthetic/cultural/discursive/performative) as able not only of producing contemporary realities but also a new understanding of subjectivity and subject. These are subjects that emerge from computational, artistic and cultural processes immanent to our contemporary condition and exemplified in events such as 'Curating YouTube'. Goriunova's take on current cultural practices, 'meaningless and idiotic in their automatism and randomness', finds a resonance in Kittler's media inscription techniques of noise, randomness and combinatorics for discourse networks. This significant piece shows how software replaces writing and analogue media to produce a different assemblage for the new millennium, that of the software engineer-curator/algorithm (Turing machine). The focus on the generic and its connectivities to seriality, relationality and multiplicity, also via Deleuze's thesis on *Difference and Repetition*, allows the author to claim the subject's emergence back out of its Kittlerian oblivion (and Foucauldian production) and through 'the database's operationality in aesthetic terms'.

Finally, Jussi Parikka's 'Postscript' situates Kittler's work, and the particular theoretical desires it produces in media theory to ponder its implications not only for a renewed media studies but also for a more useful analysis of the present. This final chapter completes the endeavour of the book to trace and extend 'a current drive for a radical revisiting of media as a transversal field of investigations of relations' between different spheres. Parikka notes Kittler's contribution in radicalizing media theory not only as part of the oeuvre he produced in his writings about technology but also, importantly, as demonstrated in his own transformation from classic literature analyst to 'software programming theorist' par excellence. The author shows how Kittler was a master of disciplinary intersections, demonstrated by the ways in which his writings in digital culture are at the same time 'a genealogy of writing and technology'. This indeed is the in-between zone that all technologies, from writing to the Internet, can be understood to occupy from a media philosophical perspective. The chapter points to the key idea, proposed by the authors of this book, that 'the grey areas' of media are where we should be looking if we want to effectuate a change from a depressing sociocultural analysis of media texts to 'media as techniques, or operations, which produce differences'.

A few years after Kittler's death, this edited collection examines the implications of his thought and its potential power in probing the ever-changing condition of media and in theorising such an uncertain relational field. As the chapters in this volume explore widely in the pages that follow, drawing a transversal line between Kittler and media theory has ultimately less to do with celebrating a particular figure—or indeed relying on any particular style or culture to define and refine media studies—and more with exposing media vectors (texts/theories/objects) as speculative, pluralising, autogenerative, capable of generating their own worldview.

NOTES

1. For a distinction between anthropocentrism and anthropomorphism, see Rosi Braidotti who, drawing on N. Katherine Hayles, suggests: 'You can be a posthumanist and post-anthropocentric thinker. In fact, in advanced capitalism, in which the human species is but one of the marketable species, we are all already post-anthropocentric. But I don't think we can leap out of our anthropomorphism by will. We can't. We always imagine from our own bodies', 'Borrowed Energy', Issue 165, September 2014, inter-

view by Timotheus Vermeulen, available at www.frieze.com/issue/article/borrowed-energy/.

2. This is from an email conversation between Ernst and the present author but it is also developed in his article in this book.

3. In relation to his term 'optical unconscious' and affinity of technology with the unseen and unknown, Benjamin writes: 'It is after all another nature that speaks to the camera than to the eye, other primarily in the sense that a space informed by human consciousness gives way to a space informed by the unconscious. [. . .] Photography, with its devices of slow motion and enlargement, reveals it to him. It is through photography that he first discovers the existence of the optical unconscious'.

4. As is noted by some of the authors in this volume, early on in his career Kittler seeks to turn away from 'media analysis' (the German dominant approach to media studies at the time) in what he called 'The Exorcising of the Spirit from the Humanities' [*Austreibung des Geistes aus dem Geisteswissenschaften*] (1980). Through this collection of essays, Kittler highlights a need to escape philosophy's overshadowing of the other disciplines. As Bernhard Siegert put it, in our email correspondence, to Hegel's 'we do not bow before religion anymore' Kittler declares 'we do not bow before philosophy anymore'.

5. Discussing 'the *accusation* of technodeterminism' in an interview with Annie van den Oever, Geoffrey Winthrop-Young remarks that it 'is one of the most pathetic yet unfortunately also one the most handy devices in the vast arsenal of intellectual dishonesty. It is a gratuitous and more often than not misinformed mixture of ideological moralizing (to be a technodeterminist is, somehow, a politico-moral failing) and supercilious laziness (now that I have determined that *X* is technodeterminist, I can happily disregard *X* and go back to sleep). When you hear the t-word, remove your gloves'. The problem with the critique against technological determinism can also be traced in what Bruno Latour calls 'the anti-fetishist' position in critical theory, which argues that objects are merely concepts onto which human agency is projected. This 'fact position' is for Latour illusory and leads to a disregard of the actual powers and roles of nonhuman actors. See 'Why Has Critique Run out of Steam? From Matters of Fact to Matters of Concern', in *Critical Inquiry—Special Issue on the Future of Critique*, vol 30(2): 25–248, Winter 2004.

6. Certainly, attempts to revisit and reconceptualise the media question are not confined to these two worlds, the English and German theoretical spheres. Intriguing new approaches are currently emerging within a wide range of cultures and places, from Brazil to Japan and beyond, which the Media Philosophy Series will endeavour to summon and put forward in the future, but which are not in the scope of the present project.

BIBLIOGRAPHY

Benjamin, Walter. (1979) *One-way Street and Other Writings*. Trans. Edmund Jephcott and Kingsley Shorter. London: New Left Books.

Bostrom, Nick. (2014) *Superintelligence: Paths, Dangers, Strategies*. New York; Oxford: Oxford University Press.

Braidotti, Rosi. (2013) *The Posthuman*. Cambridge: Polity.

Brewster, Scott et al., eds. (2000) *Inhuman Reflections: Thinking the Limits of the Human*. Cambridge, MA: MIT Press.

Carr, Nicholas G. (2010) *The Shallows: How the Internet is Changing the Way We Think, Read and Remember*. London: Atlantic.

Couldry, Nick. (2012) *Media, Society, World: Social Theory and Digital Media Practice*. Cambridge: Polity.

Cramer, Florian. (2013) *Anti-Media: Ephemera on Speculative Arts*. Rotterdam: NAi.

Crutzen, Paul J. et al. (2014) 'The Anthropocene Project', Haus der Kulturen der Welt, HKW, available at www.hkw.de/en/programm/projekte/2014/anthropozaen/anthro pozaen_2013_2014.php.

Crutzen, Paul and Eugene Stoermer. (2000) *Global Change*. International Geosphere-Biosphere Programme.

Deleuze, Gilles. (1990) *The Logic of Sense*. Trans. Mark Lester. London: Continuum.

———. (1997) *Negotiations*. Trans. Martin Joughin. New York: Columbia University Press.

Feenberg, Andrew. (2001) *Transforming Technology: A Critical Theory Revisited*. New York; Oxford: Oxford University Press.

Fuller, Matthew and Andrew Goffey. (2012) *Evil Media*. Cambridge, MA: MIT Press.

Galloway, Alexander R., Eugene Thacker and McKenzie Wark. (2014) *Excommunication: Three Inquiries in Media and Mediation*. Chicago; London: University of Chicago Press.

Goriunova, Olga, ed. (2014) *Fun and Software: Exploring Pleasure, Paradox, and Pain in Computing*. New York: Bloomsbury.

Grusin, Richard, Mary Mullen et al. (May 3–5, 2012) 'The Nonhuman Turn', annual conference The Center for 21st Century Studies, Milwaukee, WI.

Hansen, Mark B. N. (2004) *New Philosophy for New Media*. Cambridge, MA; London: MIT Press.

Haraway, Donna. (5/9/14) 'Anthropocene, Capitalocene, Chthulucene: Staying with the Trouble, the Arts of Living on a Fractured Planet', talk at the University of California Santa Cruz.

Harris, Michael. (2014) *The End of Absence: Reclaiming What We've Lost in a World of Constant Connection*. London: Penguin.

Hayles, N. Katherine. (1999) *How We Became Posthuman: Virtual Bodies in Cybernetics, Literature, and Informatics*. Chicago; London: University of Chicago Press.

International Union of Geodesy and Geophysics (IUGG) Electronic Journal, Volume 12 No. 7 (1 July 2012).

Johnson, Steven. (2010) *Where Good Ideas Come From: The Natural History of Innovation*. New York: Riverhead.

Keen, Andrew. (2012) *Digital Vertigo: How Today's Online Social Revolution Is Dividing, Diminishing, and Disorienting Us*. London: Constable.

Kelly, Kevin. (2010) *What Technology Wants*. New York: Viking.

Kittler, Friedrich, ed. (1980) *Austreibung des Geistes aus dem Geisteswissenschaften. Programme des Poststrukturalismus*. Paderborn: Schöningh.

Kittler, Friedrich. (2001) 'Experience in the Era of Information' in Annette W. Balkema and Henk Slager (eds.), *Exploding Aesthetics*. Amsterdam: Lier en Boog

Kittler, Friedrich. (2014) 'No Such Agency' *Theory, Culture & Society*. Vol 31(2–3). Available at available at theoryculturesociety.org/kittler-on-the-nsa/.

Kurzweil, Ray. (2005) *The Singularity Is Near: When Humans Transcend Biology*. New York: Viking.

Lanier, Jaron. (2011) *You Are Not a Gadget: A Manifesto*. London: Penguin.

Latour, Bruno. 'Why Has Critique Run out of Steam? From Matters of Fact to Matters of Concern', in *Critical Inquiry—Special Issue on the Future of Critique*. Vol 30(2): 25–248, Winter 2004.

Lovink, Geert. (2011) *Networks Without a Cause: A Critique of Social Media*. Cambridge: Polity.

———. (2014) 'Hermes on the Hudson: Notes on Media Theory After Snowden', e-flux Journal, Issue 54, April 2014, available at www.e-flux.com/journal/hermes-on-the-hudson-notes-on-media-theory-after-snowden/.

Lyotard, Jean-François. (1991) *The Inhuman: Reflections on Time*. Cambridge: Polity.

Mackenzie, Adrian. (2010) *Wirelessness: Radical Empiricism in Network Cultures*. Cambridge, MA: MIT Press.

McLuhan, Marshall and Quentin Fiore. (1967) *The Medium Is the Massage: An Inventory of Effects*. New York: Bantam.

Munster, Anna. (2013) *An Aesthesia of Networks: Conjunctive Experience in Art and Technology*. Cambridge, MA: MIT Press.

Palfrey, John and Urs Gasser. (2008) *Born Digital: Understanding the First Generation of Digital Natives*. New York: Basic Books.

Ronell, Avital, interview with Benjamin Walker. (27/12/11) 'The Big Ideas Podcast: Friedrich Kittler's Computer Wars', *The Guardian online*, available at www.theguardian.com/commentisfree/audio/2011/dec/27/big-ideas-podcast-frederich-kittler.

Shaviro, Steven. (21/01/14) 'Spike Jonze's HER', The Pinocchio Theory blog, available at www.shaviro.com/Blog/?p=1186.

Sheehan, Paul. (2003) *Becoming Human: New Perspectives on the Inhuman Condition*, Westport, CT; London: Praeger.

Turkle, Sherry. (2011) *Alone Together: Why We Expect More from Technology and Less from Each Other*. New York: Basic Books.

Turpin, Etienne, ed. (2013) *Architecture in the Anthropocene: Encounters Among Design, Deep Time, Science and Philosophy*. Ann Arbor, MI: Open Humanities Press.

Virilio, Paul. (2012) *The Administration of Fear*. Trans. Ames Hodges. London: Semiotext(e).

Winthrop-Young, Geoffrey. (2011) *Kittler and the Media*. Cambridge: Polity.

Winthrop-Young, Geoffrey and Annie van den Oever. (2014) 'Rethinking the Materiality of Technical Media. Friedrich Kittler, Enfant Terrible with a Rejuvenating Effect on the Parental Discipline. A Dialogue' in *Technē/Technology, Researching Cinema and Media Technologies—Their Development, Use, and Impact*, Annie van den Oever (ed.). Amsterdam: Amsterdam University Press.

Part One

Chapter One

Secret Passages

Media After Kittler and the Typeface of Love Letters

Martin McQuillan

A POST CARD FOR KITTLER

Sam came to pick me up at the station, and then we went for a long walk in the forest (a man came up to greet us thinking that he recognized me, and then excused himself at the last moment—he must be suffering, as I am, more and more, from prosopagnosia, a diabolical impulsion to find resemblances in faces, to recognize, no longer to recognize). I said a few words about my post cards, asking him to keep it as secret as possible. This morning, in Freibourg, to which he accompanied me by car, I understood that he had immediately spoken of it to Kittler, my host here, and perhaps to his wife (psychoanalyst). The secret of the post cards burns—the hands and the tongues—it cannot be kept, q.e.d. It remains secret, what it is, but must immediately circulate, like the most hermetic and most fascinating of anonymous—and open—letters. I don't cease to verify this.

S. was to summarize and translate my lecture (at the *studium generale*). I stopped at the places that he himself had chosen and checked off in my text (still on '*La folie du jour*,' the title this time), and he took this as a pretext to speak longer than I did, if not, I couldn't judge, to divert the public's attention, or even the sense or letter of my discourse. We laughed over it together and between us laughter is a mysterious thing, that we share more innocently than the rest (somewhat complicated by the strategies), like a disarming explosion and like a field of study, a

> corpus of Jewish stories. On the subject of Jewish stories: you can imagine the extent to which I am haunted by Heidegger's ghost in this city. I came for him. I am trying to reconstitute all his paths, the places where he spoke (this *studium generale* for example), to interrogate him, as if he were there, about the history of the posts, to appropriate his city for myself, to sniff out, to imagine, etc. To respond to his objections, to explain to him what he does not yet understand (this morning I walked with him for two hours, and then I went into a bookstore, I bought several cards and reproductions, as you can see (I'm also bringing you back an album, *Freiburg in alten Ansichtskarten*), and I fell upon two books of photographs that cost me a great deal, one on Freud, very rich, the other on Heidegger, at home, with Madame and the journalists from the Spiegel in 1968). So that there it is, back at the Hotel Victoria (that's where I called you from), I laid down to flip through the albums and I burst out laughing when I found that Martin has the face of an old Jew from Algiers. I'll show you.

This is the entry marked as 9th May 1979 in Jacques Derrida's 'Envois' section of *La Carte Postale* (Derrida, 1987: 188). It describes a trip by the narrator to a conference in Freiburg at which he meets someone called Sam Weber and is hosted by a character with the name of Kittler. I could rehearse all the means by which the text of the 'Envois' offers every opportunity and no possibility to be read as a roman à clef, as if there really was someone called Sam Weber or a real person called Kittler. Let us not be so naive. Upon inspection, and not very close inspection at that, all of the dates and locales of the 'Envois' are out of synch, it is as much about the production of a convincing and undecideable reality as it is a confession of the autobiographical. The affirmation of the undecideable would be the quality of the pretense. So, let us not imagine that in this passage we are confronted with the real Sam Weber, Friedrich Kittler and Jacques Derrida.

The last time I sat at this desk in the Bolivar Hall in the Venezuelan Embassy in London,[1] I was speaking on the issue of debt, sitting next to the real Samuel Weber. At least I think it was the real Samuel Weber, he spoke about the onto-theological origins of the so-called credit crunch although like the man in the forest who approaches the narrator of the 'Envois' I may have been suffering from prosopagnosia, an inability to recognize faces. I might have been sitting next to the 'S' of the 'Envois', this avatar who acts as confidante to the narrator and who betrays his secret within minutes to Kittler. Perhaps, it was an entirely different Sam, the son of Sam, another theoretical Sam, a Beckettian character, or the ghost of another Weber, a name maxed out by the theoretical family. I can no longer remember. I am unable to recognize the face. Like the solitary walker in the forest at Freiburg I can only come up close to Sam and to Kittler and to Derrida and then excuse myself at the last moment. As much as I would like to find or have a 'diabolical impulsion to find resemblances' in these faces, I am forced to turn away rather than risk an introduction. A simple greeting would be too much to venture. Perhaps, for fear of rejection; perhaps to avoid a social awkwardness, perhaps out of genuine uncertainty. The introduction is impossible. How to begin a conversation with figures such as these? It would be the madness of the day, the madness of the everyday, an everyday madness. I cannot introduce myself or introduce them. Instead bashfully I will turn away and carry on my lonely walk through this passage. The narrator says that he is also increasingly suffering from prosopagnosia. The turn away is mutual. We might approach either other, convinced that we see a resemblance in one other only to withdraw at the last moment, performing a swerve or a U-turn, our steps creating the loop of the invaginated fold that Derrida describes in his reading of '*La folie du jour*' as the structure of narrative, a story with a single permeable skin, with no inside and no outside and only inside and only outside (see Derrida, 1980). This madness, this neurotic compulsion to narrativize results in misrecognition or a failure to connect, a meeting in a clearing [*holzweg*] that does not go anywhere.

So, instead let me say a few words about my post cards. Not the same words that the narrator of the 'Envois' asks Sam to keep secret and which he so quickly passes on to Kittler. Here we might ask the question, what would it mean to betray a confidence to Kittler, to tell Kittler our secrets, to speak to Kittler today and to make a revelation or to pass on some gossip? As soon as we are among the post cards we are once more in the question of media, one more method of inscription and circulation, another mediation, in media res, in-betweeness, the human condition from Socrates to Freud and beyond. The secret of the narrator passes around the academics of Freiburg like a post card, from one facteur to another, each reading it in turn before its next posting. At the same time it remains 'as secret as possible', as if secrecy were possible, and not the impossible condition of all media. 'As secret as possible' which is to say that the narrator has a doubt concerning the absolute secrecy of the secret. This might have more to do with the garrulous nature of his chosen confidante than it does with the possibility of absolute secrecy: 'I understood that he had immediately spoken of it to Kittler, my host here, and perhaps to his wife (psychoanalyst)'. Derrida's wife was also a psychoanalyst. The psychoanalytic partner, the silent observer of an everyday madness, a keeper of secrets, as well as a reader of symptoms, of messages and envois. The one who always receives even if they are not the intended or final destination. The producer of the domestic-analytic scene, or the one who turns the domestic scene inside out into an analytic moment: a site of transference and countertransference, of media and mediation. 'The secret of the post cards burns—the hands and the tongues—it cannot be kept'. There can be no possibility of keeping the secret of the post card, it must by definition be passed on to the next facteur who in turn will read it and move it along. And yet it remains secret, unreadable, undecideable, like the relation between Kittler and Derrida, Kittler and philosophy, Kittler and media. This media that we say comes after Kittler, or that Kittler is in some way after, a mediation that is in the manner of Kittler, after Kittler as we say a painting is in the style of an old master, media after Kittler.[2] This relationship burns the hands and the tongue, it cannot be held and yet it must be spoken. 'Media after Kittler' must circulate among us like a post card that we must pass on from one to another but do not hold on to it for too long, pass the parcel and do not be caught out when the music stops. Never cease to verify this impossibility.

Media will always accompany Kittler like Sam Weber accompanies the narrator in the 'Envois', chauffeur and acolyte, driver and driven, automobile and autobiographer, translator and transformer: 'S was to summarize and translate my lecture', a trans that contains within itself the sense of beyond (from Socrates to Freud and beyond) a movement from one side to the other but which never arrives at its destination, the in-betweeness of translation, another form of media, a beyond that is only ever mediation. No jump from media to Kittler, no beyond or after, only the in-between of a sustained thinking of media and the object itself. The object that is also the vehicle of its analysis, no outside to this scene of analysis. No media after Kittler. Here the after or the beyond is only another mediation. Let us not speak of 'Media after Kittler', rather if this after is just another stage or posting of an extended and interminable in-between, then let us say 'Media media Kittler'. Kittler in media res, Kittler in the middle, Kittler between philosophy and media studies, Kittler as the third term of an interminable and impossible analysis, Kittler as the in-between, a post that receives the secrets of the post card, the secrets of media that burn the hands and the tongue. Kittler, pass it on. Kittler as a mediation between philosophy and media. Let us not then speak of Kittler after media or of 'Kittler media media' but of 'media, media, media'. The three terms of our scene today all turn around the same impossible secret that there is no outside to the scene of analysis, nothing but the endless exchange of the letter, from one burned hand to another, media, like a hot potato, passed on without end.

Here the translation lasts longer than the original address, like Sam's summary of the narrator's text: the critique outweighs the object. The in-between stretches as far as the eye can see. Like the two characters in the 'Envois' we can laugh about this and this laughter between us will be a mysterious thing. The narrator describes it as being 'like a disarming explosion and like a field of study'. One could read this sentence too quickly, the analogy is not 'like a disarming explosion in a field of study', the field of study is equivalent to the explosion: a 'disarming explosion', one that demilitarizes all ordinance. As elsewhere in the 'Envois' we must take this order of metaphoricity seriously. Derrida is at pains to note that the post card is not a mere metaphor for meaning, the relationship is not to be understood in an allegorical way with one half of the metaphor subordinate to the description of the other. Rather, the circulation of meaning is as much an analogy for the passage of the post card as vice versa. Equally, the field of study and the explosion are equivalent. What if we were to understand media studies as just such an explosion? A 'disarming explosion' that left us with no more weapons. Media studies would be the only field of study that identified its own impossible condition as its object. Here I am not referring to a media studies that concerned itself with the weak anthropology of the popular, something like television and film studies in which the idea of study is merely the application of established academic protocols to a new object, often unable to justify the weight of an academic scrutiny. Rather, this would be an understanding of media after Kittler, the most profound engagement with the conditions of mediation, inscription, technology and the abyssal prosthetic origin of thought, human and nonhuman life. A field of study that recognized only the field and understood study to be the active and critical practice of being within that field without horizon or boundary. This media after Kittler would be a dis-enclosure, to use a term translated from Nancy [*la déclosion*] (see Nancy, 2008), of all the borders and categories of academic classification, running the question of media, mediation, and mediatisation through the university as a problem for the university, perhaps the very condition of the university and of academic life. We might say, following the narrator of the 'Envois' that: in the beginning was media and I will never get over it. No university without media studies, equally no media studies without the university, no approach to the wider field of digital, celluloid, print media without a critical framework for understanding. No media studies without Kittler. No media studies without the philosophy of media. Not that philosophy can be asked to speak to media or be used to explain media in a utilitarian way, because media itself is a philosophical concept, perhaps the only philosophical concept, the only thing worth thinking since *Khora* and since the cave. If the narrator and Sam share the mysterious laughter of a corpus of Jewish stories it is because at their best such stories are a philosophy, they are a repository for a knowledge of their object, a mediation of that object in which the object becomes the media itself as an articulation of its own understanding. Equally, with Kittler today we might share the laughter of a mysterious thing called 'media after Kittler', a disarming explosion, a corpus of philosophical stories, a field of study that would not be recognizable as the media studies in our universities today. That media studies, so often the *bête noir* of ill-informed politicians and media commentators who in an act of self-loathing cannot recognize their own work as a suitable object for academic study and so decry the corruption of academic purity by the study of their own practice. Perhaps, such denunciations of media studies are a warning, an attempt to make the academy back off from its enquiry into the media: a smokescreen of indignant verbiage that says, do not look behind the curtain, do not inquire further into the construction of globalized meaning and how we the media produce it. While such a media studies is absolutely necessary if we are to stay alert to our present conditions of artificatuality, media after Kittler is something more. It is more than the toolkit of ideology critique and semiotic analysis that media studies so often contents itself with. Certainly, this 'after' is not a 'beyond' that will transport us to the other side of media studies, but it is a critical mediatisation that takes us through media studies as just another symptom of the mediatic effects that it first diagnoses. Study here is just one more mode of the in-between, a mediatisation that acts as if it stands on one side of a divide when in fact it is the very act of division itself. Let us not speak of 'Media Studies', rather of 'Media Media', media's own mediatised scene.

What would it mean then to pass on a secret to Kittler today? To do so too quickly, fresh out of the car from the forest of Freiburg like the loquacious Weber. Media after Kittler, today Kittler is our host just as he was for the narrator of the 'Envois'. As the etymology runs he is both our host, the one who brings us all together here, and our guest, the one that we invite into our midst and whom we must treat with the upmost hospitality. He is host and guest and ghost today. You can imagine the extent to which I am haunted by Kittler's ghost in this city. Kittler plays host to the narrator of the 'Envois' not just in any city but in Freiburg, the scene of so much of Heidegger's media effect. Here the narrator seeks out the haunting effects of Heidegger and walks with his ghost ('this morning I walked with him for two hours, and then I went into a bookstore'). The setup here is one of classic elegy in which the poet is reunited with the dead in the landscape with which their lives were most keenly lived, and the poet walks with the dead until dawn. The deceased loved one must always return to the underworld before dawn breaks or the narrator turns into a bookstore, one more false exit into a world of media. He buys two books of photographs, one of Freud and one of Heidegger, as well as a book for his lover of Freiburg in old post cards. Between Freud and Heidegger he introduces a slip worthy of comment. He says of the Heidegger book that it shows the philosopher 'at home, with Madame and the journalists from the Spiegel in 1968'. Once again we are in the scene of the domestic and the observant, analytic spouse. However, this living arrangement is shared with journalists. That is to say, with the media.

I am reminded here of Derrida's other, short and under-read text of media studies, from a book edited by Sam Weber, 'Above All, No Journalists!' on the passing of the commandments to Moses in which he suggests that the condition under which the Law can be handed down on the top of Mount Sinai is that there are no witnesses present: there can be no revelation, no divine authority or onto-theology with the media (Derrida, 2001). As soon as we have mediation the Law and everything that depends upon it is ruined. However, perhaps more interestingly in this scene of Heidegger among the journalists is that Derrida makes a slip on the date of the Spiegel interview known in English as 'Only a God can save us now'. It took place in 1966 not 1968, significant dates for any follower of European culture. Perhaps, this is not a slip at all; perhaps it is in keeping with manipulation and falsification of dates that characterizes the 'Envois' in general. The narrator is not Derrida; the real Jacques Derrida would know the correct date of the Spiegel interview. Perhaps, it is another affirmation of the undecideable that sits so seductively and problematically at the top of every page of the 'Envois' as a false mark in this story of dating. The

Hotel Victoria to which the narrator returns to look at his books of photographs may be another comic lodging like the Russell Hotel in London from which Derrida launched a philosophical and historical hoax in the text 'Racism's Last Word' (Derrida, 1985). The Russell Hotel is of course also the scene of another mediatisation that those who work in media studies in the UK know well. But for the moment let us imagine that this is some other interview given by Heidegger to the media, one not on the God of a hopeless onto-theology but on media itself. 1968 after 1966, media after Kittler, from Socrates to Freud and beyond. Such an interview waits to be invented, a discourse to come, that will require all the resources of our poetic imagination, just as the thinking of media after Kittler asks us to imagine another way of working and representing thought and media itself. A gesture as bold as the 'Envois' will be required to find a suitable vehicle for this project. A suitable elegy for Kittler, one that was up to the task of thinking media after Kittler, might not require us to walk with his ghost in the early morning but to pick him up from the station in a fast car and to be the first to spill his secrets before we have reached our destination. He has so much to tell us and we cannot help but pass it on, it will burn our hands and tongues otherwise.

ON THE TYPEWRITER AND ITS RELATION TO LITERATURE

Someone must have been spreading lies about K . . . for having saluted Kittler and recognized the importance of his thought not only for a rigorous reflection on media but for all that this means for the university and the disciplines of the humanities, I will now identify my worries about his writing *on writing*. I will, then, send a post card of my own to Kittler, arriving late in the day, in the evening post, after Kittler has left the house and is unable to pick up this correspondence. It is an invoice requesting payment on behalf of literature. The sort of literature that Derrida spoke of in his lecture in Freiburg and which Kittler deals with repeatedly in two related works *Discourse Networks 1800/1900* (1990) (*Aufschreibesysteme 1800/1900*, 1985) and *Grammophon, Film, Typewriter* (1999).

Kittler is a historian of media, perhaps the first historian of media, perhaps the last historian of media: the historian who takes seriously the history of media as a history of mediatisation and history itself as mediatisation. In these two volumes published one year apart on the cusp of the digital epoch of a new crisis in destination, of email, the Internet, mobile communication and so-called social media, Kittler outlines a history of European culture that shifts from an age of writing by hand to an age of technological inscription. He schematizes these two moments in German thought and culture as the epoch of Goethe and the time of Nietzsche. These revolutionaries anchor Kittler's periodization of the different networks of 'technologies and institutions that allow a given culture to select, store, and process relevant data' (1992: 369). These two periods, for Kittler, orientate themselves, give or take twenty years on either side, around the turn of the nineteenth and twentieth centuries. In the former he makes the claim that 'technologies like that of book printing and the institutions coupled to it, such as literature and the university, thus constituted a historically very powerful formation, which in the Europe of the age of Goethe became the condition of the possibility of literary criticism' (369). In the latter he tells us that three technologies of inscription—the gramophone, film—and the typewriter, broke the monopoly of writing creating a new autonomous relation between the human and meaning as a machinic process, freeing information flow from the rigid grid of the symbolic and in so doing transported Europe from a Romantic subjectivity into a modern idiom of alienation. In an arresting aphorism he notes 'around 1880 poetry turned into literature' (Kittler, 1999: 14).

As with any such summary of a sweeping historicization I am unable to do justice to Kittler's archival account of this switch from Western print culture to an analogue Europe. As with any such sweeping historicization, Kittler pins his argument down through the citation of facts and dates, but I would contest is unable to do justice to an archival account that would attend to the texts, as texts, that make up that archive. What Kittler gives us, for all his scholarship and precise, exemplary citation, is a history without reading. This is significant not only for the discourse analysis Kittler inhabits as a historiological method but for the history of media itself which for Kittler is only a phenomenology of media and not a reading of media. A history of media, worthy of the name, both the name of 'media' and the name of 'history', should only ever be a history of reading. There can be no media without reading, no history without reading. A history of media without reading is only a typology of technologies of storage that cannot do justice to the singularity of the 'information', to use Kittler's term, which is stored. This is not to say that Kittler does not *read*; he is a scholar with considerable reading, he is as we might say 'well read'. These two volumes refer to Hoffmann, Schlegel, Fichte, Mallarmé, Stefan George, Benjamin, Freud, Goethe, Nietzsche, Rilke, Herder and so many others. However, they do not read any of these authors, these thinkers of media, in a way that understands the critical and figurative dimensions of their writing as writing, in order to appreciate the resources within that writing, which render the idea of media itself a problematic and divided resource for the Western tradition. Reading in this sense would be the presentation of an irreducible undecideability as the condition of meaning, the destabilisation of any stable or seemingly settled discursive system, as a challenge through aporetic tension that emerges not as a reductionist demasking but as a performative dynamic that cannot be escaped by any text regardless of its technological mode of inscription. Ultimately, Kittler's periodization of the epochs of discourse may tells us more about the discursive epoch in which Kittler himself writes, which perhaps Kittler himself invents, as a historically powerful formation within the university and a condition for what we call media studies. Such an accusation against K will require a presentation of evidence and the making of a case against his discursive method. Allow me then to present exhibit A, the case of literature, although we might equally and on another occasion choose the case of philosophy, assuming that we could, even if we wanted to, draw a coherent border between these two idioms that define so much of the history of the period that Kittler puts into analysis.

In the section on the typewriter in the 1986 (1999) book, although the chapter on Nietzsche from *Discourse Networks*, for example, is very much a representation of similar material, Kittler proposes that the typewriter 'inverts the material basis of literature' (183) by nullifying handwriting and rearranging the gender relations of literature from a cadre of male poetic secretaries to a pool of female typists. As a product of war, the patent for the typewriter was lodged by Remington, an American arms manufacturer attempting to diversify its product range following the end of the Civil War. The typewriter, says Kittler, improved administrative efficiency and, along with celluloid and the phonograph cylinder, opened the new century onto an information age. Such a seductive narrative must necessarily operate on a certain level of generality that does not attend to literary and philosophical writing by women during the nineteenth and eighteenth century and previously. However, Kittler has a stronger claim to make by way of Heidegger. Kittler recalls that for Heidegger man 'acts [*handlet*] through the hand

[*Hand*]' and 'the hand is, together with the word, the essential distinction of man' (198): the animal, for example, does not have a hand. Derrida has provided an extensive gloss, which Kittler does not cite, regarding the relation between *greifen* and *begreifen* in Heidegger (see Derrida, 1989), the essential relation between pre-hension and comprehension, grasping and understanding, that places the Word firmly in the hand of Man as the script of handwriting. The typewriter, for Kittler, 'tears writing from the essential realm of the hand, that is, the realm of the word' (198). In other words, mechanical writing deprives the hand, and therefore man, of the privileged relation to meaning by transforming the word from the signature of man into a means, we might say 'type', of communication. After Remington we are all typewriters, reduced to the same indistinguishable typeface, no longer identifiable by our unique handwriting and now reduced to mere word processors. This argument has a superficial appeal, but it is curiously ahistorical, given that the history of scribe culture and of national educational systems is precisely the history of an attempt to standardize handwriting. The font adopted in early print from Caxton onwards reproduced an already homogeneous script used in the reproduction of manuscripts by hand. While printed books from the very beginning have always presented a systematized and anonymous version of a written text.

However, the interest in Remington's invention for this present argument lies in the claims that Kittler makes with regard to the specific literature of the *fin-de-siècle* period that emerges from these typewriters. He identifies Nietzsche as the first philosopher of the typewriter, who, as an early adopter of Hansen's writing ball to overcome his increasing blindness, wrote poetry with a hammer, or at least hammer keys, giving rise to an aphoristic, telegraphic and staccato style that both opened philosophy to a new idiom of thought and the discipline of philosophy to the female students who acted as secretaries, and sometime lovers, to the sage. In *Spurs*, Derrida also offers a substantial thinking of Nietzsche and the questions of both style and sexual difference (see Derrida, 1981). Kittler only ever committed to print one extended consideration of his contemporary in the text '*Derridas Didaktik*' (Kittler, 1989). (For a consideration of the textual intersection between Kittler and Derrida, see Peter Krapp, 2011.) We have no record of the conversations between Kittler and Derrida in Freiburg, and Derrida only merits a handful of mentions in Kittler's two volumes but it would be a reasonable assumption to make that their time together gave rise to a set of mutual interests beyond the secrets of the post cards relayed via Sam Weber.

Kittler also takes from Nietzsche two of his most often quoted aphorisms that humans are 'perhaps only thinking, writing and speaking machines' (1999: 17) and that 'technology is entrenched in our history' (1999: 200). He appeals to other early adopters of the typewriter such as Mark Twain and T. S. Eliot as the authors of a new opening in literature in which the scene of writing for modernism 'designates the turning point at which communications technologies can no longer be related back to humans. Instead, the former have formed the latter' (1999: 211). For Kittler the medium is not only the message but the messenger as well. Just as the blind Nietzsche wrote by touch, separated from his script, the typist does not look down at the keys but proceeds through memory of the location of letters on a standard keyboard, also writing blind. The typist is dictated to, *diktiert* in the German of Kittler and Heidegger, related as Kittler acknowledges to the *dichten* that poetizes in the age of Goethe (1999: 198). The typist is also the secretary who introduces a new relation between *dichten* and *diktiert* into literary production. Kittler says:

> That is why the world of dictated, typed literature—that is, modern literature—harbours either Nietzsche's notion of love or none at all. There are desk couples, two-year-long marriages of convenience, there are even women writers such as Edith Wharton who dictate to men sitting at the typewriter. Only that typed love letters—as Sherlock Holmes proved once and for all in 'A Case of Identity'—aren't love letters. (1999: 214)

I am old enough to remember the days when secretaries would type up the hand-written manuscripts of professors, which is to say I am also old enough to remember when to be a professor meant to have a secretary. I have also spent long hours working on the transcription of a handwritten manuscript by Paul de Man from 1973 for online publication in 2009 (as a professor I had a talented research assistant who was the real secretary to this text) (see de Man, 2009). Now in the digital epoch the secretary has been replaced by the laptop even if voice-recognition software still allows for the possibility of dictation straight to machine. However, when it comes to literature there can be no 'once and for all', even if it is declared definitive by either Sherlock Holmes or Friedrich Kittler. I would now like to spend a moment attending to the text of Conan Doyle's short story, in a way that Kittler does not, in order to suggest how the act of reading might problematize the history of media that Kittler proposes.

The story makes an issue of the typist and of typewriting but unlike the text of Nietzsche or Eliot it was not itself written on a typewriter. The hand-written manuscripts of Conan Doyle are held in a range of public and private collections, although the location of 'A Case of Identity' remains a mystery. The singularity of literature lies beyond its utility as an archive of social history, the story may work for Kittler as a sociological document that records the rise of the financially independent female typist and the challenge this poses for Edwardian patriarchy, but it is not in itself the sort of typed literature that Kittler suggests opens the modern period. The case, in brief, which Holmes considers 'rather a trite one' concerns the engagement of a typist Miss Mary Sutherland to a Mr Hosmer Angel and his subsequent disappearance on their wedding day (Conan Doyle, 2009). The couple had meet at a ball where they became betrothed, thereafter they communicate by letter. Mr Angel only provides his place of work as a postal address and types his love letters including his signature because 'if they were sent to the office he would be chaffed by all the other clerks about having letters from a lady', so Mary offers to typewrite hers, 'like he did his, but he wouldn't have that, for he said that when I wrote them they seemed to come from me, but when they were typewritten he always felt that the machine had come between us. That will just show you how fond he was of me' (153).

When Mary's protective stepfather Mr Windibank, 'only a few years older' than she, departs for France, Hosmer Angel visits the house to propose that they marry immediately. On the day of the wedding Angel is unsettled and tells Mary that if anything happens to him she must be loyal to him for the next ten years. He disappears from the cab in which he is travelling in convoy with Mary and her mother. Holmes makes short work of solving the mystery when Mr Windibank accepts an invitation to Baker Street by typewritten response. Holmes exposes Windibank as the true Angel Hosmer, who had disguised himself and played upon his stepdaughter's shortsightedness to deceive her at the ball. His typewritten love letters further disguised his identity since Mary would have been familiar with his handwriting. This deception was motivated, in connivance with his wife, to prevent Mary inheriting her fortune, allowing Windibank to continue to enjoy the economic benefits of living off his older wife. Duplicitous as his behavior might have been, Holmes knows the law cannot touch Windibank and he leaves Baker Street a free man.

Mary, like Nietzsche, is myopic and so earns a living 'by the machine', it is the first deduction that Holmes makes when she enters Baker Street; typewriters were first introduced for use by the blind. It is the same blindness that allows her to be fooled by Windibank in this 'affaire de coeur'. However, while Mary is deceived, Holmes as an expert reader is not:

> 'It is a curious thing,' remarked Holmes, 'that a typewriter has really quite as much individuality as a man's handwriting. Unless they are quite new no two of them write exactly alike. Some letters get more worn than others, and some wear only on one side. Now, you remark in this note of yours, Mr Windibank, that in every case there is some little slurring over the e, and a slight defect in the tail of the r. There are fourteen other characteristics, but those are the more obvious.' (157)

Holmes uses a magnifying glass, normally a corrective for myopia, to note the details of the unique typing and while exposing Windibank Holmes comments 'I think of writing another little monograph some of these days on the typewriter and its relation to crime. It is a subject to which I have devoted some little attention' (157). Holmes here is a committed media historian. This story is then a poor piece of evidence in the case that Kittler would like to construct about the machinic anonymity of the typewriter. It rests upon the opposite claim that Kittler makes, namely that no two typewriters are the same. An irreducible trace remains for those who can read in dark and who follow Holmes's advice to Watson 'Never trust to general impressions, my boy, but concentrate yourself upon details' (155). The universality of a media history will always be undone by the singularity of the text.

While Holmes and Watson encounter the typist and owner of a Remington Mrs Lyons in *The Hound of the Baskervilles*, and at first mistake the musician Miss Violet Smith with 'spatulate finger-end[s]' for a typist in 'The Adventure of the Solitary Cyclist', and also receive a typed letter from Inspector LeStrade in 'The Adventure of the Cardboard Box', there is never a suggestion in the stories that Dr Watson, Holmes's Boswell, uses a typewriter himself, even when tracing the tracks of the missing German school master Herr Heidegger in 'The Adventure of the Priory School'. On the contrary, 'The Final Problem' opens with the line 'it is with a heavy heart that I take up my pen to write these last words . . . I shall ever record' (403). Equally in the two stories narrated by Holmes himself, 'The Blanched Soldier' and 'The Adventure of the Lion's Mane', there is no suggestion of the use of machinic writing.

The mystery that 'A Case of Identity' presents us with is not that love letters are not love letters if they are typed but love letters are not love letters if they can be read otherwise, or, we might say, if they are literature. The typed envois to Mary Sutherland gives rise to a risk of something like incest, certainly an impropriety, the short-circuit of a desire gone awry, a letter that arrives at some other destination. Even if Mr Windibank has not broken any law, Holmes is of the opinion he 'will rise from crime to crime' (158) and end his days on a gallows. Did Oedipus still love Jocasta? Did he continue to love her even after he knew she was his mother? Did Myrrha not always love Cinyras? However, this was not an attempted seduction, but the pretense of a seduction for economic benefit. Holmes can read the envois for what they are, as promissory notes, invoices, against future payment of Miss Sutherland's inheritance. However, for the unaware Mary the typed letters will always be love letters and she resolves to be faithful to the absent Angel for at least a decade. The correspondence is simultaneously love letters and not love letters, depending on how they are read, one possibility does not exclude or depend upon the other, the relation is asymmetrical. Holmes refuses to rob Mary of her hermeneutic illusion, he advises her to forget the incident: 'Let the whole incident be a sealed book, and do not allow it to affect your life' (154). Do not read too much into these letters and the disappearance of their author, but like Marlow and the beloved in Joseph Conrad's *Heart of Darkness* he decides, quoting a Persian saying, '"There is danger for him who taketh the tiger cub, and danger also for whoso snatcheth a delusion from a woman." There is as much sense in Hafiz as in Horace, and as much knowledge of the world' (158). Holmes justifies his own interpretative deception of Mary not from the classics but from the Quran, another book of the Abrahamic tradition. Watson does not inform Mary either, he, like Miss Sutherland, is a secretary and so a keeper of secrets, as well as the observant domestic 'spouse' who like Madame Heidegger makes the *mis-en-scène* of the entire domestic scene under observation. The secret of the love letters remains to be read but it is an open secret, there on the page in front of Mary should she open her eyes to her own blindness.

The narrator of Derrida's 'Envois' offers a thesis within the same ambit to that proposed by Kittler. He writes: 'An entire epoch of so-called literature, if not all of it, cannot survive a certain technological regime of telecommunications (in this respect the political regime is secondary). Neither can philosophy, or psychoanalysis. Or love letters' (Derrida, 1987: 12). I have puzzled over the meaning of this passage elsewhere, more than once (McQuillan, 2009 and 2012). My response to it today, apropos of Kittler, would be that what this case of literature, 'A Case of Identity', tells us is that the literature of the information age, of the typewriter, of the epoch of the technological regime of telecommunications, is no less or more literary than the handwritten poetry of the age of Goethe because such eighteenth-century (or 'pre-modern') writing, despite Heidegger's assumptions, enjoys no more or less a privileged relation to the mastery of meaning by the subject. It is the singularity of literature that it depends, and we take this as read, as it were, upon the possibility of entertaining a double relation between reference and denotation. The reader is able to distinguish between the Baker Street in London and the Baker Street in Conan Doyle.

However, Kittler is correct to identify in literature a machinic element that separates its author from its production. The machine of literature throws up random meanings that confuse the reader, who is no more master of the text than its author. (For a commentary of the machine of reading see Derrida, 2002.) In this sense, reading itself is as every bit as machinic as Nietzsche's haptic production. The 'case of identity' at stake in this story is in fact not so much that of Mr Windibank but that of literature itself. Not only do Holmes and Watson open this adventure with a discussion on the nature of fiction, arguing over which is the more unbelievable, reported real-life crime or detective stories, but the story itself unfolds as an act of literary fiction reporting a mundane act of domestic wrongdoing that would supposedly be beyond the imagination of any writer. The referential loop falls back upon itself, this story can, like the typed letters, be read both ways, as fictional fact and as in fact a fiction. Its identity is undecideable; the challenge is not to be a type reader, one who would read literature literally as an archive of historical facts as mere information, a row of ones and zeros that has significance by virtue of its storage prior to or anterior to reading. It is not that Kittler is wrong in what he says about so-called modern literature but that this is true of all literature, or philosophy, or psychoanalysis, or love letters.

Kittler himself in the same chapter goes on to present an example of a typed love letter, from Kafka to Felice Bauer, a couple who like the future Mr and Mrs Hosmer Angel attempted to sustain an engagement through correspondence. In a final letter that Kittler quotes with good humour an exasperated Kafka declares to his departing love 'How on earth did anyone get the idea that people can communicate with one another by letter!' (1999: 225). His dismay is well founded as the Angel letters demonstrate, and at the risk of channeling Paul de Man, it might be said that one should not take too lightly the impossibility of writing a love letter. Nor should we doubt that it is in acts of reading, divisible and impossible reading, that histories such as Kittler's are generated. However, when we read and in so doing give the text of Kittler a life of its own, as an automaton or machinic assemblage of stories and (hi)stories, what if we were to read these trials of K as if it were a novel? What if we were to read these two volumes, like Derrida's *La Carte Postale*, as a great postmodern novel of intertwining narratives in the tradition of, say, Thomas Pynchon or Douglas Hofstadter? In that case we might recognize the identity of both *La Carte Postale* and Kittler's volumes, as just another piece of literature that aims to put an end to all literature.

NOTES

1. This text was first given as part of a session with Sam Weber at 'Media After Kittler', Bolivar Hall, London 09.10.2013, organized by Eleni Ikoniadou and Scott Wilson for the London Graduate School. I have retained this marker of its original context for obvious reasons.
2. See Nicholas Royle's comments in his *After Derrida* (1995).

BIBLIOGRAPHY

Conan Doyle, Arthur. (2009) 'A Case of Identity' in *The Complete Sherlock Holmes*. Harmondsworth: Penguin. Also available at sherlock-holm.es, p. 155.

de Man, Paul. (2009) *Textual Allegories*, ed. Martin McQuillan, transcribed by Erin Obodiac, UCI Special Collections; also available at ucispace.lib.uci.edu/handle/10575/1092.

Derrida, Jacques. (1980) 'The Law of Genre'. Trans. Avital Ronell. *Critical Inquiry*, 7(1): 55–81.

———. (1981) *Spurs: Nietzsche's Style*. Trans. Barbara Harlow. Chicago: University of Chicago Press.

———. (1985) 'Racism's Last Word'. Trans. Peggy Kamuf. *Critical Inquiry*, 12: 290–99.

———. (1987) *The Post Card: From Socrates to Freud and Beyond*. Trans. Alan Bass. Chicago: University of Chicago Press.

———. (1989) '*Geschlecht II*: Heidegger's Hand'. Trans. John P. Leavey in *Deconstruction and Philosophy: The Texts of Jacques Derrida*, ed. John Sallis. Chicago: University of Chicago Press.

———. (2001) 'Above All, No Journalists!' in *Religion and Media*, eds. Hent de Vries and Samuel Weber. Stanford, CA: Stanford University Press.

———. (2002) 'Typewriter Ribbon: Limited Ink'. Trans. Peggy Kamuf, *Without Alibi*. Stanford, CA: Stanford University Press.

Kittler, Friedrich. (1989) '*Derridas Didaktik*', *Jahrbuch de Deutschdidaktik*: 31–41.

———. (1990) *Discourse Networks, 1800/1900*. Trans. Chris Cullens and Michael Metteer. Stanford, CA: Stanford University Press.

———. (1999) *Grammophon, Film, Typewriter*. Trans. Geoffrey Winthrop-Young and Michael Wutz. Stanford, CA: Stanford University Press, 1999.

Krapp, Peter. (2011) 'On Collegiality: Kittler Models Derrida', *Thesis Eleven*, 107(1): 21–32.

McQuillan, Martin. (2009) 'Tele-Techno-Theology' in *Deconstruction After 9/11*. New York: Routledge.

———. (2012) 'Toucher II' in *Deconstruction Without Derrida*. London: Bloomsbury.

Nancy, Jean-Luc. (2008) *Dis-Enclosure: The Deconstruction of Christianity*. Trans. Bettina Bergo, Gabriel Malenfant and Michael B. Smith. New York: Fordham University Press.

Royle, Nicholas. (1995) *After Derrida*. Manchester: Manchester University Press.

Chapter Two

The Calculable and the Incalculable

Hölderlin After Kittler

Samuel Weber

Allow me to begin with a recollection, which takes me back to the years around 1980, when Friedrich Kittler and I saw each other regularly and during which time we collaborated on a number of projects. Friedrich was then still an assistant professor at the University of Freiburg, preparing his Habilitation, which a few years later would be published in 1985 as *Aufschreibesysteme*, and which in 1990 would then appear in English under the significantly different title of *Discourse Networks* (1900). In the early 1980s I was spending part of each year in Strasbourg, and so Friedrich and I were able to visit each other fairly often and discuss common concerns, of which there were many. For both of us had been invigorated by the emergence of French post-structuralism, in particular by Lacan, Derrida and Foucault, whose writings at the time seemed to pose a serious challenge to traditional ways of thinking as well as to the institutions that perpetuated them.

A few years earlier, in 1977 Friedrich had coedited with Horst Turk a collection of essays that was to be quite influential at the time, entitled *Urszenen* (Kittler and Turk, 1977), in which he published a text entitled 'The Phantom of the I and the Psychology of Literature' dealing with E. Th. A. Hoffmann's story 'The Sandman' in the light of Freud's reading of it in his essay on 'The Uncanny,' and of Lacan's subsequent discussion of both. But as the Hoffmann story and the psychoanalytic theory of the uncanny might have suggested, this 'phantom of the I' was not to be as easily exorcised as many of us at the time expected. Friedrich's next major publication, another essay collection, but this time edited on his own, stated in bare terms the program that he was to follow in the coming years. Its title, roughly translated, was 'The Exorcising of the Spirit from the Humanities,' with as subtitle, 'Programs of Post-Structuralism' (Kittler, 1980). If the subtitle is easily rendered in English, the main title is not. But since the problem of translation here touches on certain aspects of Kittler's later work, let me dwell on it for a moment.

In German, the title is: *Austreibung des Geistes aus den Geisteswissenschaften* (1980). One of the untranslatable words is of course *Geist*: in English, spirit, mind or intellect. But none of these even begins to render the multiple connotations of the German word. Languages, which are singular systems, are often incommensurable in their most neuralgic moments. There is no adequate English correspondence for *Geist*, and even less for the disciplines that study them: *Geisteswissenschaften*. 'Humanities,' which is how I rendered the title, is surely related to *Geist* but by no means identical with it. The German rendition of 'humanities' or 'sciences humaines' is *Humanwissenschaften.* It sounds as artificial as 'sciences of the spirit' would in English.

All of this is not merely a linguistic accident, nor is it trivial in its implications and consequences. I am dwelling on this issue among others for the following reason: I am convinced that writers in general, and in this very singular case, the writings of Friedrich Kittler, gain enormously when they are read as *responses* to determinate situations, to distinct and not necessarily universal traditions and conventions, which can vary enormously from one linguistic area to another. Academic discourse traditionally—at least in the three languages with which I am familiar, but presumably in others as well—lives and thrives on the axiom of its *universality*. Given however the vastly different, not to say incommensurable, intellectual and institutional histories of the German and English-speaking countries—areas that already are highly diverse *within* themselves—the assumption of such universality, which is the precondition of the expectation of perfect translatability—results frequently in an extreme parochialism, insofar as the universality that is presupposed turns out to be nothing but the projection of a very particular set of experiences and structures upon very different situations. Let me add that this situation is something of which

Kittler was acutely aware, even if he did not address it often explicitly. Here however is one striking and exemplary exception:

> A medium is a medium is a medium. Therefore it cannot be translated. To transfer messages from one medium to another always involves reshaping them to conform to new standards and materials. In a discourse network, which this requires an 'awareness of the abysses that divide the one order of sense experience from the other,' transportation necessarily takes the place of translation. Whereas translation excludes all particularities in favor of a general equivalent, the transposition of media is accomplished serially, at discrete points. (Kittler, 1990: 265)

Let me highlight one of those 'discrete points' of what, in translation, Kittler refers to as 'transportation' but which in German involves a word that is much larger in its connotations, namely: *Übertragung*, the literal German equivalent of the Greek 'metaphor'. The word in both Greek and in German strongly connotes not just a change of place, as it does in English, but rather a change in what is changing place. In this sense, a better translation in English would be *transfer*, or even *rendition*, rather than *transportation*, or another possibility, *transport.* To be sure, Kittler is characteristically referring to the transition from 'one order of sense experience' to another one—but the word he uses suggests that the 'abyss' mentioned divides not merely '*one* order of sense experience from the *other*' but moreover and primordially *each* individual 'sense experience' from itself, which is to say, from its conventionally determined form. As a result, it can be argued that 'translation', impossible in the sense of identical reproduction, actually goes on all the time not just between different languages and media, but *within* them—but that it also tends to obscure and conceal the transformative nature of the process. In doing this, it avails itself of a number of traditional devices, not the least of which being the belief that so-called proper names—for instance, that of 'Friedrich Kittler'—necessarily guarantee the self-identity and constancy that the process of transfer, translation and transport constantly belie. Another related device, closely linked to the notion of the proper name, especially where persons, subjects or authors are concerned, is precisely that 'Phantom of the I' apostrophized in the subtitle to Kittler's first essay collection *Urszenen.* The belief in a unified medium or in the unity of a particular 'sense experience' is thus closely tied to the belief in the unity of that I or ego that the *Urszenen*, whether Freud's or Kittler's, sought to call into question.

This belief or expectation of a unity of sense-experience or of the medium associated with it is related to another phantom, against which Kittler argued from the start: that of self-identical, universal and unchanging *meanings* as the object or product of what Friedrich Kittler addressed as *Geist*. *Geist*, as the title of his second essay collection proclaimed, was to be 'exorcised', or more literally, 'driven out'—expelled—of the institution that perpetuated it, namely the *Geisteswissenschaften*, which, once they had been purged of this *Geist*, could then return in a substantially altered, more materialistic form, namely as *Medienwissenschaften*.

At the time—and indeed ever since—I was and remain troubled by the second word that is difficult to translate, but that is decisive for a major part of Kittler's writing, the word: *Austreibung*. The word is not innocent, and its English renditions—exorcising, exclusion, expulsion—hardly do justice to its historical resonances. In German, it is difficult to separate it from one of the many traumas that haunted German society in the postwar period, namely that of the German populations that were 'expelled'—the German word used was (and is) *vertrieben* rather than *ausgetrieben* (exorcised)—from areas in which they in part had lived for centuries as the political map of Central Europe was redrawn following the Second World War. In short, there was a theological, even 'spiritistic' violence in the notion of *Austreibung* that concerned me then as now, but that I also felt corresponded to the violence of recent German and European history.

Not that I felt that the allusion to violence in academic or intellectual matters was something to be avoided on principle. Such avoidance, it was and is clear to me, often serves as a cover to label as violence only that which is less firmly institutionalized—that of individuals for instance—and to legitimate, by implication, forms of institutionalized violence. One of these—and here I was certainly of the same opinion as Friedrich Kittler—was surely associated with the notion and word 'Spirit', for reasons that subsequently Derrida deployed in his little book *Of Spirit*, whose subtitle reads: *Heidegger and the Question* (1987).

Rather, what worried me at the time and what continues to concern me is the suspicion that exorcism itself could constitute a form of avoidance. For although I had no illusions about the dangers involved in a culture that placed a universalizing concept of *Geist* at the summit of its values, I was even more concerned with the project of 'driving (it) out'. For it was clear that this title announced not an accomplished fact but an ongoing project and program. It did this by forming the substantive out of the infinitive, using the form *Austreiben* rather than *Austreibung*. To me at least this underscored the *unfinished*, ongoing nature of the process and defined itself as a call to action, an appeal. This was to emerge as a constant characteristic of Kittler's prose: behind its many declarations, often decried as apodictic, stood an appeal to action—here, the action of driving out a 'spirit' that had outlived its usefulness. Or at least, of driving it out of its institutionalized cover in the academy.

However, it was not this call to action that concerned me, then as now, but rather its efficacy. For I was reminded of a remark made by Adorno in an essay on Kafka that I had translated some years earlier from his book *Prisms*: 'No sooner has the surveyor expelled (*vertrieben*) the annoying apprentices from his room in the country inn, then they return through the window, without the novel bothering to dwell on this apart from simply reporting the fact; the hero is too tired in order to expel them again' (Adorno, 1997: 258). By contrast with Kafka's antiheroes, Kittler never grew too tired to renew his effort to exorcise—*auszutreiben*—what he felt had outlived its usefulness. And that began, but did not end, with the academic conventions that dominated the institutions in which he had to function, the German university. It is here that I feel it indispensable that readers of his work recall or are informed of the particular situation of the German university against which Kittler was reacting. If he began by seeking to limit if not deprive the *Geisteswissenschaften* of their indispensable object, *Geist*, it was also because he had had to endure the power of the Academy to limit critical thinking that called its basic principles into question. The desire to make a clean break with the past—felt to be an impediment to the future—drew him to Lacan and Derrida, but especially to Foucault, who at the time had popularized the notion of the '*coupure épistémologique*' borrowed from Gaston Bachelard to emphasize the fundamental discontinuity between historically distinct discourses and systems. This in turn would encourage the kind of periodization that informed Kittler's first two major books: *Discourse Networks* (*Aufschreibesysteme*) (1990), which bore the subheading *1800/1900* and the follow-up publication *Grammophon, Film, Typewriter* (1986). The latter title, designating a pure sequence without any sense of completion—no 'and'—thereby suggested the technical devices that would supplant the notion of a 'spirit' guiding the development of history according to a more or less transparent teleological pattern. As a result, the academic *Geistes-*

wissenschaften would be reorganized as sciences of technical media. But in turn, such media techniques would be defined in part at least through the manner in which they would exclude and transform a long tradition dominated by discursive semantics claiming to draw their authority from the universality of meaning.

From Kittler's many pronouncements on the subject of media, the following has the virtue of being both short, and sweet; from an essay originally published in German in 1988 entitled 'The City as Medium': 'Media exist to process, record, and transmit numbers' (Kittler, 1996: 720). And a little further on in the same essay:

> Media record, transmit and process information—this is the most elementary definition of media. Media can include old-fashioned things like books, familiar things like the city and newer inventions like the computer. It was von Neumann's computer architecture that technically implemented this definition for the first time in history (or as its end). [. . .] This network of processing, transmission and recording, or restated: of commands, addresses, and data, can calculate everything (based on Turing's famous proof from 1936) that is calculable. [. . .] And this is reason enough, moreover, to decipher past media and the historical function of what we refer to as 'man', as the play between commands, addresses and data. (Kittler, 1996: 722)

Thus, on the one hand the 'break' between new and older 'media' was presented as a clear and distinct discontinuity, on the other hand it was to provide a basis for seeing the development of history as a continuum whose structure only the newer media allow us to comprehend fully; or as Kittler puts it in the passage just quoted, permits us to 'decipher' ('this is reason enough . . . to decipher past media . . . as the play between commands, addresses and data'). It is in thus deploying as a key to historical understanding this notion of 'deciphering' that a point is attained where those 'annoying apprentices' to which Adorno refers in his Kafka essay return massively, through the rear window—or rather, to use Kittler's vocabulary, return transported by the 'bus' of the circuit board, through the 'gates' or 'ports' of Boolean algebra and of the circuit board, 'gates and ports' which, as Kittler notes, can be considered to constitute 'simplest elements' of the computer insofar as they 'have no memory'—and are therefore dependent on the 'built-in memory' of the 'bus' in order to be operational (720).

In what consists then this 'return'? I want to suggest that it consists in the unquestioned epistemological authority of the writing subject that signs his texts 'Friedrich Kittler' or sometimes more simply, 'FAK', which in part at least seems to me based on the distinction of functions that are only functional insofar as they are interdependent: that of storage, processing and transmission of something called 'data'. I am reminded a bit of Saussure's famous attempt to justify the priority and independence of the synchronic over the diachronic state, by referring to the game of chess. What Saussure forgot—and his own notes to his lectures show that he was fully aware of this—was that the so-called synchronic state is structurally divided by the 'move'—by the fact that one of the two players has the move and the other does not. In short, a certain diachrony intrudes on the apparently self-contained chessboard precisely insofar as it is a game. What I want to suggest is that a certain diachronic overlapping of functions breaks down the clear-cut distinctions into processing, storage and transmission, since each is implied and involved in the others, which limits their distinct self-identity.

Thus, in a lecture on 'Universities: Wet, Hard, Soft and Harder', Kittler seeks to interpret the functions of the medieval institution according to his triadic mould, as 'the data-processing lecture, the data-storing university library, and the data-transmitting mail' (Kittler, 2004: 245). But a lecture or seminar can be considered as much 'data-transmitting' as 'data-storing,' and mail and the library also can be considered to 'process' the data by the ways they store and transmit it. Similarly, the notion of 'address' is not simply an aspect of 'storage' but can also designate a form of transmission or at least of movement: it applies both to the library and to mail, for instance. It can be a factor orienting or directing the flow of such information as much as designating its more or less fixed location and retrievability.

I want to suggest that despite the unquestionable global dimensions of the technicity with which Kittler was concerned, that his 'addressing' of it was very much a response to the specific traditions of German humanistic scholarship—and that his thought is therefore not entirely separable from the notions embodied in words such as *Geist* and even *Geisteswissenschaft*. Kittler was initially trained as a literary scholar, and the field of literary studies was—and to a certain extent still is—dominated in Germany by what is called the 'hermeneutic tradition', which portrays literary texts as the articulation of meaning, generally fulfilling the intentions of the writing subject qua 'author'. This ultimately theological tradition, going back to the Biblical account of the creation of the universe through a single Deity, became sedimented in the rules of Biblical textual '*Auslegung*'—explication or unfolding of meanings that are held to have been contained in or symbolized by the sacred text. As the direct authority of the Church was weakened, first through the Reformation and then through what is called the Enlightenment, the explication of texts, and of artistic works more generally took up the slack as it were, becoming the exemplary instances through which an initial, authorial and creative meaning was to be recuperated and reappropriated by world-bound finite and mortal 'spirits'. The cult of authority, imposing itself through intentional meaning and action, thus found one of its strongest defenses in this hermeneutic tradition, whether in its Hegelian form of an Absolute Spirit qua Knowledge, or in its more cautious Diltheyian form distinguishing between scientific—causal—'explanation' and humanistic 'interpretation'. This then constituted one of the first, negative 'addresses' of Friedrich Kittler's writing, understandably, since it dominated the institutional context in which he had to work, and which would provide the condition of further research. Recent revelations about the opposition to his Habilitation on the part of certain senior faculty members only underscores the reality of the power-relations in and against which he had to work—and of course not just he.

Kittler's fascination with war as the medium both of historical and of technological-medial development can be seen therefore as in part at least a response both to the more immediate reality of recent German history—which in his case as in so many others had directly affected his family and his childhood—and to the hostile power-relations that pervaded the academic context of his writing, and which threatened during his Habilitation-process to put an early end to his career—as it had done a half century earlier to the academic career of one Walter Benjamin.[1]

Thus, although Kittler from the start was intent on driving the *Geist* out of the *Geisteswissenschaften* and thereby opening the way for their transformation into *Medientechnik-* and also *Kulturwissenschaften* (media-technical and cultural studies), his reliance on a paradigm borrowed from contemporary media, as the storage, processing and transmission of information, threatened at times to introduce a new dogma into the soon-to-be established sciences of media, and one which, somewhat but not entirely paradoxically, would wind up reinstating the epistemic authority of the scholar as founder of a cult or school. For the process of *Austreibung* implies or entails an exorciser, with priestly qualities, but also as what Lacan once called the subject supposed to know. The spirit as absolute knowledge thus returned to haunt the extraordinarily erudite and remarkable stylist that was Friedrich Kittler, establishing yet another, if highly innovative 'school' after the many 'schools' and 'circles' that marked German cultural, intellectual and artistic life since at least 1800: another continuity that the advent of the digital age apparently has not disturbed. The existence of such schools, and above all the demand to which they respond, appears to transcend the undeniable alterations brought about by the rise of new, electronic media—a fact that I am not certain the triad of data storage, processing and transmission alone can 'address', which does not mean that this triad cannot be helpful in developing an interpretation of the persistence of this phenomenon.

This 'reactionary' dimension marking the return of an authority, that in many ways was no less absolute than those of the *Geisteswissenschaftler* it was supposed to supplant, was neither peculiar to Kittler nor by any means the only aspect of his prodigious writing. But it does pose a problem that demands attention in evaluating the scope and ramifications of his work—work that has no doubt profoundly and durably altered our understanding of what C. P. Snow many years ago called the 'two cultures' and what today is designated as the 'digital divide'.

It has to be added, however, that alongside a certain totalizing tendency in his presentation of the historical significance of technical media, his writing often expresses a sense of necessary limitation to what can be thought and said of their impact. Of this an interesting instance can be found in his essay, 'The City as Medium'. I have already quoted these lines, but they doubtless passed by without receiving much attention, so let me repeat them: They refer to von Neumann's 'computer architecture' which leads to the microprocessor: 'This network of processing, transmission, and recording, or restated, of commands, addresses and data, can calculate everything . . . that is calculable' (Kittler, 1996: 722). The question that remains unasked, although implied, is: Are there limits to the calculable? And if so, then can we think or experience what is incalculable and how does it relate to what can be calculated?

There is in the literature that Kittler surveyed in his first book, a highly significant attempt to introduce a certain calculus into the writing and theorisation of poetry, and in particular of tragedy. I am thinking of the famous opening comments of Friedrich Hölderlin's 'Remarks on Oedipus'. Given the relevance to what we have been discussing, and given the density of the passage, I take the liberty of quoting it at length:

> It will be good—in order to assure the poets, including ours, a decent existence (*eine bürgerliche Existenz*)—if poetry, including ours, subtracting (*abgerechnet*) the difference of times and constitutions, can be elevated to the *μηχανη* of the ancients.
>
> Also other works of art, compared with those of the Greeks, are lacking in reliability (*Zuverlässigkeit*): at least they have until now been judged more for the impressions they make than for their lawful calculus and other procedural modes through which the beautiful is brought forth. Modern poetry however is particularly lacking in schooling and handwork (*an der Schule und am Handwerksmäßigen*), so that their procedural modes (might be) calculated (*berechnet*) and taught, and once learned, reliably repeated in their exercise. One has, among humans, with each thing, above all to attend to (the fact) that it is some thing (*daß es Etwas ist*), i.e., that in the means (*moyen*) of its manifestation it is recognizable (*erkennbar*), that the way, in which it is conditioned (*bedingt*), can be determined and taught. Therefore and out of higher grounds poetry requires particularly certain and characteristic principles and limits.
>
> That is where that lawful calculus belongs.
>
> Then one must be attentive to how the content distinguishes itself, through which procedures and in the infinite but thoroughly determined context particular contents relate to the universal calculus, and the goings-on (Gang) and that which is to be set in place (*das Vestzusetzende*), *the living sense* (*der lebendige Sinn*) that can not be calculated, is brought into relation to the calculable law. (Hölderlin, 1992: 309. *My translation—SW*)

Hölderlin, schoolmate and friend of Hegel and Schelling, formed through an intensive confrontation with the German idealistic philosophy of Kant and Fichte—Hölderlin here does what according to Kittler all of metaphysics, from Plato through Hegel and beyond, refused to do, namely, to introduce technics and calculus into the determination of poetry as something other than as the act of a subject. In so doing, Hölderlin is also well on his way to overcoming the polarity of 'form and matter' that Kittler, following Heidegger, sees as one of the hallmarks of traditional metaphysics. This gesture of Hölderlin's seems to me profoundly related to Kittler's demand to include knowledge of 'the technical state of the art' in any effective 'ontology of media'. Such knowledge would concern the 'technical state of the art,' which Kittler associates with the 'blueprints, layouts, mainboard designs, industrial roadmaps and so on . . . namely the hardware of high tech' (Kittler, 2009: 29–30) and in particular with its numerical dimension, 'a mathematical medium' that, as 'the early modern invention of real numbers and general exponents, brought forth an acoustic medium' (2009: 29–30). When Hölderlin in the passage cited makes the production and understanding of tragedy dependent on the knowledge of certain general laws and their application, which he interprets as a 'calculus,' he construes 'tragedy' as inseparable from rules that can be taught and transmitted, which in turn make the writing of tragedies in part at least into something like a 'handwork' and not just the result of genial 'inspiration' or 'creation'. Compare this to the following general assessment to be found in Kittler's essay, 'Number and Numeral':

> The principal difficulty resides in not submitting our world made up of *mathematical calculus, epistemic things and technological media* to a supreme being, be it God, Meaning, or Man—something the early modern age was incapable of doing. From Leibniz to Kronecker, the simplest of numbers (binary or natural) were said to be a gift from God; and from Descartes and Hegel to Dilthey the 'meaning' imposed by subjects on objectivities or media was a covert resistance against thinking about technology. Evidently numbers had to leave humans behind and become part of machines that run on their own in order for technology to appear as a frame that conjoins being and thought. This turn was completed by Alan Turing. (58)

The 'turn . . . completed by . . . Turing' was not one that Hölderlin sought to take—not at least in his 'Remarks on Oedipus and Antigone', written after having translated both plays. Indeed, he warned against taking certain turns, which sought entirely to overturn existing systems of values, however much he sought to have them altered and transformed; and this was because his 'world' was not that described by Kittler in the passage just read, and attributed to all of us: 'The principal difficulty resides in not submitting *our world made up of mathematical calculus, epistemic things and technological media* to a supreme being'. However much Hölderlin argued for a revalorization of technique, general principles and 'lawful calculus' in their application, he also was aware that his world did not consist exclusively of 'mathematical calculus, epistemic things and technological media' for the simple reason that not all things could be considered strictly from the perspective of the *episteme.* And this is also where his notion of the medium—for which he invokes the French word *moyen*—certainly diverges from the one invoked by Friedrich Kittler, namely, in reserving an irreducible place to their *singularity*: For if he demanded that in the practice of poetry 'each thing' be seen as a 'something', which is to say, recognized with reference to the general conditions of its emergence, he also insisted on the irreducible gap separating those general principles, and all calculability, from what he called 'the living sense'—not to be confused with the notion of a universally valid 'meaning' which Kittler justifiably identifies as presenting perhaps the major obstacle to a rethinking of technology and media that would no longer be dependent on the paradigm of a Supreme Being, God, Creator or autonomous subject. No, the 'living sense' of which Hölderlin writes is that which precisely is set off by and against the general calculation as that which resists resolution in an equation even while it presupposes equations and algorithms in order *at the same time* to comply with them and to resist them.

The singularity of this 'living sense' thus involves a movement that is neither linear nor circular, neither strictly sequential nor strictly parallel. Kittler concludes his essay 'Towards an Ontology of Media' by recounting the 'dream most dear to solid state physicians', namely one of 'computers based on parallel and tiny quantum states instead of on big and serial silicon connections,' and notes that if this 'rosy dawn' should ever really arise, 'I, or rather my successors, shall withdraw this paper'. Without claiming to fully understand the implications of this dream or the likelihood of it 'dawning' some time soon, rosy or not, I would like to believe that the shift—not turn—from sequential to parallel (quantum) thinking, although not computing, is already at work in the poetry, translations and *Remarks* . . . of Hölderlin.

At the close of his *Remarks on Antigone*, Hölderlin seeks to confirm his theory that tragic presentation (*Darstellung*) is designed to preserve a certain 'equilibrium'—*Gleichgewicht* is the German word he uses—which in *Antigone* means a certain balance between Antigone and Creon. But it is a balance that is preserved only through imbalance. This summed up in Hölderlin's use of the German word, '*gleich*', which is rather 'like' our English word, 'like', stressing similarity but retaining difference. What is *like* is never simply equal or identical. The implications of this *equivocal* 'like' are unfolded when Hölderlin, toward the end of his *Remarks*, comes to articulate the *political* import of the tragedy. But before citing this passage, it may be useful to point out that Hölderlin also employs a tripartite structure somewhat 'like' what Kittler, in 'Towards an Ontology of Media' designates as a 'new trinity' destined to replace the old polarity of 'form and matter', namely the triad 'made up of commands, addresses, and data'—whereby the question remains of whether Kittler's 'new trinity', however ironically the term is meant, does not carry some of the implications of the 'old' trinity, by *likening* the notion of 'medium' to that 'Supreme Being' he also wishes it to replace. Hölderlin, for his part, seeking to analyse 'tragic presentation,' acknowledges that some sort of relationship of bodies to the 'godlike' is constitutive but this relation is hardly one of 'submission' as Kittler puts it: rather it entails striving, conflict and tension. It is this tension that then results in the triadic structure that I want to juxtapose with Kittler's 'new trinity'. Here then is the relevant passage, quoted *in medias res* as it were:

> Preeminently however tragic presentation (*Darstellung*) consists in the factical word that, more context than (actually) enunciated, destined (*Schicksalsweise*), goes from beginning to end; in the mode of provenance (*Hergang*), in the grouping of persons against each other (*gegeneinander*), and in the form of reason that constitutes itself in the terrible muse of a tragic time. (374–75)

Hölderlin's 'new trinity' here clearly takes its distance both from the traditional polarity of form and matter (or content), and from the no-less-traditional trinity, since it begins not with an origin or Creator, but with a *Hergang*, which is to say, with the question of *provenance*, the 'where-from', and hence with the trajectory that has been followed in arriving 'here'—*her*: If this can be compared to the process of 'storing' data, in the case of the tragic 'medium'—and more specifically of *Antigone*, such 'storage' is shown to be highly unstable and inconstant, since it consists in what Hölderlin goes on to designate as an 'upheaval' (*Aufruhr*: an 'uproar'), which in turn is the result of an 'infinite overturning' (*unendliche Umkehr*). Unlike the 'turn' that Turing is said to have 'completed', for Hölderlin such a turn can never be consummated, not at least for man as a 'cognizant being': 'A complete overturning in this is however—like complete overturning generally, without anything to hold on to (*ohne allen Halt*) is not permitted for humans as cognizant beings' (375). In such situations, 'where the entire figure of things changes' and where 'nature and necessity, which always remain, incline toward another figure, whether to savagery or a new figure' what is possible for man is the feeling of being profoundly *shattered—Erschütterung*—and this in turn impels the shattered persons to redefine themselves, or as Hölderlin puts it, to 'formalize themselves' as 'persons of rank' (*Standespersonen*).

In short, the experience of a shattering turnover of all values and realities drives those whom it affects to transform their self-understanding from that of individual persons to that of members of a class—and hence, as dependent variables. In this sense, the second category of Hölderlin's triad emerges out of this initial experience of being both shattered and of belonging to a larger group, a 'Stand' or 'estate'. Hölderlin calls it a 'grouping'. But here again, the 'grouping' can be 'likened' (although not identified) to what Kittler's 'addresses' insofar as it designates the way in which individual elements or 'data' are localized—namely, in interdependent but discrete relation to one another. Hölderlin describes this relation of dependent variables as agonistic, and more particularly, with respect to *Antigone*, as a 'contest of runners' in which 'the one who first gasps for breath and collides with the opponent *has lost*' (376). Hölderlin, it should be noted, does not tell us how such a race is *won*, but only how it is *lost*, as if in this kind of (tragic) 'race' there are no winners, but only losers—which of course is a pretty good description of *Antigone*. This losing race where it is not permitted to touch the opponent or to breathe heavily could be likened to the processing of discrete data that has been collected through its '*Hergang*'.

But to see how strained and excessive these 'likenesses' are, and also how their discrepancies serve to bring out what is *un-like* in the two 'trinities,' we need only proceed to the third branch of Hölderlin's triad, namely what he calls the 'rational form'—*Vernunftform*—which for Socrates in *Antigone* he considers to be 'political and namely republican.' Here, as with Kittler, it is necessary to keep in mind that against which and to which Hölderlin is here responding and reacting, namely the prevalent monarchical form of government that prevailed in most of Germany at the time. Republican, as non-monarchical, requires a certain plurality or diversity in governance. In the play *Antigone* this takes the form of the conflict 'between Creon and Antigone,' which Hölderlin also describes, chiastically, as that between the 'formal (Creon) and anti-formal (Antigone)'. And now comes the decisive phrase, which I will translate as literally as possible, and hence awkwardly—'the equilibrium—*das Gleichgewicht* (the aim of the tragic caesura)—'is held *too like*'—*zu gleich gehalten ist.* Normally, the two words used by Hölderlin are written together, as one word, namely: *zugleich*, which, when written as one word, is how it is usually used, signifies 'at once' or 'at the same time'. However, by introducing a space between the two words, *zu* and *gleich*, Hölderlin has them say—process or transmit—a supplementary meaning, which although less common is also more literal. The republican form of 'reason'—a political reason—is indicated at the end of the tragedy by Sophocles 'by the fact that at the end, Creon is practically mistreated by his servants' (376)—in other words, by the fact that his social and political form is degraded, just as that of Antigone has been through his punishment of her. In this separation of the mortal living being, whether Antigone or Creon, from their formalized social rank, the balance or equilibrium—*das Gleichgewicht*—is upheld, but precisely through a certain excess. By becoming 'too (a)like' in their destinies, the two figures maintain a balance between singularity and generality, between mortality and endurance, that consists more in an excess of likeness than in a simple equation.

This then seems to be that 'living sense' that Hölderlin demands from tragic presentation and that presupposes the laws of its calculus—through which a certain equilibrium is first imposed by the caesura on what could be called the death-drive of the 'tragic transport'—but only in order then to set off what remains incalculable, *unberechenbar*, since it is inseparable from the singular dimension of the living—which is to say, from their mortality. This singular dimension cannot be equated with an 'epistemic object,' because, like the uproar and overturning that is its medium, it can only be 'felt' but not cognized, only experienced as an overwhelming shock, but never entirely calculated or recognized.

It is this self-limitation of a certain cognitive experience and authority in the name of the incalculable and of a certain feeling that, I submit, fascinates Friedrich Kittler who also reacts to it through his effort to replace the dominion of a Supreme Being with the reign of computers, numbers and of a recursivity that defies all sense. 'A medium is a medium is a medium' he wrote famously in his magnum opus, *Discourse Networks*. I would like to suggest that this insistence on the untranslatability of the medium in relation to other media, upon which each nevertheless depends, calls for another, equally gnomic statement in order to be made fully operable, this time from Jacques Derrida. That statement is truly untranslatable, so I will have to quote it first in French, and then try to paraphrase it in English: '*Tout autre est tout autre*'—'Every other is entirely other.'

Media theory and analysis *after* Kittler may thus also include a rereading of texts that ostensibly belong to a period that is long since past. But it may also be one that turns out to coexist 'at once'—*zugleich*—with the extension of calculability that is one of the hallmarks the digital age. It coexists with it by raising the question of whether that *zugleich* may not *at the same time* be *zu gleich, too alike*, and therefore singularly *unlike*. Perhaps this is the subtext, or at least question haunting the 'rosy dream' of parallel computing, which Kittler acknowledges ironically, but perhaps did not entirely share.

NOTE

1. For a journalistic account of the controversy surrounding Kittler's Habilitations-process, see the following article from the Frankfurter Allgemeine Zeitung: www.faz.net/aktuell/feuilleton/friedrich-kittlers-habilitationsverfahren-spucken-hilft-nicht-herr-kollege-11727699.html (consulted on Oct. 3, 2013).

BIBLIOGRAPHY

Adorno, Theodor W. (1997) 'Auszeichnungen zu Kafka' (Notes on Kafka) in *Prisms,* Gesammelte Schriften 10.1. Frankfurt am Main: Suhrkamp.

Derrida, Jacques. (1987) *De l'esprit: Heidegger et la question.* Paris: Galilée.

Hölderlin, Friedrich. (1992) Anmerkungen zum Oedipus' (Remarks on Oedipus), *Sämtliche Werke und Briefe*, ed. Michael Knaupp, vol. 2. Munich: Carl Hanser Verlag.

Kittler, Friedrich. (1980) 'Autorschaft und Liebe' in *Austreibung des Geistes aus den Geisteswissenschaften*, ed. Friedrich Kittler. Munich; Wien; Zurich; pp. 142–73.

———. (1986). *Grammophon, Film, Typewriter.* Berlin: Brinkman & Bose.

———. (1990) *Discourse Networks 1800/1900.* Stanford, CA: Stanford University Press.

———. (1996) 'The City as Medium', trans. Matthew Griffin. *NLH* 27(4): 717–29.

———. (1998) *Daten Zahlen Codes*. Leipzig.

———. (2004) 'Universities: Wet, Hard, Soft and Harder'. *Critical Inquiry* 31(1): 244–56.

———. (2006) 'Number and Numeral'. *Theory, Culture & Society* 23(7–8): 51–61.

———. (2009) 'Towards an Ontology of Media'. *Theory, Culture & Society* 26: 29–30.

———. (2012) 'Götter und Schriften rund ums Mittelmeer', transcript of a seminar session, summer term 2010, published in TUMULT 40: *Friedrich Kittler. Technik oder Kunst?* Wetzler.

Kittler, Friedrich and Horst Turk, eds. (1977) *Urszenen* (Primal Scenes). Frankfurt am Main: Suhrkamp.

Chapter Three

Kittler-Time

Getting to Know Other Temporal Relationships with the Assistance of Technological Media

Wolfgang Ernst
Translated by Yuk Hui and James Burton

KITTLER AS PHILOSOPHER OF HISTORY

This text does not aim at a historicization of Kittler's quest for knowledge [*Wissensimpuls*], not here, not yet.[1] Nor is this an attempt at a hermeneutic reconstruction of 'Kittler as philosopher of history';[2] this would require a fundamental survey not only of his publications, but first and foremost of his unpublished texts, now stored in the Literature Archive in Marbach. This chapter aims, rather, to carry further the knowledge of a brother in spirit—and, accepting the risk that comes with this, to smuggle in an original critique of history in the name of Kittler.

The current text does not seek to provide a reconstruction of Kittler's model of (media-)history, but rather to highlight within it the points at which he flashed upon other possible ways of modeling emphatic time—yet which he did not further develop, since they only barely related to his central research interests. Nonetheless, an implicit philosophy of history may be assembled from Kittler's diverse writings. This reading identifies a critique of history that the author only peripherally touched upon, allowing only its edges to appear, since it stood outside the scope of his main concerns.

Kittler planned to end his cycle of works on music and mathematics with a volume on Turing-time. Now that time itself has caught up with him in a galaxy shared with Turing (in the ahistorical *Typographeum*, the temporally invariant symbolic order of the archive), it is time to reconsider the concept of (media-)history critically associated with Kittler. This is not an attempt to historicize the thought of Kittler, but rather, in the spirit of the appeal he made in October 2011, on his sickbed in the critical care unit of the Virchow Clinic in Berlin ('knowledge purge'), to advance and disseminate through critical debate the knowledge of the machinations [*Machenschaften*] of the media in time.

HEGELIANISM IN DISGUISE: KITTLER AS HISTORICAL MATERIALIST

Is there, behind the evidence of the 'technical *a priori*' (harking back to Immanuel Kant's term) of all discourses, which Kittler (in a decided intensification of Michel Foucault's insights) alleged to be a feature of technological determinism, also a Hegelian philosophy of history pulling the strings? A dim memory: In the course of Kittler's Bochum lecture on the occasion of the candidature of a local professor, at a time when I was engaged in doctoral research on the theme of the reception of Antiquity among historians, this suspicion came to me. Is a *non-human agency* (as Bruno Latour might well put it, see Latour, 1999: 145–214) stepping on to the stage of the world spirit of cultural development in the name of a media-technical a priori? It is not only the time of *human* history that media underlie: 'without the mathematics of frequency and the physics of electromagnetism, "technics" would by no means be able to historically shape the human—who indeed is no longer its creator' (Kittler, 2000a: 232).

In an article on museology, Kittler recalled that the chronological order of the hanging of paintings (for example in the Alten Museum of Berlin which, significantly, can be seen from the house in which Hegel lived) corresponds with the concluding passage of Hegel's *Phenomenology of Spirit* (Kittler, 1996: 68; see also Ernst in Hensel and Köstler, 2005). It is precisely this order that is undermined through the recombinant depth of the virtual, thus mathematized, museum (data *plus* algorithms):

> Digital archiving could break up the alliance that the museum has maintained with history or even historicism since 1800. The chronological sequence, as the emptiest of all kinds of order in which stored things are to be put, could be replaced by an order of co-presence once their combinatory connections were located. (Kittler, 1996: 75)

In the report and counter-report, recently made publicly available on Kittler's Freiburg Habilitationsschrift *Aufschreibesysteme* ['inscription systems', though commonly rendered in English as 'discourse networks'], Gerhard Kaiser perceived a certain Hegelianism. Was there a new a priori world spirit hiding in the background? 'One might easily understand [. . .] this writing system 1900 that concludes itself in Kittler's analysis, in a Hegelian sense, as the last, from which all the preceding are accordingly to be deciphered' (Kaiser, 2012: 131). For 2000, the medium that provides the model is, then, the computer.

What inscribes itself here is a dialectical figure of thesis, antithesis and synthesis. The ancient Greeks established the multiple alphabet (for linguistic, musical and mathematical notation); in the course of the development of the isolated sciences, this unity breaks apart: the Fall of Western knowledge. However, in the 'Turing-time' of the symbol-processing computer, with the alphanumerical machine, this original unity is reestablished, or established again in a new form.

Thus Greek antiquity becomes a past loaded with 'now-time' [*Jetztzeit*], as defined by Walter Benjamin in chapter XIV of his theses 'On the Concept of History.' Furthermore:

> The historical index of images doesn't just say, in fact, that they belong to a specific time; it says above all that they become readable in a specific time. [. . .] Image is that wherein what has been [*das Gewesene*] comes together with the now and, lighting-fast, forms a constellation. [. . .] while the relation of the present [*Gegenwart*] to the past is purely temporal, the relation of what has been [*Gewesene*] to the now is dialectical [. . .]. (Benjamin, 1972–1989: 577f)

HISTORY BY THE HOUR

In the unpublished preface to the *Aufschreibesysteme*, Kittler states 'that an archaeology of basic structuralist assumptions emerges from historical facts. [. . .] For the transposition of philosophical theories into historical findings, the technological vocabulary is the appropriate one' (Kittler 2012: 121). However, this technical vocabulary is not to be understood as something purely technological, but rather as radical (in the sense of root-oriented) media archaeology. Kittler represents a materialism of the history of Being, which in the end has less to do with Hegel and Benjamin and is formulated rather on the basis of Martin Heidegger's critique of time.

A media-archaeological question already presents itself: How to write a media history of the clock, that would question its own form of representation—historiographical narration as information about time—so that clocks would form a rival model of time? With Christiaan Huygens's pendular clock, which elementarizes temporal measurement all the way down to the level of the second, the *Dasein* of physics itself was subjected, through the double-clock experiment of 1655, to a temporality of measurement—a time which is not emphatic history, but rather opens up a world of microtemporal economies of synchronisation (see Pikorsky, 2003).

Friedrich Kittler noted in his *Kulturgeschichte der Kulturwissenschaft* [Cultural History of Cultural Science], that Heidegger in §80 of *Being and Time* (1927)—that is, in the 'clocks' chapter—shifts from fundamental ontological to positivist cultural-historical description. Heidegger's dilemma: 'A history, which is essentially time, intersects with those other histories that themselves traverse the machines of temporal measurement. Clocks are ontic, thus apparatuses subjected to fundamental ontology, which nevertheless bring forth historically different ontologies' (Kittler, 2000a: 235f). Kittler demonstrates that Heidegger (who was after all a former student of mathematics) 'cannot correlate this line from Plato via Aristotle to Hegel with the line from Ptolemy via Kepler to Huygens' (Kittler, 2000a: 235f); in this light, a 'historical media archaeology' turns out to be an oxymoron. That is, media archaeology cannot be fully merged with the model of history. This insight does not result in, for example, a posthistorical aesthetics, but rather in a perception in which the two modes have a common interest: proceeding in time, the thinking-together of the past; that is, absence and time, but also of alternative forms, different levels and various modes of time-writing. Aristotle understood time and number as causally linked—and thereby formulated the puzzle of re/counting [*Er/zählung*], in which the rupture between history and media archaeology already graphically appears. Does clock-time then form the rationale for—in the media archaeological sense—an 'ahistorical "deep time"' rather than a history? (Sconce, 2000: 10). Or can the incisions and discontinuities only be explained as functions of 'differing historical and technological contexts?' (Sconce, 2000: 10). Is clock-time a cultural construction, or is culture for its part shaped by a temporality that is not solely determined by relevant social circumstances?

In his middle period, Kittler saw the epoch of the *posthistoire* being fractured by high-tech media, and previous history therein suspended [*aufgehoben*]—absolutely in the sense of Hegel, who in his time formulated the end of art history for aesthetics. Today Kittler's own urn lies in the Dorotheenstadt Cemetery in Berlin, close to G. W. F. Hegel's grave. The later Kittler, however, reconsiders temporal signs. By this point the *posthistoire* is seen as already beginning in ancient Greece, with the disciplinary breaking apart of the hitherto wondrous unity of phonetic script, mathematics and musical notation within a single symbolic alphabet. From the moment of the dissociation of music and mathematics, there begins a forgetting that recursively carries itself forward [*sich fortschreiben*] as history. Here Kittler follows Heidegger:

> [It is] also symptomatic that Kitter had originally intended the title of the fourth volume to be '[the] Turing galaxy and Heidegger's Enframing'—an ultimately erased reference to Heidegger's philosophy of technics, which would however have had to be reinterpreted: for Heidegger, modern technics (the 'en-framing' [*das 'Ge-stell'*]) was the final phase of the total forgetting of being. (Bayreuther, 2012: 108)

BETWEEN MEDIA ARCHAEOLOGY AND MEDIA HISTORIOGRAPHY

The philosophy of history tends toward narration, and thus evolutionary-historical perspectives acquire a seductive power. Was even Kittler's media archaeology of the historical figure underlain by an ineluctable techno-teleology, a 'negative eschatological force'? (Reck, 1996: 231). Did Kittler, despite all his criticism of classical (media-)historiography, remain caught, in his turn, in the narrative discourse of history, therefore ensnared in history? 'Generally speaking, even media historiographies are grand narratives,' (Mazza, 2001) for they make what has happened [*das Gewordene*] merge into (hi)stories [*Geschichten*], which are then put into circulation—even if 'the literature of the writing system itself becomes historical, and must allow itself to be overtaken by a post-history [*Nachgeschichte*] of the technical media of reproduction' (Mazza, 2001, unpaginated). Genuine media historiographies, however, are no longer simply written archivo-graphically, but rather deposited in technical blueprints, diagrams and source codes. Kittler was aware of this cul-de-sac of classical source-based research [*Quellenforschung*]. The new secret files of power are signal- and datastreams, whose archival sediments barely register as alphabetical writing on paper. History becomes the mode of straightforward differences between observers: 'in this site only flashbacks remain and this means narrations. [. . .] That such narrations cannot replace a history of technics, is obvious' (Kittler, 1986: 4). Technology on the level of its actual operativity escapes in its own micrological temporality the relativizations referred to as historical context.

CINEMATOGRAPHIC MONTAGE IN PLACE OF HISTORICAL NARRATION

As one peers into nonhistorical modes of temporality, horror obscures the view. Before undertaking the epistemological adventure of writing the passage of time and the past in an alternative manner to history, it is therefore usually preferable first of all to (re)write history otherwise. How might this look? In his *Archaeology of Knowledge*, Michel Foucault pleads explicitly for a history that keeps the caesurae in view, and no longer focuses on the obvious continuities, which only serve to stabilise the fiction of the subject. For this reason, Foucault wrests discourse from the law of historical becoming and outlines a series of discontinuous timelessnesses, which follow in sequence like the cinematographic play of fixed images, consecutively fading into one another. Kittler comments in *Grammophon, Film, Typewriter* (1986), in which he wrote his media history from the heart: 'Contemporary theories, like discourse analysis, would be determined by the technological apriori of their media' (Kittler, 1986: 180). Although a movement in time results from this, it is no longer that of history. Indeed, Foucault doesn't explicitly equate historiography with cinematography, yet epistemologically such thinking is only thinkable and writable against the background of a film-technical media culture. With montage, film itself very quickly develops a nonlinear technique (Griffith, Eisenstein), which as time line manipulation subverts the narrative model of history itself. In his talk on the twenty-fifth anniversary of the *Deutsches Museum* in Munich, on 6 May 1928, W. von Dyck invokes an alternative to the archivally maintained minutes of meetings and administrative reports and describes the technical memory of the technological museum:

> One could, in order to be totally modern, [. . .] think about presenting the course of development in the form of a film, and indeed as process seen in slow-motion. Whence the slow maturation of the idea of a technological museum [. . .] would be laid out, the steady struggle for the realisation of the master plan [. . .] More felicitously however, through such a prolonged representation of the scenario, it would perhaps be possible to run the historical film of the development [*Werdegang*] of the museum at an abbreviated tempo, whereby on the other hand we would be made aware of just how rapidly [. . .] the walls were erected. (von Dyck, 1929: 2f)

Where history no longer presents itself to be read in book format (as codex), but rather as images *scrolling* [*abrollen*] before the eyes of the observers (the museum paradigm), it loses its philosophy: 'When the film called history rewinds, it becomes an endless loop' (Kittler, 1986: 12). And so the chrono-technical time-mode of film questions its own classification within so-called media history: "it is arbitrary to say where the development of [. . .] moving pictures began' (Münsterberg, 1916: 3).

SIGNAL-TIME IN PLACE OF SYMBOLIC ORDER: THE NEW ARCHIVE

History as academic discipline is a predominantly text-based, that is, symbol-based science—in contrast to those sciences that (since photography and phonography) have to do with signal processing and thus with the physical traces of the preceding present [*vergangender Gegenwart*] (see Siegert, 1999: 175). With film and sound recording as technical memory, just as with technically encoded script (telegraphy, pulse-code modulation), discourse analysis reaches its limits. Concomitant with the establishment of the modern (on the basis of general alphabetization in schools) is the establishment of its tele-communicational postmodern; the French National Assembly in 1794 decided in the same moment in favour of public school education for everyone and optical telegraphy for military staff. Media as messages, however, disappear beneath their contents like the operations of battle beneath the noise they create—so history is only ever possible on the basis of a deferral: the thematic absence of its writing systems [discourse networks] (Ernst and Kittler, 1992: typescript).

Retentional power, since the time immemorial of alphabetic writing, and conclusively with the Gutenberg epoch, is bought at the price of the radical translation of all contingent worldliness into the symbolic order. Yet nothing is more deconstructive than the symbolic order of the archive itself: 'history being delirious is already a possibility, except that the records to which I have oriented myself are also delirious. Who knows which of the two possibilities causes more trouble?' (Kittler 1984: letter).

REAL TIME AND/OR HISTORY: AESTHETICS OF THE *POST-HISTOIRE*

With Hegel the end of history became thinkable even in a non-eschatological sense. In place of the world spirit in its dialectical self-fulfilment, Kittler introduced the agency of technical media as the fulfilment (or end) of history. From linear historiography via the transformation into cinematographic montage, in the end time becomes a time of discrete media:

> The age of media, in contrast to history—which it puts to an end—runs spasmodically like Turing's ticker-tape. From the Remington via the Turing Machine to microelectronics, from mechanisation via automatisation to the implementation of a writing consisting of figures rather than meaning—it has taken just a century for the age-old monopoly on recording to migrate from writing to an omnipotent electronic circuitry. (Kittler, 1986: 33)

Kittler does not write historically, but as a radical archaeologist of the present—a present whose situation is determined by its Turing-completeness [*Turingmächtigkeit*]. We can observe everywhere the way digital modelling is gradually appropriating every historical object. 'Digitalisation retroactively dissipates from the end of history to all epochs,' suggests Rainer Bayreuther in his critique of history, going on to say, 'one is now obliged to log in to the digital "absolute knowledge as endless loop," and already no longer looks backwards with the Rankeian historical perspective' (Bayreuther, 2012: 108; Kittler, 1986: 8).

This applies especially to the techno-mathematically conceptualised forms of musical existence. It is the privileged alliance of sonic and media-technical implementation in the time channel that also produces macro-historical consequences:

> Music was always the interface between my technical and historical interests. Perhaps for the simple reason that music is ideally understood as simply a variable of time, and was therefore already electrifiable in the early seventies. It was then that I began to build musical electronics. (Kittler 2000b: 117)

The concrete employment of electronically generated noise on the micro-level of contemporary critique results in insight into the ahistorical essence of emphatic time (see Stockhausen, 1957).

> Hence his peculiar interweaving of digital posthistory with the Hölderlinian/Heideggerian talk of the return of the Gods, which seems more convincing to Kittler given that the reflections of Turing and Heidegger were formulated at almost exactly the same moment: in the year 1936.[3] (Bayreuther, 2012: xxx)

'The day corresponds to floundering and error, the long-term to success and achievement' (Johann Wolfgang von Goethe). Media scholars know better than anyone that it is possible to outsmart, and even undermine time; it was with technical media in the first place that a wonderful world of time-axis manipulation became accessible. 'Craftiness', so books tell us, is one of the meanings of the ancient Greek *mechané.* The essence of the technical is nothing simply technical, we learn from an inspiration of Friedrich Kittler in Freiburg. In the end the Gods outsmart the human drama as a technological phenomenon. This is presented to us to be thought not as media history, but as its alternative. Turing-time achieves the total simultaneity of all that was previously historically non-simultaneous:

> All the circulating theories that want to make a distinction between historical and electronic time, as between deferral and simultaneity, are myths. Real Time Analysis means just one thing, that deferral or delay, dead time or history, will be processed quickly enough to be able to pass directly and in timely fashion to the retention of the next time slot. Since the electrical telegraphy of 1840, which, for the very first time, transmitted the alphabet encoded into actual time-characters, one long and one short, effective even when reversed, it has been possible to increase

> the transmission rate (in accordance with Shannon's famous theory) by caching. It is only when the long and short telegraph signals are not sent instantly, but recoded in a way that takes into account their time consumption, that the data rate reaches its optimum. (Kittler, 1993: 201; see also Siegert, 1993)

The temporal dimension of history is accordingly nothing other than the stretched version of that which occurs microtemporally in the transmission process. 'The conceptual opposite of real-time is [. . .] not historical time, but merely a time of simulation, in which it is either impossible or unnecessary to keep pace with the simulated' (Kittler, 1993: 201). Yet history, in contrast to the 'runtime' of signals, is not a physical parameter that can be outwitted by techno-mathematical intelligence, but a symbolic construct.

TECHNOLOGICAL INVARIATIONS? RECURSION IN PLACE OF HISTORY

In the two volumes of his *Hellas*—work on *Music and Mathematics*—Friedrich Kittler has given us the task of thinking temporal processes in terms of recursion. In such a thinking, from every departure there comes a return. 'The return as recursion' is the name of an unrealized (now held in the Kittler archive in Marbach) subsection of Part 1 ('Romans and Christians') of Kittler's partially completed second volume of *Music and Mathematics*, *Roma aeterna.* In computer science, recursion is precisely defined as the reapplication of a processing instruction to a variable that is itself already the (intermediary) result of the same processing instruction. The value of the variable thus changes with each running of the loop; recursion combines repetition and variation in order to bring forth something new (Winkler, 1999: 235). Does this also function as a denial of media history? Staying with the sounding of time, phonography as a recording of signals is, in the manner of a chronic Möbius strip, the technical folding [*Falte*] of ancient Greek gramophony (vocal notation), but as such no longer a historical figure of Western history, rather a structural time relationship (see Ernst, 2006). It then makes a fundamental difference whether the harmony of integer relations (Pythagoras) is discovered on the monochord, or whether dynamic vibration as a form of time becomes mathematically inscribable through that same string. But frequencies undermine the elementarizing gesture of ancient Greece, for it means absolutely nothing to the human ear to explain in this way a pure tone or the composite sound of a single microtemporal oscillation (period). Here we are dealing, rather, with microtemporal events that break with the musical horizon of thought of ancient Greece. If in that context, vowels are written down, they really indicate the musicality of language. In contrast, in digital code, alphanumerics do not in any way comprise a written/graphical *phonē.* Here, at a fundamental level, the physical world meets the symbolic order of cultural technics. However, in Kittler's late work—following his almost Heideggerian turn (the reversion from the technical a priori to the knowledge of ancient Greece)—the figure of recursion returns to the position of historical/dialectic materialism. Recursion is not a Hegelian dialectics, but an updated temporal figure with a Hegelian dimension. Spectral analysis as a perversion of the temporal tones in tabular mathematics causes vibration—following the interlude of analogue phonographic acoustic recording—to assume a numerical existence once again, in a return to alphabet-based epistemology, and thus the ancient linkage between number and sound comes back under a different sign (that of dynamic proportionality). The Möbius strip of media time does not mean development, but intertwining and recursion: 'It comes back to the alphabet, in order to sink it ever deeper: the two sirens into the octave, octaves into polyphony, polyphonies into overtones (harmonics), overtones into Fourier series—and so on and on, all the way to the signal processing of today' (Kittler, 2009: 80). The media-archaeological approach anchored recursion not within human culture as a historical figure, but rather exclusively in the autonomy of electrophysics, logic and mathematics, which it treated as technical media. It is a genuine operativity of hi-tech media that suggests an alternative form of time-writing: algorithmic time, the temporal logic of programming, using loops and conditions. Recursion is an application of a media-induced modelling of the time formerly conceived as historical:

> For this new kind of history writing, there is only one way, one name: recursion. We attend to the return of the same—and indeed do so to the same extent that it is transformed in its historical being. We 'run backwards' in time, from today to the Greeks, but simultaneously also forwards in time, from the very beginning all the way to its recurrence in distorted form. Thus we push the addresses of functions little by little into a stack, which we then poke again. Harmony is always new, and yet [. . .] always the same. This is what references to forwards and backwards ought to suggest. At one moment the threads branch out like a

> fork, at another moment the separated threads intertwine themselves again into a mesh. (Kittler, 2009: 245)

Whether what results is a form of history writing at all, and not, rather, its alternative, remains to be seen. In any case, the current flourishing of interest in the operational temporal figure of recursion is an indication of a new epistemological situation: a discontent with the model of media history which stands for the denial of the technical time of recursion. Thus the recursive interpretation of media-technical modes of time reaches not only backwards, into the past, but always forwards as well. Human culture in its undoubtedly historical development and transformation is continually invoked by a Same belonging to the laws of physics and logic, which underpin all media-technical structures. Yet to think the emphatic time horizon of technical media truly archaeologically does not require that we reduce their *epistēmē* to the status of a history of decay. Media time should, rather, be dealt with as an ongoing reconfiguration of isomorphic challenges, oscillating between theory, theory-driven experimentation, scientific analysis, mathematical modelling and philosophical reflection on all of these repeated attempts to analytically penetrate a media event. When technicians and computer scientists refer to one another in this respect, it is quite evident that this does not take place in historical consciousness, according to the model of the evolution of knowledge, but as an ongoing renegotiation, which can more plausibly be described in terms of the dynamics of an electromagnetic field than as a history-of-knowledge narrative. Understanding media history in such a way means seeing it not as having a philosophical and historiographical form, but rather as consisting in the incessant effort to mandate an operationally and materially implicit knowledge, which repeatedly invokes itself, and accordingly seeks to include itself within the deepest of its own conditions, a formulation that paraphrases Michel Foucault's remarks on the genealogy of science (see Foucault, 1968).

At first glance, this seems to recall G. W. F. Hegel's philosophy of history; the spirit becoming self-conscious in the gallery of world history resembles a recursive function. But the repeated return of former knowledge is ultimately not due to the accumulating linearity of the Western tradition; the laws of physics and mathematics are equally insistent in the cultural unconscious, and always force epochs to fit equi-primordially within their logic, as soon as they allow themselves to become caught up in the demand for technical knowledge. Thus the corresponding experiments inevitably bring about parallel effects—in ancient Greece as in early modernity. Fractals realize this macrotemporal figure of self-similarity microtemporally, though this was only first appreciated on the screen, encapsulated in computer graphics, in contrast to the purely numerical symbolic writing of mathematics.

Recursions do not only befall us as the formative time-figure of computerized music; on the contrary, they also prove to be the *form of time* (see also Kubler, 1962) of musical knowledge in the macrotemporal horizon. The (media-)technically grounded bifurcation, through Aristoxenus and Euclid, of *mathesis* and music—which in the Archaic period of ancient Greece had originally been thought together (see Carlé, dissertation and 2007)—for Friedrich Kittler indicates the doom of the history of Being, in a dimension thus reminiscent of Heidegger's 'oblivion of Being'. But in contrast to Heidegger, here the divisiveness ends with a reconciliation: 'Leonard Euler [. . .] will twine their two meshes together again. [. . .] Europe is a game of recursions which is always already tuning us as the history of Being' (Kittler, 2009: 246). An algorithmic phenomenon here becomes a metonym for the macrotime of musical knowledge. However, mood is not narratable, but merely neuro-physiologically countable.

Recursion is an unhistorical temporal figure for the description of past events. In the sense of a mathematical operation (and in a way that is foundational for the computer), recursion means the recalling of a function through itself. When epistemologically generalized, this leads to an 'approach which makes it possible for completely different times and lines of development to relate to one another, without having to presuppose a world spirit of Hegelian proportions' (see Ofak and Hilgers, 2010: 11; see also Ernst, 2010). At this point my text runs definitively into danger, (mis)using fragments of Kittler's text to support my own current chronopoetics of technical media (see Ernst, 2012). But in fact, Kittler is here the kindred spirit of McLuhan, who configured the law of media in emphatic time no longer in a historical–philosophical, dialectical manner, but in the figure of the tetrad. In an interview with Bruce Powers, he summed this up:

> The intensification of any human process, artifact, or creation will have four simultaneous consequences: it will enhance something, it will cause something to become obsolescent, bring something back, and pushed to the limit flip into an opposite effect. (McLuhan and Powers, 1995: 139. See also McLuhan and McLuhan, 1988)

McLuhan and Kittler part company, however, in their diagnosis of the electronic age. While Kittler did not give up the mathematical, time-underpinning components of Shannon (1948), McLuhan condensed the theory of information into a metaphor for technologies in the historical tradition:

> All Western scientific models of communication are—like the Shannon–Weaver model [of sender-channel-receiver]—linear, sequential and logical as a reflection of the late medieval emphasis on the Greek notion of efficient causality. [. . .] [But] for use in the electric age, a right-brain model of communication is necessary to demonstrate the 'all-at-onceness' character of information moving at the speed of light. (McLuhan and Powers, 1995: 3)

Kittler writes the metamorphoses of harmonic analysis, from Pythagoras to Turing-time, in a continuation of Heidegger, explicitly as history of Being [*Seynsgeschichte*]. In modernity, noises and sounds also allow themselves, when analysed through the powerful mathematical tool of Fourier integrals, 'to be recognised as harmonic. So often, so long ago and so recently, have the two sirens returned with their single harmony, only to sink more and more deeply, all the way into the vibrating core of quarks and superstrings' (Kittler, 2009: 246). Yet it is not a question of recovering a contemplation of an originary insight, but rather, of the simultaneously arising insistence of a sonic knowledge in/of nature itself, which continually calls to the human ear, wants to be heard—and not as the mere function of a historical, thus relative, knowledge. Kittler remains trapped in historical discourse at this point. But perhaps the issue no longer has anything to do with alternative 'media' or 'musical' (both muse-related) historiographies, but with an alternative to historiography itself, of another form of writing (with) time [*Zeit(mit)schrift*].

NOTES

This text was first published in German in Walter Seitter, Michaela Ott and Wetzlar, eds. (2013) TUMULT. Schriften zur Verkehrswissenschaft (Vol. 40: 2012) and Friedrich Kittler. Technik oder Kunst?, Büchse der Pandora: 100–107.

1. See Max Ettlinger, Leibniz als Geschichtsphilosoph (Munich: 1921). This is not simply an allusion to the title of this publication; rather, the significance lies in the fantasy, replicated within it, expressed by Gotthold Wilhelm Leibniz (Apokatastatis panton) of a combinatorial play of signifiers, which would underpin the linearity of alphabetical historiography.

2. Against a putative technological a priori as 'timeless expression', Sconce points to 'a culture's changing social relationship to a historical sequence of technologies' (Sconce, 2000: 10), thus the autonomous time of technical media subjugates the discourse of history, as nothing more than heraldic periodization.

3. In the same year Alan Turing (1932) published his paper 'On Computable Numbers, with an Application to the Entscheidungsproblem', Martin Heidegger gave the lecture 'Hölderlin and the Essence of Poetry'.

BIBLIOGRAPHY

Bayreuther, Rainer. (2012) 'Friedrich Kittlers Bedeutung für die Musikwissenschaft' in *Die Musikforschung* 65: 99–113 (here referring to the page numeration used by Fink Verlag in 2005, before the actual publication of the first volume).

Benjamin, Walter. (1972–1989) *Gesammelte Schriften*, ed. Rolf Tiedemann and Hermann Schweppenhäuser, 7 Bde., Bd. V, 577f. Suhrkamp, Frankfurt am Main.

Carlé, Martin. (dissertation) 'Augmented Phenomenology', Humboldt-Universität zu Berlin, Philosophische Fakultät III.

———. (2007) 'Geschenke der Musen im Streit ihrer Gehörigkeit' in *MusikTheorie. Zeitschrift für Musikwissenschaft*, 4 ('Zur Aktualität des antiken griechischen Wissens von der Musik', ed. Sebastian Klotz): 295–316.

Ernst, Wolfgang. (2005) 'Medienkulturelle Halluzinationen. Das Museum zwischen Gedächtnisort und Wissenssystem' in Thomas Hensel and Andreas Köstler (eds.), *Einführung in die Kunstwissenschaft*. Berlin: Reimer, pp. 95–116.

———. (2006) 'Homer gramm(at)ophon' in Wolfgang Ernst and Friedrich Kittler (eds.), *Die Geburt des Vokalalphabets aus dem Geist der Poesie. Schrift, Zahl und Ton im Medienverbund*. Munich: Fink, pp. 299–314.

———. (2010) 'Der Appell der Medien: Wissensgeschichte und ihr Anderes' in Ofak and von Hilgers (eds.), *Rekursionen. Von Faltungen des Wissens*. Munich: Fink, pp. 178–97.

———. (2012) *Chronopoetik. Zeitweisen und Zeitgaben technischer Medien*. Berlin: Kulturverlag Kadmos.

Ernst, Wolfgang and Friedrich A. Kittler. (1992) 'Editorial: Medias in Re(volution)s', unrealized publication project 'Media–Revolution–History' (typescript).

Foucault, Michel. (1968) 'Réponse au Cercle d'épistemologie' in *Cahiers pour l'Analyse*, No. 9 (special issue on the theme of 'Généalogie des sciences'), Paris.

Kaiser, Gerhard. (2012) (Albert Ludwigs Universität Freiburg, Deutsches Seminar, 31 August 1982), Gutachten zur Habilitationsschrift von Herrn Dr. Friedrich A. Kittler, *Aufschrieibesysteme 1800/1900* (typescript), in *Zeitschrift für Medienwissenschaft* 6(1): 127–33.

Kittler, Friedrich. (1984) Letter to Wolfgang Ernst, Freiburg, 12 March.

———. (1986) *Grammophon, Film, Typewriter*. Brinkmann & Bose.

———. (1993) 'Realtime Analysis und Time Axis Manipulation' in *Draculas Vermächtnis. Technische Schriften*. Leipzig: Reclam, pp. 182–207.

———. (1996) 'Museums on the Digital Frontier' in *The End(s) of the Museum*, ed. Thomas Keenan. Barcelona: Fondació Antoni Tápies, pp. 67–80.

———. (2000a) 'Zwölfte Vorlesung (über Heideggers Kehre)' in *Eine Kulturgeschichte der Kulturwissenschaft*. Munich: Fink, pp. 229–46.

———. (2000b) 'Weil das Sein eine Geschichte hat. Ein Gespräch mit Friedrich Kittler' (interview with Alessandro Barberi) in *Österreichische Zeitschrift für Geschichtswissenschaft* 11(4): 109–23.

———. (2009) *Musik und Mathematik*, Vol. I: Hellas, Part 2: Eros. Munich: Fink.

———. (2012) Kittler, Preface to *Discourse Networks 1800/1900*, date unknown [1982/83], now printed in *Zeitschrift für Medienwissenschaft* 6(1): 117–26.

Kubler, George. (1962) *The Shape of Time: Remarks on the History of Things*. New Haven, CT: Yale University Press.

Latour, Bruno. (1999) *Pandora's Hope*. Cambridge, MA: Harvard University Press.

Mazza, Ethel Matala de. (2001) 'Maupassants Vermächtnis'. Review of Stefan Andriopoulos, *Besessene Körper. Hypnose, Körperschaften und die Erfindung des Kinos* (Munich: Fink, 2000) in IASLonline (published online 16 October 2001); accessed 3 July 2012, at www.iaslonline.lmu.de/index.php?vorgang_id=2269.

McLuhan, Marshall and Eric McLuhan. (1988) *Laws of Media: The New Science*. Toronto: University of Toronto Press.

McLuhan, Marshall and Bruce R. Powers. (1995) *The Global Village: Transformations in World Life and Media in the 21st Century*. Oxford: Oxford University Press.

Münsterberg, Hugo. (1916) *The Photoplay: A Psychological Study*. New York: Appleton.

Ofak, Ana and Philipp von Hilgers, eds. (2010) *Rekursionen. Von Faltungen des Wissens*. Munich: Fink, pp. 7–25.

Pikorsky, Arkady et al. (2003) *Synchronization: A Universal Concept in Non-Linear Sciences*. Cambridge: Cambridge University Press.

Reck, Hans-Ulrich. (1996) 'Inszenierte Imagination: Zu Programmatik und Perspektiven einer historischen Anthropologie der Medien' in Wolfgang Müller-Funk and Hans-Ulrich Reck (eds.), *Inszenierte Imagination. Beiträge zu einer historischen Anthropologie der Medien*. Vienna, pp. 231–44.

Sconce, Jeffrey. (2000) *Haunted Media: Electronic Presence from Telegraphy to Television*. Durham, NC: Duke University Press.

Shannon, Claude E. (1948) 'A Mathematical Theory of Communication' in *Bell System Technical Journal* 27 (July/October): 379–423; 623–56.

Siegert, Bernhard. (1993) *Relais: Geschicke der Literatur als Epoche der Post*. Berlin: Brinkmann & Bose.

———. (1999) 'Das Leben zählt nicht: Natur- und Geisteswissenschaften bei Dilthey aus mediengschichtlicher Sicht' in Claus Pias (ed.), *Medien. Dreizehn Vorträge zur Medienkultur*. Weimar, pp. 161–82.

Stockhausen, Karlheinz. (1957) '. . . wie die Zeit vergeht . . .' in *Die Reihe: Information über serielle Musik*, 3, universal edition (Wien; Zürich; London): 13–42.

Turing, Alan. (1932) 'On Computable Numbers, with an Application to the *Entscheidungsproblem*' in *Proceedings of the London Mathematical Society* 42(2): 230–65.

von Dyck, W. (1929) 'Wege und Ziele des Deutschen Museums'. Berlin (VDI). Deutsches Museum. Abhandlungen und Berichte, Vol. 1.1.

Winkler, Harmut. (1999) 'Rekursion. Über Programmierbarkeit, Wiederholung, Verdichtung und Schema' in *c't*, 9: 234–40.

Chapter Four

The Humming of Machines

To the End of History and Back

Mai Wegener
Translated by Robin Cackett

In 'Dracula's Legacy' Friedrich Kittler quotes Jacques Lacan saying to his seminar participants,

> From now on you are, and to a far greater extent than you can imagine, subjects of gadgets or instruments—from microscopes to radio and television—which will become elements of your being. You cannot now understand the full significance of this; but it is nevertheless part of the scientific discourse, insofar as discourse is something that determines a form of social cohesion. (Kittler, 1997: 53; Lacan, 1999: 82)

This remark by Lacan in his seminar *Encore* from 1973 always pleased Kittler, he quoted it every so often. That we are today subjects of—and that is, as Kittler instantly makes clear, also subjected to—gadgets or instruments—and that through the course of history we have always been subjects of the appliances produced or built at each time, but much more so today—this is one of Kittler's fundamental tenets. And Lacan, at least, had been observant of this fact. Both agree on not conceiving of appliances and machines as tools made by man as a means to aid him or her, as an extension of his or her possibilities and evils; indeed neither of them takes up a human point of view at all, both take their point of departure outside the human being: be it in language (as Lacan did) or in specific machines or media (as Kittler did) to the effects of which each human being is singularly subjected. Nevertheless, Kittler was passionately interested in these instruments and gadgets, and on their basis created his theory of the media. One might even say that Kittler passionately subjected himself to selected instruments. Again and again he submitted himself to the hardware and the programming of synthesizers and personal computers, subjugated himself to their laws and listened to their ways of functioning. It was only logical to include this aspect of Kittler's work in the publication of his collected works as is now being done. Lacan, on the other hand, showed little interest in specific machines. In his lecture 'Psychoanalysis and cybernetics, or on the nature of language' from 1955, Lacan stated,

> I'll tell you right away. I won't be talking about those varieties of cybernetics which are more or less fashionable, nor will I be talking about the big or the little machines, I won't be calling them by their names. I won't be telling you about the wonders they accomplish. In what way could all of that be of interest to us? . . . Our concern will be to find an axis by means of which some light will be shed on a part of the signification of [psychoanalysis and cybernetics]. That axis is none other than language. (Lacan, 1988: 295)

For Lacan, the 'cybernetic machines'—the common term for such appliances and various forms of machinery because until the 1970s the word 'computer' was rarely used—offered a possibility to understand how language was constructed. 'From the point of view of language, the machines are humming new tunes to us', he says. They are humming that they are made of language. For every machine can be described as an 'articulation', that is, as a chain and substitution of parts. 'The most complicated machines are made only of words [*paroles*]' (Lacan, 1988: 47). On the basis of cybernetics he could even go a step further and discover the fundamental linguistic alternation of presence and absence even within the machines. He states that 'every machine can be reduced to a series of relays, which simply consist of *plus* and *minus*', and adds: 'Everything in the symbolic order can be represented with the help of such a succession.' This, in short, is Lacan's theory of machinery. 'The symbolic world is the world of the machine' (Lacan, 1988: 47). In 1989 Friedrich Kittler made this formulation of Lacan's the title of one of his articles (Kittler, 1997: 130–46) and he had already quoted it ten years earlier in a beautiful short text, which is relatively little known and which was written before his opus magnum *Aufschreibesysteme [Discourse networks]*: 'Lullaby of Birdland' (Kittler, 1979; 15). The sentence belongs to the basic inventory of his media theory. I am not so sure, however, whether it meant quite the same for him as it did for Lacan . . . it certainly didn't lead them into the same direction. In the following I would like to pursue the *drive* this sentence unfolded with Kittler.

I would like to make clear that the distinct presence of Lacan in this chapter is due to my personal approach and focus. I came to Kittler because I found his reading of Lacan excitingly provocative. I don't wish to throw both into the same basket or even represent Kittler as a clandestine Lacanian. Kittler never had an easy relation with psychoanalysis, not even Lacanian psychoanalysis. There was vying, philandering and challenging, but there was no truce. I am interested here in a tension, a kind of *drive* that I perceive in Kittler's texts on media theory. My only claim is that there are indeed some points of crossover on which I may rest my case.

When Friedrich Kittler came to Humboldt University in Berlin in 1993 the historical emergence of computers and their logical predecessor, Alan Turing's universal machine, was at the centre of his concerns. It was quite clear to him—not only to him, but with him it received special emphasis—that this was an epochal break, something really fundamentally new. There was a sense of new beginnings at the department and a general ambition to theorize this break, in which we now find ourselves, to think through both its consequences and what had paved its way. Kittler's obsession was highly contagious. The hypothesis of the disappearance of script/writing was circulating at the time. The emergence of the new media was characterized by the waning of writing. I don't remember how this hypothesis came about. It strongly worried me at the time and I remember that Kittler hardly ever has disputed it orally. It almost seemed to me that he liked the irritation it caused. Ironically in writing, however, he took a rather different stance. Ever since computers had become real, he said, 'a new epoch has dawned for scripts that will multiply their power to unheard-of dimensions' (Kittler, 1998: 19). This is quite the opposite of disappearance. Kittler didn't claim that writing was in decline, but he insisted that ever since computers had become real something very fundamental had happened to writing. He pinpointed this break and alarmingly noted: 'As one knows without saying, we do not write anymore' (Kittler, 1997:

147), writing (again ironically) in order to say that from now on machines would do all the writing and reading. Due to the emergence of this new writing, which circulates as a formal script at the basis of every computer, writing has now been radically 'uncoupled' from the possibility of pronunciation and from the field of meaning (Kittler, 1998: 11). I once tentatively called these processes the 'ex-carnation of the symbolic' (Wegener, 2004: 59). Kittler in this context explicitly insisted on the word 'writing' and emphasized it would be much more appropriate to speak of 'programming scripts' rather than 'programming languages' (Kittler, 1998: 19).

This emphasis wasn't a passing fancy but a red thread running through his media theory. Much later, after his Greek turn, Kittler explicitly emphasized that

> the most fundamental and elementary of all media, the most elementary of all cultural technologies is writing. This is so because our mother *tongue*, our *spoken* language is no medium but our true house of being. But writing is where mediality begins, so to speak. (Kittler, 2012: 127)

This was his wording in a seminar session in summer 2010, the transcript of which has recently been published (2012). Writing, as I have said before, in the course of history has undergone crucial changes. In the twentieth century, it was stripped bare of imaginary layers of meaning in order to get down to its structure and have it run through machines.

> What runs within the machines is a writing before and after all writing, a writing that gets immediately [*umstandslos*] short-circuited with the crystalline qualities of certain chemical elements like silicon and with the genetic codes of any kind of organism like Homo sapiens. (Kittler, 1998: 21)

It is a writing with imperative characteristics and direct effects; matter is subjected to it 'immediately' *umstandslos*, as Kittler says, and by using the term 'short circuit' he evokes the image of a discharge of sparks and of blown fuses.

To jump from programming languages to the DNA is one of those Kittlerian promptings that already point to the *drive* developing in his text. I will return to it, but for now note that the direct effect of writing on bodies had already preoccupied Kittler much earlier, long before the advent of the computer and long before his discovery of Greece. In his early article on 'authorship and love', which begins by spelling out the break between Dante's *Divine Comedy*, where reading aims at the body, and Goethe's *Werther*, where it addresses the soul, Kittler already spoke of 'the violence books have over bodies' (Kittler, 1980: 144). Again and again in his texts we are confronted with the materiality of writing, a pleasure in literalness: in the 'great Lalula' (Kittler, 1990: 40), in the stupidity of the signifier (Lacan, 1999: 12), in entropy and random noise, in the effects the enjoyment of writing has on a particular body. He even harked back to a language that predates writing, back into the vestibule of media technology, so to speak: back to the voice. For the voice too 'has effects . . . on levels affecting the speechless body' (Kittler, 1979: 15). In *Lullaby of Birdland*, that beautiful early essay to which I referred before, he deals with the voice of 'mother nursery rhyme', whose 'parameters' are the '*melos*, sound, rhythm of breathing' (1979: 15). At and before the threshold of writing, 'breath and voice are the real of language' (1979: 7). There is a group of voices, especially female voices, meandering through Kittler's texts, but they are not only maternal, not always lulling to sleep, they rarely prove to be harmless. Just think of the Sirens!

To return to Kittler's essay 'The World of the Symbolic—A World of the Machine', in order to trace the *drive* developing in this text I would like to jump to its conclusion. In the final sentence of this paper everything is present, all of Kittler's subjects are brought together: the state of war or between wars, machines, language, music and sex. The final sentence reads as follows:

> Thus, according to Lacan's most concise statement on Aesthetics, there remain only three things for subjects who do not speak any formal languages: dance, jazz and libido. At least for an inter-war period. (Kittler, 1997: 146)

We are all 'subjects who do not speak a formal language', because no subject ever speaks a formal language for the simple reason that formal languages are processed rather than spoken (even seminars on programming, as Kittler used to hold them, don't produce such subjects). Human beings therefore are left with the threesome of jazz, dance, libido, and we cannot be sure whether this is a pitiable rest left over for humans by the machines or whether it is a triumph, a feast of non-machines over the exact and stupid rule of a 'universal programmability' (144) completely devoid of pleasure. This is the ambiguity at which the final sentence aims. Everything 'human' takes place within the shadow cast by the rule of formal languages or machines marking the end of history.

Indeed, there is a Hegelian undercurrent here and it becomes all the more obvious as we follow Kittler's reference to Lacan. The reference deals with Hegel's idea of the conclusion or end of history in the form of absolute knowledge incarnated in fully completed discourse, that is in a discourse that has reached agreement with itself and which thus basically renders all further speech superfluous (Lacan, 1988: 72). This discourse is located on the side of the masters, it functions as the 'sceptre and property of those who know' (71). Nothing implies that absolute knowledge is for everybody. With Lacan we read:

> When the scientists [*las savants*] [. . .] succeed in bringing human discourse to a close, they are in possession of it, and those who don't have it have nothing left but to turn to jazz, to dance, to entertain themselves, the good fellows, the nice guys, the libidinal types [*les braves, les gentiles, les libidineux*]. That is what I call elaborated mastery (*maîtrise élaborée*). (Lacan, 1988: 72)

This precisely is the sentence Kittler alludes to in his concluding statement. To those excluded from absolute knowledge—or to speak with Kittler: who do not speak a formal language—there is nothing left but jazz, dance, agreeable (*brave*) libidinal entertainments. The reading of Hegel indirectly alluded to here by Kittler via Lacan is, of course, a dissected one. Lacan had borrowed from Hegel the idea of fundamental alienation without following the World Spirit all the way to the end of history. According to Lacan, Hegel had shown 'that the reality of everything human, if one can say so, is in the being of the other' (72). But Lacan cancelled the sublation (*Aufhebung*) of alienation that Hegel had aimed at. While for Hegel this alienation or discord, which he unfolded as a relation between master and slave, was resolved at the end of history, Lacan's reading remains completely unreconciled. For him, there is no reason to suppose that power relations should dissipate. According to Lacan the above scene can be further developed following the logic of master and slave:

> Think how little effect the elaborated discourse will have on those who are busy with jazz at the corner café. And how much the masters will be aching to go and join them. While conversely, the others will consider

> themselves wretches, nobodies and will think—*how happy is the master in enjoying being master?*—whereas, of course, he will be completely frustrated. (Lacan, 1988: 72)

The masters regard their power curtailed by the amused little crowd, while the little crowd in turn imagines an overwhelming enjoyment on the part of masters—deprivation both here and there. Kittler again takes up this ambiguity and lack of reconciliation: One doesn't know which part carries 'true' victory meaning satisfaction; the logic of the machine or the dancing subjects. In one point, however, Kittler's vision is unambiguous: The victory of power will be with the machines.

The dissection of Hegel and the specific emphases that lie at the bottom of this train of thought, had of course been spelled out by Alexandre Kojève, whose echo can be heard here in the Lacan quotation that forms the substance of Kittler's concluding sentence in 'The World of the Symbolic' (1997). I would therefore like to invite you to yet another short detour.

It was Kojève who made the relation between master and slave the centre of his interpretation of Hegel and who at the same time foregrounded a definition of the 'I' as desire. For Lacan, who listened to Kojève's legendary Hegel lectures in Paris (1933-1939) this reading of Hegel was pertinent. I don't wish to insist on this only too well-known Kojève, except maybe to recall his formulation that human desire is not directed towards a thing but towards another desire—a formulation famously rephrased by Lacan as: *The desire is always the desire of the Other.* Which again can be related to the scenario of master discourse and slave jazz that I have just described. What I would like to stress here is another side of Kojève, namely his conviction that the end of history already had broken. It is Kojève who, as you will see, lies at the source of *jazz, dance, libido*. In a couple of shorter texts—footnotes, book reviews, interviews—Kojève was more precise about his diagnosis of the imminence of the end of history. There is one text in particular which is overwhelmingly comical—and whose comical element in my opinion can be traced right down to Kittler's final sentence. The text I am referring to combines the unreserved concreteness and verve of Kojève's reading of Hegel with his friend Raymond Queneau's surreal humour and sense of the absurd.

Kojève in this delightful little text reviews three novels by Queneau that he certifies to be at very much of the moment: they grasp the world as it is after the end of history. These novels are: *Pierrot mon ami* (1942), *Loin de Rueil* (1945) and *Le Dimanche de la Vie* (1952). 'Le dimanche de la vie' (The Sunday of Life) is a quote from Hegel and a metaphor for the world after the end of history. The protagonists in Queneau's world move wisely but their wisdom may easily be overlooked because the way these heroes pass through their trivial everyday world always borders on the ridiculous, as if they were absurd clowns or, to use Kojève's expression, '*voyous désoeuvrés*' (idle rogues/lazy rascals) (Kojève, 2007: 15), characters like the antimilitarist soldier Bru, who at one time gives way to his ardent desire to visit the battlefield of Jena in Germany and who, at the end of the novel, may not be enjoying jazz at the corner café but has found his own way of 'immediately getting in touch with concrete sensual reality' (24) by helping three young girls with climbing through a window. Kojève writes, 'Certainly the Sabbath of humankind . . . may seem unglamorous and banal, not to say ridiculous. But ridiculousness only kills those who really want to be killed' (25). The quiet happiness of these characters, whose satisfaction is as complete as it is completely conscious, which is what turns them into wise people (and serves the pleasure of everyone, concerned readers included)—the happiness of these characters according to Kojève should be 'faced without any prejudice, that is as a philosopher' (25). 'In short, if the new and, since it emerged from the last war, last world is the world of Queneau's novels, one may, I think, say without irony, that it is "*brave*". Or even "brave" in English' (25). In English, however, we are only a very short step away from Huxley's *Brave New World*, and thus the short French word '*brave*', which surfaced in Lacan's sentence and disappeared again in Kittler's, is subject to an enormous, even monstrous oscillation.

The (idle) inactivity of Queneau's main characters is, of course, essential since it bears witness to the impossibility of action after the end of history, to the end of action in a strong sense, as a negation of what is given. The essential quality of man has thus disappeared and, in a strictly philosophical sense (but different from Foucault), man himself is disappearing. Kojève registers this disappearance in a crucial footnote added to the published edition of his lectures on Hegel, which was of course edited by Queneau. Here is the crucial passage of this footnote:

> The disappearance of Man at the end of History, therefore, is no cosmic catastrophe: the natural World remains what it has been for all eternity.

> And therefore, it is not a biological catastrophe either: Man remains alive as animal in *harmony* with Nature or given Being. What disappears is Man properly so-called—that is, Action negating the given, and Error, or in general, the Subject *opposed* to the Object. (Kojève, 1989: 158–59)

Consequently there are no revolutions any more, no wars, but also no philosophy—no real, that is negating actions and no reflection on them. For man, who was defined by such negation, this new state, in which he or she remains identical with him- or herself, can only result in boredom

> Man, who—like a thing, like an animal, like an angel—is identical with him- or herself, doesn't negate, doesn't negate him- or herself, i.e., he or she is not active but bored. And only man can be bored. (Kojève, after the middle of the second chapter: 48-89. 1989)

This however is said in a completely different context, at an entirely different place in his lectures. In the aforementioned footnote Kojève rather seems to be bent on pursuing nature and happiness: 'But all the rest Everything else, however, [that is: everything but war and philosophy—M.W.] can be preserved indefinitely: art, love, play etc., etc., in short everything that makes Man *happy*' (Kojève, 1989: 159). This is Kojève's version of *jazz, dance, libido.* And I think it was the model for Lacan, who blended it with a shot of Queneau and stripped the three of all philosophy. This version again is taken up by Kittler.

Now, the passage I quoted is also rather disturbing, for isn't it contradictory to first have man disappear and then look forward to what makes man happy? And shall we attribute *art, love* and *play* to man because they 'make him/her happy' or shall we rather attribute it to the animal that man finally has turned into? Are *jazz, dance, libido* characteristic of animals? (For after all Kojève claims: 'In man there is one percent humanity, the rest is animal' Kojève, 2007a: 65.) Kojève's claim about happiness quite obviously remains incongruous. He notices this incongruity later and in 1959 he adds a new footnote—it is the well-known footnote to the footnote in the second edition of his lectures after his journey to Japan. I only quote the passage that refers directly to the above.

> One cannot say that all this 'makes Man *happy*'. One would have to say that post-historical animals of the species *Homo sapiens* (which will

> live amidst abundance and complete security) will be *content* as a result of their artistic, erotic and playful behavior, inasmuch as, by definition, they will be contended with it. (Kojève, 1989: 159)

Kojève here distances himself from the happy human animal and gets a little closer to boredom, which, by the way, also plays a significant role in Queneau's novels, except that its role there is funny enough to keep us entertained while dealing with it.

To return to Kittler after this excursion to Kojève. *Jazz, dance, libido*—Lacan's or rather (as we now have seen) Kojève's 'concise statement on Aesthetics', meaning man in post-history—is admittedly rather free of pathos. Kittler here takes a completely this-worldly stance, he positions himself as standing on the side of his cheerful surrealist and Oulipo friends while others 'wanted to spend their Sundays in more sacred ways. In the forest, in secrecy, always in the face of death', as Andreas Hiepko states with regard to Georges Bataille (Hiepko, 2007: 81). But Kittler's sentence is not without pathos after all, it is just located at a different place. To quote it again: 'there remain only three things for subjects who do not speak any formal language: dance, jazz and libido. At least for an inter-war period' (Kittler, 1997: 146). The pathos here lies in the threat, the scenario of the end of time or, more precisely, in the vision of a closure. Our excursion has brought to light that the formulation is based on an interpretation of Hegel that is genuinely Kittler's. As if Kittler had said: Today the only possibility to interpret the figure of *absolute knowledge* that Hegel has brought into the world is to combine it with precisely that kind of history that Hegel wasn't interested in at all: the history of machines. If there is anything that might realize *absolute knowledge* it will be the rule of formal languages. What Hegel called 'absolute knowledge' would be a knowledge that, in Kittlerian terms, could be known neither by any subject nor by the 'world spirit' (who, totally superfluous by now, wouldn't even have to be exorcised). Such knowledge, deeply incorporated in machines, according to an idea Hegel couldn't possibly have entertained would be functioning rather than meaning.

However, Kittler doesn't present this conclusion as an interpretation of Hegel—but as a vision of the world to come. Before arriving at his final sentence he talks about machines outdoing man in future competition, in gambling and fighting his or her wars with automatically directed weapons. It is Kittler who sees the end of history coming here.

One might object that I am overemphasizing this particular sentence. But in my opinion sentences that speak to us cannot be taken seriously enough. Furthermore I discovered to my great surprise how many of the 'technical writings' Kittler had gathered in his anthology *Draculas Vermächtnis* (Dracula's Legacy) conclude with such a vision (Kittler, 1993). I shall give you three such endings. The essay 'On the Take-Off of Operators' (written in 1990) ends as its title already suggests with the statement that 'Alan Turing, no sooner than he had gotten the first computer running, delivered the oracle that we should already now prepare ourselves for the take-over of machines' (1993: 160). 'Protected Mode' (written in 1991) concludes, 'Hugo von Hofmannsthal once ascribed the ability to read "what has never been written" to the "wonderful being" called Man. Similar crypto-analyses must become universal and mechanical in the chaos of codes that begins with the world-historical dismissal of everyday languages in favour of a universal discreet machine' (Kittler, 1997: 168). And finally, 'Dracula's Legacy' (1982), the essay that gives the volume its name, ends with the warning 'in any event the dead tyrant Dracula has left a legacy, the full implication of which you are not yet able to grasp: that from now on you are subjects to gadgets and instruments of mechanical discourse processing' (Kittler, 1997: 84). You will have recognized the Lacan quote here. To it Kittler adds a last sentence, 'I turn off the hum of the office machine, lift my eyes and see in the fog over the bay, the Golden Gate Bridge, our hyper-realistic future.' The writer in this very last sentence significantly doesn't turn off the office machine itself but its *humming*. It occurs to me that, yes indeed, we have ceased to be able to turn off the machines long ago. Kittler's plea was that rather than suppress or turn off their humming we should listen to it and try to hear 'where the journey is going'. That's what he stood for.

At the very end, then, he presents us with his vision of 'our hyperreal future'. There is (and this is what I wanted to show) a *drive*, a push towards something, be it closure or escalation, in the face of which every reader has to decide how far he or she can go along. The eschatological perspective towards the end of history, be it in master-slave-mode or machine-man-mode, was Kittler's *spleen*. And sometimes I think, it was so much so that in the end there was nothing left for him but to make a radical turn back towards history, to the Greece of beginnings. To mathematics, lyre and libido.

BIBLIOGRAPHY

Hiepko, Andreas. (2007) 'Postscriptum' in *Überlebensformen*, ed. Andreas Hiepko. Berlin: Merve, pp. 76–81.

Kittler, Friedrich. (1979) 'Lullaby of Birdland' in *Der Wunderblock* 3. Berlin, pp. 5–19. (http://www.freud-lacan-berlin.de/res/Wunderblock/Wunderblock_Nr3.pdf).

———. (1980) 'Autorschaft und Liebe' in Kittler (ed.) *Austreibung des Geistes aus den Geisteswissenschaften*. Munich; Wien; Zurich: Schöningh, pp. 142–173.

———. (1990) *Discourse Networks 1800/1900*. Stanford, CA: Stanford University Press.

———. (1993) *Draculas Vermächtnis*. Leipzig.

———. (1997) *Literature, Media, Information Systems: Essays*, edited and introduced by John Johnston. London: G&B Arts.

———. (1998) *Daten Zahlen Codes*. Leipzig: Institut für Buchkunst.

———. (2012) 'Götter und Schriften rund ums Mittelmeer', transcript of a seminar session, summer term 2010, published in TUMULT 40: *Friedrich Kittler. Technik oder Kunst?* Wetzler, pp. 127–138.

Kojève, Alexandre. (1975) *Hegel. Eine Vegegenwärtigung seines Denkens. Kommentar zur Phänomenologie des Geistes*. Translated by Iring Fetscher, Gerhard Lehmbruch, Frankfurt a.M.

———. (1989) *Introduction to the Reading of Hegel: Lectures on the Phenomenology of Spirit*, ed. Allan Bloom. Ithaca, NY: Cornell University Press.

———. (2007) 'Die Romane der Weisheit' (1952) in *Überlebensformen*, ed. Andreas Hiepko. Berlin: Merve, pp. 7–26.

———. (2007a) 'Philosophen interessieren mich nicht, ich suche Weise. Alexandre Kojeve im Gespräch mit Gilles Lapouge (1968) in *Überlebensformen*, ed. Andreas Hiepko. Berlin: Merve, pp. 58–75.

Lacan, Jacques. (1988) *The Seminar of Jacques Lacan: Book II: The Ego in Freud's Theory and in the Technique of Psychoanalysis*, trans. John Forrester. Cambridge: Cambridge University Press.

———. (1999) *Encore*: Seminar XX, trans. Bruce Fink. New York: Norton.

Wegener, Mai. (2004) *Neuronen und Neurosen. Der psychische Apparat bei Freud und Lacan. Ein historisch-theoretischer Versuch zu Freuds Entwurf von 1895*. München: Fink.

Chapter Five

Media After Media

Bernhard Siegert

MOON OR FINGER

To give an example of the denunciatory attitude of critical thought, Bruno Latour in his book *On the Modern Cult of the Factish Gods* (2011) quotes a Chinese proverb: 'When a wise man points to the moon, the fool looks at the finger' (Latour, 2011: 42). It appears to me that this proverb resonates perfectly with an anecdote Friedrich Kittler once told about Niklas Luhmann and himself. Riding together in a taxi from some airport Kittler tried to explain to Luhmann that in contrast to social systems, switching circuits cannot exist without input and output. 'Herr Kittler', Luhmann answered, 'it was like that already in Babylonia. A messenger rides through the city gate. Some (like me) ask, what kind of message he brings. Others (like you) ask what kind of horse he rides' (Kittler, 2004b: 97).

Friedrich Kittler and others (including me) took the fool's side. The wise guys know that it is not the finger or the horse which is the message, but that their role is just to act as a medium which lets us recognize or receive the relevant object, be it the moon or be it information. Not that fools are uninterested in the moon—they are in fact a little bit too much interested in the moon (or why else do you call them lunatics?)—but it is characteristic of this kind of foolish thinking, that it has a problem accepting a notion of media or mediators (to use the term which is more common in Latourese) that ascribes them the role of humble servants that assist a subject to do what he or she wants to do but have no agency of their own. Well, the lunatics say, media like nature in Heraclitus love to conceal themselves, but that does not mean that they have no agency, on the contrary: Their foreclosure allows them to rule and make those who are subjected to their rule believe that they are autonomously acting, perceiving and thinking systems. But what is more: The fools do not even believe that, on a closer look, it was possible to distinguish properly between the finger and the moon or the horse and the message.[1]

Luhmann's answer only prompted Kittler to tell him how, in the case of systems theory, the horse was part of the message: That systems theory emerged from digital electronic machines, the feedback loops of which granted the possibility for a design of a general science called cybernetics after the Second World War, which, after it had been stripped off its embeddedness in material switching circuits and bodies, could acquire the dignity of a sociological theory or even philosophy.

Kittler was always a genealogist in the Nietzschean sense because he firmly believed that discovering the mean origins of some highly valued concept would change that concept in a fundamental way. Kittler's obsession therefore is more appropriately called media genealogy than media archaeology, for it is 'nothing less than a hardware-based reboot of Nietzsche's genealogical dismantling of all our cherished historiographical conventions'.[2] He clearly expected Luhmann to dump his whole concept of social systems, and he could not understand why Luhmann didn't do so.

'GERMAN MEDIA THEORY' SINCE THE EIGHTIES

As Geoffrey Winthrop-Young has pointed out, 'German media theory' is an observer construct from non–German-speaking countries. This applies first of all to the translation of a piratical use of the concept of media into a *theory of media* which in return then gave rise to the puzzled question of what that theory actually was.

What emerged in the 1980s and is now called German media theory or New German media theory, was never able to give itself an appropriate name. It definitely wasn't 'media theory'. One of the early candidates was 'media analysis' (*Medienanalyse*), a term designed to indicate a paradigmatic replacement of both psychoanalysis and discourse analysis (thus affirming both an indebtedness to and a technologically informed distancing from Lacan and Foucault)—but it just didn't work.

The 'soon-to-be-brand-named intellectual product' (Winthrop-Young) was not primarily concerned with the theory or history of individual media. This was already the province of individual disciplines such as film studies, television studies, computer science, radio research, and so on. Rather, it strove toward histories of the mind, soul and senses removed from the grasp of literary studies, philosophy and psychoanalysis and thus ready for transfer to a different domain: media. But because *media* were less of a focus than a change of the frame of reference for the traditional objects of the humanities—to quote Kittler's infamous words, it was a matter of 'expelling the spirit from the humanities'—the traditional objects of research that defined communication studies (e.g., press, film, television, radio) were never of great interest. Much like crew members of British ships of the line in the seventeenth century who deserted their ships only to board them again as pirates, media analysis deserted literary studies to board them again and replace the emphasis on authors or styles with a sustained attention to inconspicuous technologies of knowledge such as index cards, writing tools, typewriters, discourse operators (such as quotation marks), pedagogical media such as the blackboard, media like phonographs or stereo sound technology, or disciplining techniques like alphabetization. These media, symbolic operators and drill practices, were located at the base of intellectual and cultural shifts. As indicated by Hans Ulrich Gumbrecht's famous catchphrase of 'the materialities of communication', this changing of the humanities' frame of reference aimed to replace the hegemony of understanding, which inevitably tied meaning to a variant of subjectivity or self-presence, with power constellations or military couplings of technologies and bodies as the base and abyss of meaning (see Gumbrecht, 1988: 919; Gumbrecht, 1994: 399).

Therefore Kittler was never much interested in stories that told the history of such technologies for their own sake (like for instance in Science and Technology Studies [STS]). The genealogist is interested in the history of stereo sound—to give an example—only inasmuch as its invention could be traced back to the guiding of German bomber pilots by the means of radio beams during the Second World War. The ears of those who listen to rock music do not experience a sound which reproduces the spatiality of natural hearing but they experience that it is the implementation of command and control which disposes of the sense of hearing.

Kittler had always been a codebreaker. The fundamental drive behind his analyses had always been the basic assumption that the fictionality of literary characters, or the generality of philosophical concepts, was a mere trick to conceal a real historical person, or some power relation. Behind the masks of humanity, truth, the spirit you have to discover what in Kittler-German was called 'Klartext' (a term from cryptology), the 'clear text' of power relations and the materialities of media, which always already determine the situation, in which human beings are able to write, to love, to know, to forget. Kittler's method of knowledge was not interpetation but to present some kind of document from the archives of media history, history of mathematics or military history, and to demonstrate that and how the first text could be mapped onto the second.

The distinctive feature of this kind of knowledge, which is acquired not without a considerable pinch of critical paranoia, is the irreducible 'onticity' (if there is such a word) or facticity or worldliness of the transcendental. One could call it a materialistic transcendentalism or an ontified ontology. It is a knowledge which resolutely pitted *haecceitas* against *quidditas*, if you allow me to use these scholastic terms. It is a knowledge which intended at all times to protect the concrete from the generalities, the irreducible singularities from the universals.

THE PAST OF THE MEDIA

In one respect Kittler always remained a literary scholar if not a philologist: media basically were operations of writing and reading—including the writing and reading of numbers and analogue data. The talk of mass media or the very notion of it was politics in the sense that it served only to deceive the people about what was really going on, which are the histories of the signifier and the fate of the humans whose existence, according to Lacan, is moored to the fate of the signifier. Any approach to communication that places media within the so-called public sphere, will systematically misconstrue the abyss of power relations in and from which media operate. Against the 'communicative reason' as an alleged *telos* of mass media, and against the technophobe obsession with semantic depth, the partisans of the signifier unmoored from meaning and reference turned toward the history of communication engineering that had been blocked out by humanist historiography.

But this media analysis always already operated across a historical abyss which separated media technology from the genealogists who deciphered their secret agency in the history of literature, or philosophy, or anthropology, or art or whatever. According to Kittler something happened in the history of writing and reading and that is the emergence of inscriptions which do not only process human writing but are able to write and read by themselves.

To quote from the beginning of *Gramophone, Film, Typewriter*:

> [O]nce formerly distinct data flows [are turned] into standardized series of digitized numbers, any medium can be translated into any other. With numbers, everything goes. Modulation, transformation, synchronization; delay, storage, transportation; scrambling, scanning, mapping—a total media link on a digital base *will erase the very concept of medium.* Instead of wiring people and technologies, absolute knowledge will run as an endless loop. (Kittler, 1997: 2–3)

Since the basic notion of distinct media in the plural became questionable, the ontological status of media in the present became that of a simulation which had the only function to attach human beings to machines. The only thing that counts, Kittler wrote twenty years ago, is the implosion of a writing scene which otherwise would probably still be called, like in Hegel's idealism, the World Spirit (*Weltgeist*) (Kittler, 1997). With the miniaturization of all signifiers to the size of molecules the act of writing itself disappeared.

In an article on media of communication, Kittler drew up an even bolder design of how the computer came to mean the end of media history. First step: Convert communication systems into information systems. Because they do not only control the transmission of information but also the transportation of people and goods, communication systems involve a large spectrum of different media, from streets to language, as you can read in McLuhan's *Understanding Media.* But nevertheless communication systems can be reduced to information systems. It's easy (according to Kittler): First, information means news, and news is nothing but commands (according to the etymology of the German word for news, which is '*Nachrichten*' which literally means *danach richten*, i.e., to comply with something). Second, people, according to Niklas Luhmann, are nothing but addresses 'that enable the calculation of more communication'. Goods finally are, according to Marcel Mauss and Claude Lévi-Strauss, nothing but data in a system of exchanges between people. Now, since data give rise to the operation of recording, addresses give rise to the operation of transmission, and commands give rise to the operation of processing, every system of communication that consists of these three operations can be analyzed as a system of information. Second step: There is a history of communications media only because and only as long as these operations are *not yet* implemented in physical machines. To quote Kittler again, 'The history of these technologies comes to an end after machines not only took over the transmission *between* addresses and *of* addresses, and the storage of data, but also the processing of commands' (Kittler, 1993: 170).

The decisive historical data of this story are: (A) In his paper on 'Computable Numbers' from 1936 Alan Turing invented, first, a theoretical machine which is able to write, read and erase zeros and ones; he showed, second, that the description of such a machine could be transformed into a finite number, so that it could be read by another Turing machine; and third, proved that there is a universal machine which is able to simulate all other machines as long as these machines or programs are finite, so that the Universal Turing Machine (UTM) simulating them would come to a halt. (B) Claude Shannon's mathematical theory of communication from the 1940s proved that it was possible to scan any kind of analogue data and convert them into digital values, with an error rate, which could be made arbitrarily small. (C) With pulse code modulation—PCM—Shannon, Oliver and Pierce invented the engineering solution by which digitization could be technologically implemented (see Oliver, Pierce and Shannon, 1948). In Lacanian terms the consequence of Turing's and Shannon's accomplishments was that the Symbolic could become co-extensive with the Real, since the real—in the sense of real numbers—now could be turned into computable numbers. This is what has been called the 'physical Church-Turing hypothesis': In its bold version it claims that any physical process—anything doable by a physical system—is computable by a Turing machine (see Piccinini, 2011; for a critique of the physical Church-Turing hypothesis see Hasslacher, 1988: 420). Or in other words, the analogue world could be computed by Turing's Universal Discrete Machine and thus became part of the digital world, the world of the symbolic. If people think they still write and read, this is, according to Kittler, only a software effect. Writing—he wrote—is an apparently infinite chain of translations, which link the command codes, the extension of which is yet a hardware configuration, via assembler and the programming languages, to the natural language of the users.

After writing and reading had bid farewell to the humans these were kept as domestic animals in a huge bubble of the Imaginary called the Internet or, even worse, social media. In Kittler's thinking the term 'social media' could only be an empty tautology after the very concept of the medium had been erased: The concealment of the media led as a consequence to a software explosion which some people still confuse with the social.

What then are Media after the Media? First of all, they are still around but since Turing's and Shannon's machines and procedures have been implemented they are no longer real, they are de-ontologized. To borrow an image from Geoffrey Winthrop-Young: 'Like impoverished aristocrats reduced to work as tourist guides on their former estates, media have been moved to the boundaries of the computing machine, where they now function as subaltern interfaces between it and us. Their helpful sounds and pretty images media are concessions to sub-digital human processing capabilities'.[3] In fact, if one browses through one of the numerous books on digital culture like *Digital Material: Tracing New Media in Everyday Life and Technology* (van der Boomen et al., 2009) one cannot but notice that the concept of media has become completely identical with interfaces and digital objects that can be manipulated on the screen. Are media studies left with retrospections of past media like Kittler himself suggested? In fact there is a discourse going on that addresses media only as a thing of the past or denies their being altogether. Kittler (1997), 'There is no software'; Bernhard Siegert (1996), 'There are no mass media'; Eva Horn (2007), 'There are no media'; Claus Pias (2011), 'Was waren Medien?' ('What were media').

MEDIA AFTER MEDIA

Thus, there are good reasons to assume that media after Kittler are characterized primarily by their inauthenticity (*Uneigentlichkeit*). Methodologically their authentic meaning never was to be found within their own history, but in their 'destructive character' (Benjamin): in the 'exorcism of the spirit' or in 'the abandoning of the Human' or in the 'stop making sense'. Ontologically media exist after the implementation of Turing's Universal Machine and of Shannon's scanning theorem only as simulations of themselves.

In fact what can be observed in the years that followed the digital revolution is the dissolution of the concept of the 'medium' into a series of desubstantialized concepts that pay tribute to the recent becoming inauthentic of the media: In Germany it is first of all the neologism 'mediality'; from the United Kingdom we learn about the new plural of 'mediums', which is meant to replace the ontologically inauthentic 'media'; in France it is the concept of the 'mediateur' (brought up by Antoine Hennion and recently adapted by Bruno Latour), or it is the old but modernized concept of 'cultural techniques'. Cultural techniques are a result of the 'practical turn' in media studies, which itself is a result of the post-media-effect.

But interestingly the ontological abasement of media to simulations in the digital age resulted in a mediatheoretical revision of ontology itself, which already very early in Kittler's lifetime turned into techno-ontology. The father of techno-ontology is of course Martin Heidegger. Modern metaphysics, Heidegger taught us, founded an epoch in which being (*das Seiende*) is interpreted as objectiveness. The techniques and technologies of this epoch, that have the power to call something into being, are the techniques and technologies of representation. Only what can be represented is an object. That is, only what can be represented, is at all. Kittler's high-tech version of this techno-ontology was the formula: '*Nur was schaltbar ist, ist überhaupt*'. Only what can be realized as a switching circuit, is at all. Implementation as wiring is the precondition of being. If we take wiring (*Schaltung*) in its broadest possible meaning, then Kittler's techno-ontology resonates in a quite surprising way with Bruno Latour's ontology of scientific facts.

Like Kittler, Latour insists on the necessity to open up the black boxes of abstract concepts like The Social and to demonstrate by what inconspicuous means they are fabricated and how sociologists or philosophers are made to believe in the autonomy of concepts or facts. The Latourian version of Kittler's techno-ontology would read: Only what remains stable in the 'wiring' of the immutable mobiles, is at all. As is generally known immutable mobiles are highly specialized and therefore inconspicous media of inscription and transmission, the operative concatenation of which constitutes scientific practice: traces and imprints, sketches, maps, perspectival projections, tables, diagrams, notational systems and procedures of visualization. Kittler's 'wiring' (*schalten*) in Latour's terminology would be '*enchaînement*', concatenation. The referent of scientific knowledge, the fact, is produced by the concatenation of immutable mobiles, and that referent remains solid or 'real' as long as it survives all translations without any intolerable transformations. Such a translation would no longer carry with it the onto-historical undertone, which is audible in Kittler's formula. It would as a consequence liberate the question how being is made—

fabricated—from an onto-historical thinking in epochs. The overcoming of an onto-historical conception of media history, which was always basic to media history according to Kittler, opens up the possibility for a reconceptualisation of ontology, which one could call 'operative ontologies', that asks for the concrete ontic operations and practices that produce first of all ontological distinctions—among many others also those between image and picture or figure and ground or active and passive or message and medium, subject and object, man and animal and so on. These ontic operations are called cultural techniques.

The de-ontologizing of the media thus initiated not the end of media history as one might think and as Kittler himself apparently believed in the nineties, but a media-ontology that deconstructs the objectity of the objects. A media historicity becomes imaginable which does no longer reside in a story of modernization, the telos of which was the abandoning of 'man', but which is at the core of entities formerly known as objects and humans and which are now much better addressed as processes of assemblage. And what is true for the objects is also true for the humans: If we have never been modern, we have never been 'we', too.

The reasons why Actor-Network Theory (ANT) meets nowadays with an increasing approval in German media theory cannot be discussed here (but see Engell and Siegert, 2013). Although ANT never summed them up under the generic term of media, ANT always knew and addressed media: photography, inscriptions, the printing press, maps, scientific instruments of classification and visualization. In a recent interview Latour has tagged his famous 'immutable mobiles' without further ado as 'media' in the sense of McLuhan (Latour, 2013). Like in Kittler's materialistic media theory it is not the macro-subjects like society, the spirit, freedom, the market or progress, which fuel developments but the storage, transmission and processing of data and codes. Despite these interesting overlaps a main obstacle which restrains the possibility to simply translate ANT into German media analysis is the focus of ANT on the notion of *action*, which is opposed to the focus on the notion of *knowledge* in German media theory, which is of course a heritage of Foucault's archaeology of knowledge. The prevailing question in German media theory was not how agency is distributed among human and nonhuman actors, but the question what the distinctions are, by which juridical, medical or anthropological knowledge operates, and what the technical conditions of data processing are, on which those distinctions are based. Another problem is that in French the term 'media' designates 'mass media', which is the reason why Latour had to introduce another term, which he borrowed from Antoine Hennion: the term of the mediator. The translation formula would be: '*Medien*' (mediums) in the German sense are mediators in the sense of Hennion under the premise that this term is not restricted to human beings but comprises the whole Hermes complex in the sense of Michel Serres. I suggest therefore the term 'mediator-object'.

Nevertheless there are interesting possibilities of theoretical convergences. For instance it might be possible to interpret the '*faire faire*', which describes in Latour the agency of the mediators (and also the agency of the *faitiche*), as a weak version of the 'technical apriori'. ANT is interested in the power of mediators to make other actors spring into action. If you attenuate a bit the obsession of ANT with action one could add to the power of mediators the agency to not only make other actors do something, but to make them appear first of all, or to call them into being. Mediator-objects not only *really* do something, they make something *real*, too. If one gave up not only the concept of the network because this concept has all too often been confused with technical networks and the managements theories and utopian ideas of politics related to them, but also the concept of action because this concept attaches ANT to the tradition of hylomorphism—as Tim Ingold criticizes—one would not only have to speak of an 'Actor-Media-Theory' (as some do now in Germany), but also of an 'Onto-Media-Theory', or less grandiloquent of a 'performative realism' (Michael Cuntz). Not 'make do', but 'make present' or even 'make exist'.

It seems to me therefore that it is necessary to give up the old opposition between action and being which characterized for such a long time the difference between Anglophone and Germanophone philosophies, and on the long run to replace them with a concept of an operational being which still needs further reflection. If this could be achieved then it would be possible to productively connect to Kittler's philosophy, which—if there is one at all—consists in reentering the ontic-ontological difference into the ontic.

As you know the fool's preference for the finger or the horse has often been derided as 'techno-determinism'. With Latour this critique can be deciphered as a version of the anti-fetishism of the Moderns. To mistake the indexical mediator, the finger, as the object which possesses the agency to make the moon appear and shine, is in the eyes of the Moderns a clearly fetishist belief. In the same way to hold technical media responsible for the historically contingent concepts of art, technology, knowledge, gender, the subject and so forth can be derided as fetishist naiveté, too. Latour has deconstructed this fetishist belief as something which is produced by the critique of the anti-fetishists in the first place. Anti-fetishism like anti-technodeterminism is structured in a schizophrenic way. The so-called Moderns on the one hand consider the idea as primitive that mediator-objects possess autonomous agency, and they will explain to everybody who believes in the power of fetishes that this power is fabricated by himself. On the other hand they are highly convinced that scientific facts, after they have been established, are nothing fabricated but autonomous, notwithstanding how many mediators have been involved in their making (Latour, 2011: 71). But mediator-objects are neither facts nor fetishs nor is their agency a matter of belief or disbelief. They are rather 'factish', as Latour writes, 'the factish can . . . be defined as the *wisdom of the passage*, as that which allows one to pass from fabrication to reality' (Latour, 2011: 35); that is to say move from thing to sign, from the fabricated to the real, from horse to message and from finger to the moon and vice versa. The question is not, what is active and what is passive, what is form and what is matter, what is an idol and what is an image, but whether there exists an operationalised, indexical or deictic connection between the active and the passive, action and being, form and matter and so on. The factish thus subverts the distinction between fact and fetish, determinism and non-determinism as well as the distinction between modern and pre-modern.

NOTES

1. Friedrich Kittler always had an interest in the moon (although his interest in horses was limited). The young Kittler collected appearances of the moon in literary texts with regard to its colour (unfortunately I have forgotten to what end); the Kittler of the nineties was highly interested in the plans of the NSA to use the moon as a huge relay for electromagnetic ultra high frequency rays, not to mention his love of Pink Floyd and *The Dark Side of the Moon*. There is no moon independent of the Gods or media that only lunatics are wise or paranoid enough to hear within their heads.
2. Geoffrey Winthrop-Young, 'The Rise and Fall of German Media Theory: An Old Norse Look Back at a Look Across' (forthcoming).
3. Winthrop-Young, 'The Rise and Fall of German Media Theory'.

BIBLIOGRAPHY

Cuntz, Michael (2011) 'Objets temporel und durée oder' in Becker, Ilka, Michael Cuntz and Michael Wetzel, eds., *Just not in time. Inframedialität und nonlineare Zeitlichkeiten in Kunst, Film, Literatur und Philosophie*. München: Fink, pp. 177–220.

Engell, Lorenz and Bernhard Siegert. (2013) 'Editorial' for 'ANT und die Medien' in *Zeitschrift für Medien- und Kulturforschung—Heft* 2/13. ikkm-weimar.de/publikationen/zeitschrift/13_2_inhalt/prm/518/cs__11/index.html.

Gumbrecht, Hans Ulrich. (1988) 'Flache Diskurse' in Hans Ulrich Gumbrecht and K. Ludwig Pfeiffer, eds. *Materialität der Kommunikation*. Suhrkamp: Frankfurt am Main.

———. (1994) 'A Farewell to Interpretation' in Hans Ulrich Gumbrecht and K. Ludwig Pfeiffer, ed. *Materialities of Communication*. Stanford, CA: Stanford University Press.

Hasslacher, Brosl. (1988) 'Beyond the Turing Machine' in Rolf Herken, ed. *The Universal Turing Machine. A Half-Century Survey*. Oxford: Oxford University Press.

Horn, Eva. (2007) 'There Are No Media' in *Grey Room* 29: pp. 6–13. Cambridge, MA: MIT Press.

Kittler, Friedrich. (1980) 'Autorschaft und Liebe' in Kittler, ed. *Austreibung des Geistes aus den Geisteswissenschaften*. Munich; Wien; Zurich: 142–73.

———. (1990) *Discourse Networks 1800/1900*. Stanford, CA: Stanford University Press.

———. (1993) 'Geschichte der Kommunikationsmedien' in Jörg Huber und Alois Martin Müller (Hrsg.), *Raum und Verfahren* [*Interventionen* 2]. Basel Switzerland: 169–88.

———. (1996) 'The City as Medium'. Trans. Matthew Griffin, *NLH* 27(4): 717–29.

———. (1997) *Literature, Media, Information Systems*, ed. and introduced by John Johnston. London: G&B Arts.

———. (1998) *Daten Zahlen Codes*. Leipzig.

———. (2004a) 'Universities: Wet, Hard, Soft and Harder', *Critical Inquiry*, 31(1): 244–56.

———. (2004b) *Unsterbliche: Nachrufe, Erinnerungen, Geistergespräche*. Berlin: Fink.

———. (2009) 'Towards an Ontology of Media', *Theory, Culture & Society*, 26: 29–30.

———. (2012) 'Götter und Schriften rund ums Mittelmeer', transcript of a seminar session, summer term 2010, published in TUMULT 40: *Friedrich Kittler. Technik oder Kunst?* Wetzler.

Kittler, Friedrich and Horst Turk, eds. (1977) *Urszenen* (Primal Scenes). Suhrkamp: Frankfurt am Main.

Latour, Bruno. (2011) *On the Modern Cult of the Factish Gods*. Durham, NC: Duke University Press.

———. (2013) 'Den Kühe ihre Farbe zurückgeben. Von der ANT und der Soziologie der Übersetzung zum Projekt der Existenzweisen. Bruno Latour im Interview mit Michael Cuntz und Lorenz Engell' in 'ANT und die Medien' in *Zeitschrift für Medien- und Kulturforschung—Heft* 2/13. ikkm-weimar.de/publikationen/zeitschrift/13_2_inhalt/prm/518/cs__11/index.html.

Oliver, B. M., Pierce, J. R., and Shannon, C. E. (1948) 'The Philosophy of PCM' in *Proceedings of the Institute of Radio Engineers* 36(11): 1324–331.

Pias, Claus. (2011) 'Was waren Medien-Wissenschafen?' www.diaphanes.de/buch/detail/231.

Piccinini, Gualtiero. (2011) 'The Physical Church-Turing Thesis: Modest or Bold?' in *British Journal for the Philosophy of Science*, 3. bjps.oxfordjournals.org/content/early/2011/08/09/bjps.axr016.short.

Siegert, Bernhard. (1996) 'There Are No Mass Media' in Hans Ulrich Gumbrecht and Michael Marrinan, eds. *Mapping Benjamin: The Work of Art in the Digital Age*. Stanford, CA: Stanford University Press, pp. 30–38.

van der Boomen, Marianne et al., eds. (2009) *Digital Material: Tracing New Media in Everyday Life and Technology*. Amsterdam: University of Amsterdam Press.

Part Two

Chapter Six

The Forbidden Pleasures of Media Determining

Matthew Fuller

I want to start with something that has been taken as a motto for media theory as it has developed with and through the work of Friedrich Kittler and which, as such, graces the entrance to this book. 'Media determine our situation', is the opening statement of 'Gramophone, Film, Typewriter'. This formulation is worth attending to in the context of an enquiry into media studies after Kittler since for the mainstream of media studies such a position is something approaching a *blasphemy*. Media Studies however is often a misnomer. Under the rubric of this field we are to turn our attention to what passes through media, the significatory operations arrayed on pages or screens, the governance and political economy pertaining to them, but media themselves are firmly and determinedly *not* studied.

When he wrote, '*Medien bestimmen unsere lage*', the situation Kittler describes is that of a military situation room, that of the German Army High Command of 1941, a situation that was, at that point in time, seemingly not yet out of control, not yet too late to determine in projecting, evaluating and ramifying the fascist imperium. In Kittler, there is a subtle mourning for and an admiration of such moments, points at which media and communication systems dip below the horizon of the knowable. There is a sense of a loss of agency, of the position of knowing and declaring, that is exhilarating and melancholy, and as such, quite laughable. In such a figuration the stakes of determination become recognizable at the point at which they become indiscernible: there is a sense of only knowing at the point beyond which it is already too late to act upon what is known.

Some of this fascination, of the knowing attained at the point of loss, drives Kittler's interest as (that rare thing) a politically conservative post-structuralist. Such a position manifests in his figurations of gender which are heroically kitsch, but also for instance in his statement that he was looking forward to the Iraq war since it would be a chance for the new weapons systems to be revealed. In this, as Florian Cramer (2013) notes, Kittler has something of the punk drive to shock, saying the unsayable that is also at the core of our situation. But it is a means of knowing what it is already too late to know, of being a subject, a human, studying the humanities even, that it is already too late to be: something requiring a fatalistic humour. It is with this temperament in mind that I want to think about media determinism.

TECHNOLOGICAL DETERMINATION

Media determinism is a subset of technological determinism. This is a tendency most epitomized by historian Lynn White (1966) in his account of the effect of the stirrup on mounted combat in Europe and its concatenation of effects. The stirrup allowed for the knight to have a point of leverage at the foot, hence allowing the more effective use of using swords or lances, giving the fighter a fulcrum to turn and strike from. But attaching the feet to the saddle and thus to the horse, also had reciprocal effects on the social form of Europe, consolidating feudalism, since a social organization had to be built to keep the good knight on his trusty steed. For Deleuze and Guattari (1988), who draw on White's work in developing their theory of the assemblage, the stirrup becomes the hook around which a particular assemblage congeals. For others, it became the articulation-point of 'The Great Stirrup Controversy' around which multiple modes of techno-social genesis could come into formation. The architectural and design critic Rayner Banham talks in related terms about gizmos, small gadgets with disproportionate power, such as the Evinrude outboard motor. Self contained and exciting, these are technologies that are often available to order by mail and in their dispersal by such means across a large territory, these consumer devices formulated an American approach to technology that perhaps we can see an echo of in the ideal of the personal computer.

And there are other kinds of technological determinism such as those to be found in politics as of a mode of operation, a formula for doing things, programmatic means that accomplish a social fait accompli. In Proudhon's proposition that 'the workshop will make the government disappear' is the suggestion that a specific mode of organization, knowledge and economy obviates us from the enslaving need for central control. In the very contemporary sounding aim of Saint-Simon a variation on such a tendency was the aim: 'to replace the government of men by the administration of things'.[1] The specific formulation of such things drives a certain perhaps yet insufficient amount of inquiry and invention. The anarchist emphasis on finding and enacting the correct social form for struggles that today puts in place the society of tomorrow is related.[2] Here, workers' councils, affinity groups, industrial unions, collectives and the union of egoists are part of an inventive catalogue of anticipatory and enacted technologies of distributed power. Some contemporary formulations of such approaches are to be found in the development of software or platforms that in their programmatic nature obviate the need for centralisation. Determination here becomes a field of experiment and struggle over what may be decisive factors in social composition. Media in many senses simply *are* the social.

In this regard, where what Kittler would call 'Anglo-Saxon' media studies does have a certain edge is in the tracing of symbolic systems of representation through to political systems, such as patterns of ownership, the fabrication of identities, the staging and scripting of discourses and ideologies. In other words there is a vocabulary and set of tools ready to analyse power in relation to media, usually as a form of communication. What they often point towards but can however never quite manage to utter is that media are a constituted and constitutive form of power in themselves—as, for instance, articulated by Debord, and later Agamben—and developed by scholars with a more media archaeological bent such as Jonathan Crary. There is a lot of prevaricatory and sometimes useful work involved in media studies therefore in finding modes of resistance, of identity formation, of patiently sifting for the dust of apparent audience empowerment, of the tracing of subject-formations, in order, in part, to avoid having to address the power of media systems in themselves, or indeed to posit and map counter-powers.

But let's relate this back to the question of what Kittler in particular brings to media. One of the ways into this is somewhat banal, so it is obviously the one to select: the field of *Mediawissenschaft* that Kittler and others undertook to develop has no precise parallel in the Anglophone academy. The concept of *Wissenschaft* or the Dutch *Wetenschap*, shaped in the late nineteenth century, combines all forms of higher learning, making difficult, or more precisely, incomprehensible, the dichotomy between the humanities and sciences. One can say that Kittler, with his emphasis on technical learning (for instance teaching the programming language C), operated on the basis of the desirability of a refoundation of *wissenschaft* for a computational age. The eminent Swiss neurologist Pierre Gloor, in his survey of the work of Hans Berger, the inventor of the encephalogram, suggests that the intellectual credo of *wissenschaft* is best expressed by Goethe in *Faust*, where he declares the aim, 'That I may detect the inmost force / which binds the world, and guides its course'. Berger was a scientist whose initial interest in the brain was spurred by an apparent experience of telepathy, an interest that he repressed until he was able at least to discount it. In other words, in the framing of *wissenschaft*, all the tiresome debates about whether it is possible to have any commonality between science and the humanities are, at least potentially, rather welcomely groundless. Such a condition allows for a media studies that is at least able to acknowledge the technical.[3]

MEDIA DETERMINISM

Kittler's approach to the question of determination is something partially inherited from McLuhan, Ong and the Toronto school with their emphasis on 'the power of the media themselves to impose their assumptions upon our modes of perception' (McLuhan, 1968: 172) on the one hand and from Foucault on the other. For Foucault the genealogical point of reference would also be Nietzsche, whose alarming and exciting encounter with the clattering orb of the Malling-Hansen typewriter exemplifies media determinism in a certain sense: 'Our writing tools are also working on our thoughts' (ibid).

While media work on our thoughts, these in turn may not quite be adequate to the workings of media. A case that is classically brought up against media determinism is Edison's (1876) famous list of the uses he presumed the phonograph would afford. The inventor misapprehended the uses of the technology, which were then taken up by society in different ways—to play music rather than to record the voices of the dying. We might want to ask however, who is this Edison to speak on behalf of the phonograph? If Edison couldn't see it, who could? One answer is: *media itself*—its prehensions of the world, having resonance with the kind of cybernetic yearning that Simondon talks about. Media come into being without necessarily being recognized as such. The phonogram comes into composition with music, the domestic and with escape from it, with delight, with radio and as such exceeds the intentions of its inventor.

Part of the significance of such a condition can be summarized well by turning to the extended mind hypothesis which Andy Clark summarizes in 'Supersizing the Mind' as a condition wherein 'inner neural processes . . . are often productively entangled with gross bodily and extra-bodily processes of storage, representation, materialization and manipulation' (Clark, 2010: 169).

This would certainly imply that media are a situation and one in which a 'we' of some sort finds itself composed. The slightly wry or bleakly ironic condition that Kittler rightly ascribes to this is that, as with the inhabitants of the war room, we are no longer in a position to know about determinism. Adding to the recursivity of this condition, the position to know is lost over and over again—as for instance after 1941, with Gottfried Benn, among the sandpits of the German high command where 'it may still have been possible to take stock of the situation' (Kittler, 1999: xxxix). This is a moment that Kittler also identifies with the design of the last Intel chip to be fully comprehensible to one designer described in the essay 'There Is No Software'. In informational terms (such as those of Kolmogorov or Chaitin) we can describe this as a formulation of the status of thoughts or texts that have less content or meaning than their material substrate which preempts them and in which they are enacted. In such a way, Kittler's argument is related to the question of whole-part formulations, and it is here that we can see also that Kittler establishes a boundary: the question of the body, or experience is rather beyond knowing. Here, an attention to matter, as well as to the technical scale, will afford us certain other possibilities.

STANDARDS

Returning to the opening phrase, what we can perhaps say more precisely is that contemporarily, *standards* determine our situation. Technological media form a subset of these. Kittler sees standards as something akin to forms in the Aristotelian schema of hylomorphism. Humans are the matter that is worked on, as a residuum or side-effect. The dryness of this approach leads in turn to some humour: in *Optical Media*, Kittler approvingly cites the journalist and UFO-expert Klaus Simmering's answer when asked whether television was art, to which he coolly replies: 'Television is an internationally standardized way of seeing defined in CCIR Report 407-1' (Kittler, 2009: 218). If we are to say that a problem with media studies more generally is its penchant for the sociological practice of stating the bloody obvious, Kittler's move is to attend to grey media, technologies that are so obviously present they pass beneath the threshold of critical perception. Here there is a resonance with Foucault's formulation regarding medical statistics that 'the norm is an interplay of differential normalities' (Foucault, 2007: 63). This is something perhaps that we can see articulated in Kittler's entertainingly clumsy digressions into the erotic where we see that the true rationale for gender categories is that of slapstick. But far more exciting, and culturally forbidden as such, than mere erotics is the question of technical standards.

As part of the move to an analysis of the effects of the computational subsumption of all signifying systems guided by the work of Claude Shannon, Kittler lingers over the descriptions of cases where, in a form of transposition from one system to another, the elements and associative rules of Medium A can be reproduced in the elements and associative rules of Medium B (Kittler, 1992: 270). There is an evident lien to a Lacanian play here, where symbols and symbol systems do not and cannot refer to a real, but simply to other symbols and symbol systems. The determinations of media are encountered in the combinatorial or transpositionary limit, where the 'elementary, unavoidable act of exhaustion is an encounter with the limits of media' (Kittler, 1992: 265). Equally, to work with another reader of Lacan, Félix Guattari, the interplay of media systems in this mode of description imply and entail processes of subjectivation that obey the normal patterns of psychosis implied by each set of standards and their transposition to another. The maladaption of subjects to such standards implies anguish, invention, the minor, or the proliferations of everyday administrative humiliation; to put it another way, a set of effects that offers the allure of a release into high functionality, empowerment, training towards excellence.

In such terms, media are sets of interlacing sets of standards whose idiosyncratic effects are the result of the multi-scalar interference and phasing of their characteristics. Alongside the way in which computer use can synchronise with and amplify conditions such as obsessive compulsive disorder, the phasing of the interplay of standards can of course lead to some interesting and pleasing effects as Kittler notes in his discussion of computer graphics: 'Sampling also produces continuous and thus striking forms where the program code never intended any at all' (2001: 33). We can see a concern for related conditions in his entertaining history of the interrelation of church painting and architecture in *Optical Media* (2009), what is celebrated more is the paradoxical effects of the interlocking formalisms around painting, religious iconography, architecture and the mathematical means to arrive at each.

This acuity towards standards leads his sympathy to free software, where the construction and circulation of standards also becomes a project of learning. But the attention to standards, as something also more abstract than simple substance means that Kittler's is not an approach to technology that is technocratic, but something far more giddying, psychedelic and dark, as media forms swirl in and out of each other, apprehend, ablate, stop and address each other, in ways that have significant effects—for instance in, as Sybille Krämer (2006) notes, effecting the means of time storage, manipulation and recall in time-axis manipulation.

Kittler's is then a sophisticated form of technological determinism, that is also readily alert to the ways in which such symbolic systems effectively detourn and mutate each other in manners that are not immune to correlation with diagnoses of psychic disturbance. As with playing up an eager anticipation of new weaponry, part of this pleasure is to be found in an ironic fondness for what might be called bad ancestry: revealed in the genealogical work of finding the roots of media technologies in those of war, or the roots of the domestic video recorder in systems for shopping centre surveillance (Kittler, 1996). To some extent this fascination can be mapped in relation to Ricouer's account of the hermeneutic of suspicion, and such an irony is capable of producing highly multiplicitous genealogies of systems and entities that do not fold so readily in to such a determination by one historical factor.

In examining the nature of these precursors and bad ancestors we can return to that tricky, rather formless, set of moments before media become standardized. One can say that an effect of media art, or the work of avant gardes, is to sustain and feed this state of indeterminacy at the same time as it is to contradictorily make technological breaks that, ruthlessly or seductively, with an uncanny or childish smile, conjure or impose new systematisations. Here to, to put it simply, they proliferate ethical and ethico-aesthetic questions of power and empowerment. In other words we are at that moment where standardisations are in effect, are creating lacing and distortions among themselves, but do not fully overdetermine the situation.

This is a condition in which media consist both of experimental apparatus—*contraptions* in the words of artist Graham Harwood describing experimental witnesses and participants that are not yet stabilised as instruments—but also of highly stabilised standard objects.[4] With the general computer, there is a potential for a tendentially permanent indetermination engendered by and folding in and out of machines built upon machines; hence the importance of Shannon and Turing for Kittler, and his attention to them as an important foundation for a *mediawissenschaft* that would be adequate to the present. This too is what constitutes in part the nature of the politics of the struggle over the formation of the computer that is currently taking place.

A MEDIUM FOR THE BRAIN

In order to exemplify this to some extent, I want to return to Hans Berger and his discussion of early experiments in the electroencephalogram. Kittler's work is attentive to the sheer massification of the category of media and, like Paul Virilio whom he praises, rightly emphasises the military roots and concatenations of many media systems as *bad ancestors*. In this chapter I want to suggest that another such genealogy could be drawn through the medical. Here is an account from Berger of experiments held in 1928 (Berger, 1969: 41). The text is worth citing at length since it makes the argument very clear in the linking of procedures, to drugs, to instruments, to flesh, to metals, to currents, to readings, to anatomical knowledge and technique, in the production of an experimental contraption:

> Then last year, at a time when my observations on man, which I shall report below, were already available, I again performed three experiments on dogs. In these I used the large Edelmann string galvanometer and the double-coil galvanometer of Siemens and Halske, the latter with particularly sensitive inserts. The dogs used in these experiments had received 1.5 grams of Veronal by mouth about five hours before the experiment; then in addition, one hour before the beginning of the pre-

> paratory operation, they received 0.03-0.05 grams of morphine subcutaneously. In accordance with Einthoven's suggestion for the recording of the electrocardiogram in the animal, and in order to avoid cooling of the cerebral cortex, I substituted freshly amalgamated tiny zinc plates for the non-polarizable clay electrodes which I had used before. The zinc plates were introduced into the subdural space through a slit in the dura. (The dura is a tough membrane surrounding brain and spinal column). They measured 12mm in length and 4mm in width; their four corners were rounded off to avoid injuries; to them was soldered the well-insulated connecting wire; they had a surface area of 25 sq.mm. After they had been inserted through the slit in the dura, through which they were just able to pass, they were advanced into the subdural space far enough to come to rest in the laterally sloping region of the skull. Their surfaces were firmly applied to the pia-arachnoid covered cortex and they were pressed against the dura and the bone by the pulsating brain. The trephine opening, which was kept as small as possible, was enlarged with a Lüer's rongeur only to the extent necessary to permit easy introduction of the tiny zinc plates, and was then completely filled with the wax customarily used in brain operations in man. The well insulated wire was led through this mass of wax. The wire itself was surrounded by wax, and the skin was then closed with a few sutures over the trephine opening. Thus the brain was in no way exposed to drying and cooling.
>
> In accordance with the above findings quoted from the literature it was found that when these electrodes were applied over two areas of the same hemisphere, a current exhibiting considerable oscillations is present at all times.

This is an account of the contraption assembled in order to verify the first findings of electrical activity in the brain. That characteristic current became known as the alpha wave, later to be joined by the beta wave. Both were originally called Berger's Waves, by the neurologist Edgar Adrian who drew the first widespread attention to Berger's work as it added the language of electricity to that of the then-dominant model of the thermal qualities of the brain.

We thus have a phenomena and a technology by which it can be witnessed in some way or another. But in order to produce a standard, in order that it can then go on to be *determining*, a lot of work has to be done. Reading the extended quotation from Berger's papers above shows us a way in which this might be done.

There is, first of all, a process of *stabilisation* against loss of heat of the body of the dog. In relation to theoretical concerns: the law of conservation of energy and the dependence of biological processes upon physico-chemical mechanisms which are entirely subtendent upon thermodynamics was a key concern of models of the brain at that time. Berger is "time and again haunted by the worry" of the stability of his object, blood flow perhaps, he conjectures, causing the stability of the waves via the beating of the heart. Resorting to decortication of the dog in order to establish this as a factor or not, the brain is isolated from the organism in order to guarantee itself as a witness, just as the dog is from any external electrical influence by the use of the nonconductive material glass for the legs of the operating table.

Secondly, there is the question of the *translation* of one media to another—transduction, but a transduction that is not simply of one symbolic system to another, but of multiple kinds of matter and process, including the pertaining knowledge systems for handling them. Further on in the same paper, Berger develops questions about the instruments and methods: the sensitivity of the coil galvanometer by comparison with the spring galvanometer (in his lab the two instruments were used concurrently for cost reasons); the difference in results in placing the electrodes, or their uniformity in placement in generating experimental artefacts (confirmed by postmortem examination); the noneffect of diminishing blood flow in this dog or "total exsanguination" (Berger, 1969: 43). In another, the possibility of changing brain volume, or the artificial arousal of the dogs via injection of 0.01-0.02 grams of cocaine hydrochloride into the jugular vein.

Berger's papers are often concerned with what would now be separated out as method, the reflection on the means of the stabilisation, or the precise capture of the object of study in terms both of the physical phenomena and the experimental instrument that attends to it. The papers gathered by Gloor in Berger's account of the development and refinement of the encephalogram, its accretion as a standard, are digressive, reflexive. In fact they were written in the evening after a day's work and taken by dictation by what is described as an 'intelligent patient'. They are, in a certain sense, records of his struggle to find out what media is in relation to the phenomena he is attempting to track. Berger too is isolated, working largely alone for over a decade. Relations to the work of other researchers were bad.

As Andrew Pickering (1995) might say in his disquisition on the operation of the mangle, there is a to-ing and fro-ing between method—standardized behaviour, standard objects, and what is yet coming into more precise relation with forms of knowledge. It's not about establishing a generic network of entities, but about specificity and attention, working, *poesis*. At the same time as this however, it is something that involves existing standard objects, the development and the mobilization of complexes of them as they relate to or work in between messier or unknown forces and capacities of different kinds of matter.

TAKING EDISON'S MEDICINE

While what Berger calls 'imbeciles' display what he characterizes as more beautiful and fully demarked waveforms than people categorized as 'intelligent', it is also notable that he discovers that 'making the facial expressions associated with thinking' (Berger, 1969: 315) does not in itself result in the decrease in amplitude of the potential oscillations of the brain that he finds to be associated with that state.[5]

This is a useful thing to pretend not to know in a multitude of academic settings. In later work, the earlier concern with the correlations of mental states with conventional physiognomic traces moves to comparison of the wave patterns associated across mental states. The abstracted pattern of waves is able to comparatively mediate between them according to commonality or difference. In this working of stabilisation and translation, standards are also formed, alongside the means by which they messily, effectively or ineffectively interoperate. This interplay can be seen as a kind of determination. Stabilising and translating in cycles: picking up currents, passing them along wires, tracing them on paper, codifying them as numbers.

As numbers, Berger is able to translate the inscrutable operations of epilepsy into waves; patterns that are divulged by means of harmonic analysis such as Fourier Transforms. Electrical media mediate between mathematical techniques for transforming frequency over time and a form of seizure. In doing so they were able to verify the similarity between such seizures and artificially-induced 'epileptiform' (McCrae, 2006: 69–70) attacks induced by the use of Cardiazol (a chemical used to treat schizophrenia prior to electroconvulsive therapy) by means of a common reference to the waveform (cf Berger, 1969).

The electrical activity of the brain's correspondence to such waves, mapped by the Fourier Transform, becomes the means of verifying the state of the patient. In such a condition, media and standardized mathematical analysis indeed *constitute* our situation. One may be led to imagine a closing of the circuit between the reading electrodes of electroencephalogram and the writing electrodes of electroconvulsive therapy with the human as mere transition zone, a mediumistic substance. Kittler's antihumanism is joyfully confirmed by such moments and the anticipation of them.

Here we are drawn back to the question of media as systems of standards. For Kittler, systems of symbols are read and interpreted by the schema of other systems, 'whether from algebraic variable to note values or from letters to chess abbreviations' where nevertheless, 'every transposition leaves gaps' (Kittler, 1992: 272). There is a specific texture and system of combinatorial capacity in each media, where each such transposition idiosyncratically adds, filters and blocks characteristics. Some media are capable of a universal representation of the workings of another. For instance, it is possible to write out a textual description of what is more often rendered in musical notation, but media transpose each other with a certain parallax effect. This is where the characteristic traits of their determinism are to be found.

In the working of this parallax there is something fundamentally different in the consistency of the intervention made by the digital computer. In its universal universality of all symbol-based systems, it creates the conditions for symbol-based media systems to converge on the computational. But this is a vertiginous combinatoriality. Think of code reading before Bletchley Park and after, where cryptanalysis changed from being an art of interpretation based on human ingenuity to one of probabilistic determination based on the enormously amplified combinatorial power of the computing machine. The consequences of this change is something that which constitutes the organized critical understanding, if not the 'facts on the ground' of politics and culture have yet to catch up with.

This being the case, what Kittler attends to with a characteristically peculiar acuity is the interplay of series of norms, codes and standards in media. Such things colonise, ablate, transduct, noise and digitally remaster each other. This is not only a condition of a permanently fluid interplay of forces and organizing principles, but also a condition of power. And here we can note an aporia in Kittler who always maintains a certain reticence in talking about capitalism, something that he sets aside as the work of 'economists'. Media theory however may find it fruitful to address itself to money as a form of media in itself. If all symbolic media, and all media that can in turn be transducted into symbols converge on computing as a means to integrate symbolic systems, such systems are in turn latched onto, called to order, amplified and set to work by money. The madly sprawling patchbays of axiomatics that form contemporary capitalisms provide in turn, alongside computing, a second fundamental form of interlocution and transcoding operating between symbolic systems.

In turn, since signification is only one of the modes of operation of the symbolic, money—with its highly variable, unstable, yet uncannily repetitive characteristics as a set of beliefs and orderings of ideas and interactions and operations of valorization—provides only one example of a wider set of conditions. As Hito Steyerl's video *Liquidity Inc.* (2014) suggests, the denizens of this planet are currently experiencing a historical moment defined by multiple workarounds and abreactions to the crises in the place in the hierarchy of different systems of abstraction and concreteness; systems that wrestle over what is to count as concrete and what as abstract, what is to register as a symbol, to be traced by a sensor, or not. Computing is of course key to this, but money also, two modes of systematisation, certainly not yet complete systems, each in a state of working out the other's erogenous zones with a coldness and deliberation, a fumbling and a violence that seems to encourage the evacuation of the potential of one and enhances the stupidity of the other. At the same time, other systems of different kinds are consciously or unconsciously vying for eminence, such as ecology on the one hand and the fatal twins of humanism and religion on the other.

This is something that contemporary media theory, in an expanded sense, may well find opportunities, if not quite the institutional necessities, to size up to. Such a condition may well in turn require a form of materialism that is able to work at high degrees of immanence and abstraction, across signification, and in the midst of computational culture, but as the readings from Berger's contraptions remind us, also in the thick volume, volubility and electrically exquisite nature of flesh cast as bodily tissues recast as number.

Here then, there is a necessity to attend to the myriad kinds, states and modes of matter alongside the standards they are coaxed into yielding and inducing, corroborating and submitting to without a necessary a priori privileging of any specific scale of such. If, using a Lacanian formulation, Kittler (1992) claims that technological media transform the real (rather than the symbolic) into a code that can be manipulated, reverse, and translated among other operations, it might be moot to ask what is the status of materialism in Kittler's work. I have to say that I don't fully know the answer to this question, but it seems reasonably productive to suggest that one way through to it might be via this diagrammatic split between, if we are to use these terms, the symbolic and the real that is both operative on and shears off from its intended point of traction. This is a familiar problem forming part of the transition from structuralist to poststructuralist literatures, but it is one intensified and fundamentally mutated by the shift to computational media; a condition of which is that a materialism of the abstract comes to the fore. A crucial factor for the present historical moment is the way in which computational forms such as databases, trading systems and computational media formats internalize such relations but also generate them in ways that spiral off and into the world, determining but also constituting it. In terms of mainstream databases we can think of such constituting forces as the mathematics of sets and their instantiation as logical structure, normalization, the particular idea of the relation that they establish. These are indeed standards for the generation of standards that in turn by their interactions may produce or diagram non-standard entities. Such media generate effects, as does the interplay of their standards, and as well as the processes of normalization and channeling that they imply, these effects can be powerfully nonlinear, manifesting in numerous fashion as crashes, overflows, halting as well as proliferations of hallucinatory grandeur.

For parallels, there are correlations to simple terms within standard forms that generate the nonlinear and irrational—such as the square route of two, the ancient number Pi, or the number Omega discussed by Gregory Chaitin and Luciana Parisi (2013). It is not unconnected that such numbers were called *Alogos* when first discovered. Here determining factors operate upon themselves, and determination becomes generative and expressive. Codes transcode themselves and in doing so generate torrents of jabbering symbols; Kittler maps similar effects happening in language in *Discourse Networks.* Attempts to make the real addressable via mathematical techniques and systems of reference conjoin with such processes and in this transition overspill the bounds of the merely symbolic. Codes inflate reference to other codes, developing amplificatory patterns of feedback: The spectacular ways in which the movements of capital rend housing completely free of taint by use value, indeed from actual use, in the present bubble conditions of cities such as London, provide an exemplarily demented example of such processes. Media systems, in their computational forms become fundamental to determining and exacerbating such conditions where the evacuation of the determining human subject from media is reciprocated by their ablation as significant inhabitants of cities. The innovations that might be imagined to be saved up as shiny new best for the next imperial war are also revealed in that between classes, in skirmishes fought in stock exchanges, multidimensional variations on pyramid schemes and the dense sets of informational triggers stacked up in fields on property-trading websites. As such forces constitute, interact with and gain traction on social forms, and on each other in layers of gaming and intrigue, attempts to stabilise and to translate these phenomena manifest as the military imperatives of command, control and communication refactored as sub-tenets of capital. Stabilisation and translation involve inherent struggle, a necessity that may also be executed with a tenacious attention to diagnosis, and the tenderness of an enquiring electrode. To go back to Goethe: That which binds the world, and guides its course *is* the world, something that media are a determining part of. In such a condition, Friedrich Kittler rightly reminds his readers to pay keen attention to the mechanisms of transcoding.

NOTES

1. See, for a history of the tensions and complications of achieving such ends in the conditions of 1930s Spain, Gaston Leval, Collectives in the Spanish Revolution, online at libcom.org/library/collectives-leval-1/.
2. A strong discussion of this tendency, routing it through a reading of Debord's use of Hegel, can be found in Tom Bunyard, *History's Negative: Temporality and Praxis in the Work of Guy Debord and the Situationist International, Historical Materialism*, forthcoming. See, also, Jesper Bernes, 'The Square and the Circle, the Logic of Occupy', The New Inquiry, 17 September 2012, thenewinquiry.com/essays/square-and-circle-the-logic-of-occupy/.
3. This possibility is explicitly discounted at the end of Berger's fourteenth report. Hans Berger, *On the Encephalogram of Man: The Fourteen Original Reports on the Human Electroencephalogram*, trans. and ed. Pierre Gloor. New York: Elsevier, 1969: p. 320.
4. See, YoHa website, www.yoha.co.uk/.
5. The premise of developing facial recognition software able to read intention from momentary expression parlays such possibilities into the present. See Kelly Gates, *Our Biometric Future: Facial Recognition Technology and the Culture of Surveillance*. New York University Press, New York, 2011.

BIBLIOGRAPHY

Banham, Rayner. (1996) 'The Great Gizmo' in Mary Banham, Paul Barker, Sutherland Lyall, and Cedric Price (eds). *A Critic Writes: Selected Essays by Rayner Banham*. Berkeley: University of California Press.

Berger, Hans. (1969) *On the Encephalogram of Man: The Fourteen Original Reports on the Human Electroencephalogram*. Trans. and ed. Pierre Gloor. New York: Elsevier.

Bernes, Jesper. (2012) 'The Square and the Circle, the Logic of Occupy', *The New Inquiry*, 17 September, thenewinquiry.com/essays/square-and-circle-the-logic-of-occupy/.
Bunyard, Tom. (forthcoming) *History's Negative: Temporality and Praxis in the Work of Guy Debord and the Situationist International, Historical Materialism*.
Chaitin, Gregory. (2005) *Metamaths: The Quest for Omega*. London: Atlantic Books.
Clark, Andy. (2010) *Supersizing the Mind: Embodiment, Action and Cognitive Extension*. Oxford: Oxford University Press.
Cramer, Florian. (2013). *Anti-Media: Ephemera on Speculative Arts*. Amsterdam: Institute for Network Cultures.
Deleuze, Gilles and Félix Guattari. (1988) *A Thousand Plateaus: Capitalism and Schizophrenia*. Vol. 2. Trans. Brian Massumi. London: Athlone Press.
Edison, Thomas. (1876) 'The Phonograph and Its Future', *North American Review*. Vol. 126. May–June, pp. 527–36.
Foucault, Michel. (2007) *Security, Territory, Population: Lectures at the Collège de France*. Trans. Graham Burchell. London: Palgrave.
Kittler, Friedrich. (1992) *Discourse Networks 1800/1900*. Trans. Chris Cullens and Michael Metteer. Stanford, CA: Stanford University Press.
———. (1996) 'The History of Communication Media', *CTheory*, ctheory.net, July.
———. (1999) *Gramophone, Film, Typewriter*. Trans. Geoffrey Winthrop-Young. Stanford, CA: Stanford University Press.
———. (2001) 'Computer Graphics: A Semi-Technical Introduction', *Grey Room*, No. 2, Winter.
———. (2009) *Optical Media*. Cambridge: Polity Press.
Krämer, Sybille. (2006) 'The Cultural Techniques of Time-Axis Manipulation, on Friedrich Kittler's Conception of Media'. *Theory, Culture & Society*. Vol. 23(4): 93–109.
Leval, Gaston. Collectives in the Spanish Revolution, online at libcom.org/library/collectives-leval-1/.
McCrae, Niall. (2006) '"A Violent Thunderstorm": Cardiazol Treatment in British Mental Hospitals.' *History of Psychiatry*. Vol. 17(1): 67–90.
McLuhan, Marshall. (1968) 'Is It Natural That One Medium Should Appropriate and Exploit Another?' in Gerald Emmanuel Stearn (ed). *McLuhan Hot and Cool*. London: Penguin.
Parisi, Luciana. (2013) *Contagious Architecture: Computation, Aesthetics and Space*. Cambridge: MIT Press.
Pickering, Andrew. (1995) *The Mangle of Practice: Time, Agency and Science*. Chicago: University of Chicago Press.
Steyerl, Hito. (2014) 'Liquidity Inc.' single channel video, 30 min.
Turner, Fred. (2002) *From Counter-Culture to CyberCulture*. Chicago: University of Chicago Press.
White, Lynn. (1966) *Medieval Technology and Social Change*. Oxford: Oxford University Press.

Chapter Seven

The Computer That Couldn't Stop

Artificial Intelligence and Obsessional Neurosis

Scott Wilson

'THE MOTHER'S MOUTH'

In *Discourse Networks 1800/1900* (1990), the work that established his reputation, Friedrich Kittler undertakes a deconstruction of Freud's legacy by turning the central assumptions of Freud's heir, Jacques Lacan, into the precondition of his own emergence, as if Lacan were stood behind Freud like Plato behind Socrates in Jacques Derrida's favourite postcard, commanding him to write (see Derrida, 1987). Kittler adopts Lacan primarily as a media theorist for whom subjectivity is an effect of various technologies of language and vision, voice and gaze—sound, speech, writing, film, television, radio—symbolization generally, the regime of signifiers and images that shape the world that we perceive and experience. In *Discourse Networks 1800/1900* it is with a particular event of speech and its formation into discourse that inaugurates for Kittler the historical configuration that produces the kind of European subject that Freud both exemplifies and subverts, obsessively writing away night after night at the end of a long day's analysis with his clients, puffing at his cigar in emulation of 'his father's great capacity for work and self-control' (Wilson, 2002: 163).

This media event reorients the origin of culture away from the Word of God towards the emergence, in the sonorous speech of a nurturing mother, of natural language that provides the basis for the writing of national culture in the form of Poetry, Philosophy and the Works of Great Men like Goethe, Hegel, Nietzsche and of course Freud. At the beginning of the nineteenth century, at the heart of the period known culturally as Romanticism, the well-known association of nature and woman, nurturing and maternity (mother nature) became consolidated in state policy as mothers were charged with the responsibility for teaching their infants to speak. Pre-school education became essential so that the mother's mouth could breathe life and potency into the German language through the lallation of lullabies and bedtime stories before it became pedagogically ordered into the grammar and ABC books of the schools. Only at this point did the paternal institutions of the nascent state take over the long process of education, centered on writing, particularly handwriting, that became a privileged locus of individuation and identity.

Along with writing came reading of course, but ultimately in the highly elaborated form of hermeneutical techniques and practices associated in Germany with the disciplines of the humanities, all of which became integral to 'the bureaucratic reforms designed to mobilize and install modern, self-reflective, and self-directing civil servants in the service of the emerging nation-state' (Winthrop-Young, 2011: 40). The working life of this essentially bureaucratic subject would accordingly be determined by the various technologies of writing, reading, storing and processing information; a life multiplied throughout the nations of Europe, that would be spent in offices bookkeeping, sorting files, filling forms, entering and erasing letters and numbers in the empty spaces of grids and graph paper, even as, at the same time, the libidinal core of this activity remained tied to the demand of a pure voice enjoining the writer to express his inner nature in great thoughts and poetry. Kittler argues that the role of maternal voice, reduced to its function as pure sound and sonority was part of the 'methodological purification of speech' (Kittler, 1990: 37) designed to enable the German language to become a 'general, purified, homogeneous medium' for national culture (1990: 36). Kittler writes, 'While poetry results from this maternal gestation, the mother herself remains woman under erasure, a stand-in for nature whose function is to ensure that men can speak' (Kittler, 1990: 26). In becoming the basis for discourse, then, the 'maternal' aspect is nevertheless overwritten by 'masculine' discourse. The 'feminine' aspect is effaced but not entirely erased; however, the repression of the maternal voice rendering it unconscious as the language's object-in-desire, or *objet petit a*, to use Lacan's formula. The maternal voice becomes *objet a* of German discourse that the Romantic poet seeks to separate from the Other as the expression of his natural genius. As Kittler shows, the purification of language becomes the basis for a highly masculine culture ripe, we could add, for the production of obsessional neurotics whose 'self-reflective, self-directed' fantasy of quasi-Cartesian Romantic egotism binds being entirely to thought in either the exalted form of philosophy and poetry or the more mundane form of bureaucratic administration. At the same time, nineteenth-century women, confined almost exclusively to their domestic and maternal roles and keenly aware of their effacement, are thus located in a position ripe for the forms of somatic resistance and rebellion associated with hysteria.

In the essay 'Dracula's Legacy' (Kittler, 1997) that returns to the point of transition between the discourse networks of 1800 and 1900, Kittler acknowledges that while women called mothers were largely happy to be the paper for 'the scriptorial quills' of their sons, 'women who preferred to speak themselves were called overly sensitive or hysterical' (71). However, another role was emerging for women, that of the stenographer or typist or steno-typist, who took advantage of the handwriting fetishism of their quill-wielding male contemporaries and began to displace them with the greater efficiency of the new writing machines. Kittler adds that 'if the great word emancipation has any historical meaning, it is only in the area of word processing, which continues to employ more women world-wide than any other field' (64). In his reading of Stoker's novel, Kittler seizes on this innovation in technology and the emergence of the female 'word processor' to locate the steno-typist Mina Harker (nee Murray) as the heroine of the novel, the fulcrum through which new technologies in writing, recording, storage and transmission defeat the vampires. Less than a novel about vampires and the occult, Bram Stoker's *Dracula* is 'rather the written account of our bureaucratization' (73).

Poised between the two possibilities of typist and the vampire that she nearly becomes, Mina Harker shows that in the discourse technological conditions of 1890 women have at least two more possibilities than 'simply mother or hysteria, as the dispositive sexuality had established in classical-romantic times. Since our culture has begun to allow women into the sacred halls of word processing, far worse things are possible' (70). The mother's mouth may begin to sprout fangs in the noumenal world of the word processor.

THE PERSONA COMPUTER

The discourse networks of 1800 give rise to obsession and hysteria, then, the classic Freudian neuroses (along with phobia and perversion). With the proliferation of different audio and visual media described in *Discourse Networks* 1900 (gramophone, photography, cinema), however, physical affects of the real are rendered directly accessible to perception via analogical means that do not require mediation by language. For Lacan, the imaginary apprehension of the real that bypasses the defile of the signifier broaches psychosis, and Kittler suggests that it is this condition that characterizes the twentieth century. From 1800 to 1900, then, the 'conceptual persona' characteristic of new technical media moves from bureaucrat-poet to the schizophrenic with his or her machines (on the 'conceptual persona' see Deleuze and Guattari, 1994). The gap introduced by language and the symbolic order is closed as sound and visual media directly invade the psyche. The schizophrenic, Deleuze writes, 'lives in machines, alongside machines, or the machines are in him, in her' (Deleuze, 2006: 17).

While in *Discourse Networks*, Kittler refers again to a Freudian text and the example of the psychotic Judge Schreber, Geoffrey Winthrop-Young provides a very neat commentary on another of Kittler's examples that makes the point most effectively with reference to Pink Floyd's song 'Brain Damage' from *The Dark Side of the Moon*. Kittler reads the song as a commentary on advances of technologies of sound reproduction that culminates in the collapse of the distance necessary for aesthetic appreciation, the distance separating subject and object, listener, song and performer since everything appears to take place inside the listener's head: 'the explosion of acoustic media flips over into an implosion which crashes with headlong immediacy into the very centre of perception' (Kittler, 1982: 472; see also Winthrop-Young, 2011: 55).[1] The world of Deleuze and Guattari now seems to replace that of Freud and Lacan; neuroses are superseded by a generalized psychosis that becomes the ordinary state of the subject (something acknowledged in a different way by Jacques-Alain Miller at the end of the century; Miller, 2009) and proliferates throughout various machine assemblages.

What symptoms might characterize the conceptual persona of discourse network 2000? With the reformatting and homogenization of analogue technologies into digital code and convergence onto various platforms, new forms of subjectivity are emerging related to new media, new economic and social imperatives. For Colette Soler, 'the symptoms that we call new, which affect orality, action and mood, are almost all symptoms outside the social bond, bearers of an autistic jouissance' (Soler, 2014: 183). This 'autistic jouissance' is partly the paradoxical effect of the networked existence produced by the twenty-first century regime of telecommunications in which to use the title of Sherry Turkle's book, we are 'alone together' (Turkle, 2010). Perhaps it is no coincidence that a statistical debate is currently raging about the so-called epidemic of autism, a debate that in itself makes the case for its 'quasi-ordinary status', according to Eric Laurent.

In this chapter, however, I want to look at a different symptom, one that has returned with the rise to ubiquitous presence of the 'personal' computer in the late twentieth century and its rapid miniaturization and integration into everyday existence at a most intimate level in the twenty-first century. A product of the discourse network of 1800, the computer was then not just 'personal', he or she was actually a person: a clerk or bookkeeper, accountant or bureaucrat. A particularly humble one was Herman Melville's Bartleby the Scrivener (1853/2009) whose job was to 'copy and paste' legal documents. The computer Bartleby memorably develops a virus, a line of code or 'formula', in the phrase of Deleuze, that bears the command: 'I would prefer not to'. In the story this virus repeatedly countermands and overrides any and every request of his superiors, in spite of every effort to de-bug and fix it, with result that the company ultimately has to relocate away from the source of the virus, abandoning Bartleby and the command prompt that repeats its formula continually until the computer is sealed-off, imprisoned and terminally shuts down, finally having preferred not to eat, presumably in a drive to become inorganic.

To assess some of the symptoms of the delirious yet post-psychotic, hyper-obsessional world of the persona computer in the twenty-first century, I want to return to Kittler in his Freudo-Lacanian mode to interpret and analyze a model of the subject that finds its facilitating structure in a network of persona-computers, indispensible objects and instruments generating and exchanging data and information, and thereby establishing the discourse network and threshold of economic existence in the twenty-first century.

THE BLANK SCREEN

In his book *The Man Who Couldn't Stop: OCD and the True Story of a Life Lost in Thought* (2014), David Adam sketches a self-portrait in his attempt to convey the subjective experience of his condition. He writes, 'It is hard to communicate obsession' but in what follows offers 'the best description I have'. In this description he invites us to consider a personal computer, noting that on the screen of the computer 'various windows and separate operations' can run at the same time. Referring to his real-time activity of writing or processing in one window the words that the reader will read, Adam sketches the vignette of his subjective experience on one application while another window is in the background updating his email, and 'a separate web browser . . . tracks football scores' (8). Adam tells us that as he's writing these words, he's also toggling between the windows, minimizing them, making them bigger and so on as he checks his email and keeps an eye on the progress of Stoke City, the team he supports. This he says 'is how the mind usually handles thoughts. It shares conscious concentration between tasks, while the subconscious changes the content of each window, or draws our attention among them' (8). While Adam's mind operates like this, it is simultaneously beset by obsession.

> Obsession is a large window that cannot be made to shrink, move or close. Even when other tasks come to the front of the mind, the obsession window is there in the background. It grinds away and is ready to sequester attention. It acts as a constant drag on the battery and degrades the performance of other tasks. . . . Whenever you are awake, the window is there. . . . Sometimes, usually when you wake [up], it is absent. The screen is blank. But push a key, move the mouse, engage the brain, and it whirrs and clicks back into place. (Adam, 2014: 8–9)

What is interesting about this description, it seems to me, is not that it uses the computer as a model for the mind or brain—that is after all quite conventional. Rather, the model for the subject, that clearly refers both to its 'mind' and its 'brain' as distinct objects is here that of a computer operating another that is at the same time itself. The subject here is someone operating a computer that he says is the 'best description' of himself complete with a window of obsession that can't be closed, moved or reduced. This mirror-effect is perhaps not all that surprising given the history of computing and the computer's use as a model of the mind. Both Andrew Goffey and Warren Sack comment on this circularity in separate pieces on 'Intelligence' and 'Memory' in Matt Fuller's collection *Software Studies: A Lexicon* (2008). Goffey argues that while computing's success in mechanizing the thought-processes involved in mathematical abstractions through the manipulation of symbols persuaded a generation of cognitive scientists 'that human intelligence itself was computation', he notes Ed Hutchins's point in *Cognition in the Wild* (1995) that 'the physical symbol-system architecture . . . is not a model of individual cognition. It is a model of the operation of a social-cultural system from which the human actor has been removed' (363). In his piece on memory Sack underscores the mirror-effect that is involved in this correlation between the work of human and entirely mechanical computation. 'Cognitive science work on memory is based—ironically enough—on a willful amnesia of recent history and thus on a circularity: computer memory seems to be a good model of human memory because computer memory was modeled on human memory!'; that is to say the bureaucratic system of recording and storing information developed throughout the nineteenth century and implemented by computers like Bartleby (Sack, 2008: 186).

There is much that could be said about the Adam computer's frozen 'obsession window' that marks the limit of the subject's 'toggling' mastery of its other windows and applications. On the one hand, it is a constant distraction from the everyday work and activity of writing and flitting from email to football scores and no doubt other entertainments and networks. But it is this 'state of constant distraction' that many are increasingly arguing is making any form of serious reading and writing impossible. Tim Parks in the *New Yorker* for example, complains that the existence of all these other connections and networks 'on the very instrument you use to write' is a significant threat to the levels of concentration required of serious literature because writers are checking their email, Facebook or Twitter feed every ten minutes (2014). In this context the frozen window of obsession is perhaps some form of symptomatic resistance.

In what follows I propose to take David Adam's description of himself as a computer with obsessional neurosis or 'OCD' as a kind of 'conceptual persona' (the 'persona computer') that characterizes life in the human-machine system. As is well accepted, social and economic life in the developed world of the twenty-first century is populated by 'cyborgs', people who cannot function without their networked computers, whether they come in the form of PCs, Macs, laptops, tablets, smart phones and so on. In the future, it is suggested, this kind of technology will become an integral part of the human body as computing power continues its exponential rise and miniaturization. Nevertheless, these computers owe their origins to the discourse networks of 1800, the production of the poet-bureaucrat version of the human-machine system that becomes supplemented and accelerated by the stenotypist word processor. Like Bartleby the scrivener, the 'Adam-computer' is a computer who 'couldn't stop', clearly troubled by problem in the system. Accordingly, in this chapter, I am going to look the obsessive neurosis of computers as a primarily technological question rather than a psychological or neurological problem. This is not about brains, but about hardware, software, binary code, the interaction of formal and natural languages and the modes of interactivity and forms of subjectivity they shape and enable.

From a technical perspective, then, what could have produced the frozen window problem that is plaguing the Adam computer? It is likely to be either a bug or a virus. In contradistinction to a virus, a bug is a glitch in the system, the result of either an error or mischief in the writing of software. As Olga Goriunova and Alexei Shulgin argue, the glitch occupies the problematic zone of functionality at the 'computer's aesthetic core, as marks of (dys)functions, (re)actions and (e)motions that are worked out in human-computer assemblages' (2008: 111).

For Lacan, very similar glitches appear at the same level of the speaking being that attempts to utilize and make sense of language. Human languages (no doubt there are many other kinds) are comprised of both symbolic and imaginary elements. The symbolic is the element of pure machine. In his paper from 1955 on psychoanalysis, cybernetics and the nature of language, Lacan goes to great pains to argue mathematically and through practical demonstration the mechanical basis of the symbolic mediation of language, and indeed the 'cybernetic' operations of human thought. At the same time, he acknowledges that symbols have always taken certain shapes that have 'a specific relation with the living existence of the human being, with a quite narrow sector of its biological reality, and the image of its fellow beings' (Lacan, 1988: 319). And it is precisely this imaginary dimension that provides the 'obstacle to the progress of the realization of the subject in the symbolic order', and that supplies the 'resistance opposing the restitution of the integral text of the symbolic exchange' (319). As is well known, it is too difficult for software engineers to read lines of zeros and ones, so that the purity of binary code has to be turned into a more workable albeit formal programming language, a kind of 'short hand' that is precisely rendered more workable through the addition of characteristics of natural languages that retain these 'imaginary' elements. And just as with speaking beings, this is where the glitches crop up for computers. As Lacan writes—and his use of metaphor is very pertinent here—'we always think by means of some imaginary go-between, which halts, stops, clouds up the symbolic mediation. The latter is ground up, interrupted' (319). This appears to be what is happening with the obsession window in the Adam computer. It won't close because it is arrested by some kind of imaginary capture that means the symbols that drive it just whirr and grind away in a perpetual cycle, symptom no doubt of the very circularity that marks the relation between person and computer or rather between computer and computer. The pure function of symbolic mediation as it manifests itself in the life of the person-computer is for Lacan the function that is connotable in binary terms of presence and absence, being and non-being. In the description of the Adam computer this is starkly configured in the conjunction of the blank screen that is briefly there at the point of waking, connoting absence and non-being, and the obsession window that as soon as one pushes a key, moves a mouse, or engages the brain, whirrs and clicks back into place suggesting the unbearable presence of being in thought.

On the one hand, blankness, the relief of absence, sleep or death in the unfathomable depths of the blank screen, on the other, unrelieved presence and the obsessive window's jouissance of thought in the thought of jouissance. As Soler notes, while 'obsession is certainly a mental phenomenon that interferes with thought . . . obsessions are always thoughts of *jouissance*' (Soler, 2014: 175). And here, with its window of obsession, the Adam computer answers a question posed to computers by Lacan in the 1970s. 'I am willing to accept that a computer thinks' he says. 'But that it knows, who would say such a thing? For the foundation of knowledge is that the jouissance of its exercise is the same as that of its acquisition' (Lacan, 1999: 219). The Adam computer, we can safely assume, clearly knows something, even if that knowledge is unconscious and it doesn't know that it knows. The obsession window is an image of the computer's jouissance as it whirrs and grinds away, expending energy, running down the battery and degrading the performance of other applications for no good reason. And that, as Lacan reminds us in Seminar XX is the very definition of jouissance: 'jouissance is what serves no purpose' (1999: 3).

One possibility, then, is that the frozen window problem is the result of a glitch that is an effect of the remnant of natural language in the formal language that programmes the software, and as such, if we follow Kittler's argument about the repressed condition of the discourse network 1800 that initially shaped the computer, this glitch is caused by the maternal voice as *objet a*. In the offices of the twentieth century, this voice rapidly became integral to the system of bureaucracy in the clickety-clack chatter of the female stenographer's typewriter as it turns the speech of her employers or interviewees, via the formal or coded language of her 'short hand', into the anonymity of print.

Another possibility, however, is that the frozen window problem is a virus which means that the cause comes from elsewhere in the network—the Other where there could be manifold dangers including, in the world of cybergothic, vampires. Certainly it is the *idea* of a virus that provides the content of the Adam computer's obsession window. The obsession window contains a single phrase like Bartleby's 'I would prefer not to'. The formula for the Adam computer, however, is 'you could have Aids'. The Adam computer's obsession is that it might have a virus; it might have AIDS. Indeed it is the fear of having a virus that produces the effect of the virus itself. This is actually not an uncommon form of virus, one called a 'text virus' that usually takes the form of an alarmed email message, usually passed on from a friend or colleague's address book, informing you that 'you could have a virus'. It then informs you of a number of steps you should take in order to locate the infected file on your operating system and how to delete it. The 'virus' relies on the ignorance and fear of the average user, who dutifully deletes the perfectly good file thereby becoming 'the virus of their own operating system'. Apparently the first instance of this was the 'Magistr virus' from 2001. Another example targeted a Windows utility—*Jdbgmgr.exe*, which was a file with a teddy bear icon used in Java environments (see Deseriis, 2008: 250). Like bugs, these viruses are, as Marco Deseriis notes, again an effect of 'a machinic system characterized by a high level of commixture of natural language and computer code' (256). Accordingly, it remains at that level in the conjunction between the imaginary elements of natural language and the machine of symbolic mediation that the real of the unconscious produces the neurotic symptoms of the computer.

THE VAMPIRE-MOTHER

The Adam computer was infected by the suggestion 'you could have Aids' in November 1990 while at university, as a result of spending a night with a fellow student. Adam describes what happened:

> It was one of those frozen Leeds nights that Yorkshire folk are so proud of. The wheezing gas fire in her kitchen generated more light than heat and the cold chased us around the room like the smoke from a wood fire. Upstairs sounded good.
>
> 'Did you have sex with that girl?' my friend Noel asked the next day.
>
> 'Yes', I lied.
>
> 'Did you use a condom?'
>
> 'No'.
>
> 'You could have Aids'.
>
> 'Don't be daft'. (Adam, 2014: 18)

Initially thinking nothing of the encounter, Adam states that it was only while at home with his parents during the vacation that 'with no warning the thought came again. You could have Aids. Only this time I couldn't move past the idea, or the cramps of panic it caused. . . . My life was over before it truly had begun' (18). The unfounded suggestion nevertheless exerts its grip as Adam anticipates the mourning of his parents as they 'gently bicker across the wooden kitchen table', retreating back to his childhood bed to weep with 'his head buried in his pillows', repeating to himself the formula that would dominate his thoughts and waking life (or rather living-death) subsequently, for at least the next twenty years: 'I could have Aids' (19).

It is not my place, nor do I wish, to speculate on the etiology of David Adam's obsession which is between him and his therapists, although I will, as here and in places, use some of the statements he offers to readers to illustrate a few general points about the structure of obsessive neurosis in Freud and Lacan. Adam's book is part memoire, part description and reconstruction of his obsession, and part reflection on the various cures and treatments he has undertaken in his attempts to free himself of his condition. All this factors into the description of the assemblage that constitutes the Adam computer that provides the focus and model for this chapter. Adam's account of his various treatments range quite widely, but also include forms of psychodynamic therapy that he associates with Freud. Adam has rather a strange attitude to Freud that is at once hostile, dismissive yet intimate, referring to him by his first name. 'Sigmund Freud said that OCD was down to repressed guilt about childhood masturbation. Thanks Sigmund' (45). This is of course simplification to the point of misrepresentation. Freud does refer to masturbation with regard to his obsessional patients but simply to report their 'unanimous belief' in the idea that their commitment to onanism 'was the root and origin of all their troubles' (Freud, 1909/1993: 43). Freud does not suggest that masturbation, which he reminds us is 'a quite typical occurrence', is responsible for neurotic disturbances (43), however, he did believe that it was important to listen to the words of his patients.

In his 'Notes upon a Case of Obsessional Neurosis' (1909), otherwise known as the case of the 'Rat Man', onanism is regarded as significant where it pops up in unexpected places, provoked by situations that combine, Freud suggests, both 'a prohibition, and the defiance of a command' (45). Such a conjunction we might add seems to characterize the morbid obsession that marked much of the European attitude to masturbation in the nineteenth century where, as Foucault discusses in *The History of Sexuality Vol I: The Will to Know* (1984), dormitories were precisely designed around the pleasure of a gaze that both prohibited and yet facilitated the masturbation of pubescent children in a 'perpetual spiral of power and pleasure' (45). This combination wherein the jouissance of a transgression is 'commanded' is of course the structure of the superego and it certainly seems that this structure continues to dominate the current attitude to masturbation, particularly in the context of the Internet and the ubiquity of pornography. On the one hand, since pornography has been at the vanguard of the technical, aesthetic and commercial development of the web, it was an imperative in the 1990s particularly, almost a duty to masturbate as much as possible in order to facilitate the growth of the online economy. On the other hand, masturbation in the wrong place or at the wrong time could cause problems—at one's place of work for example, in the office on the firm's time. Indeed, to return to the Adam computer's frozen window problem, how awful would it be if one could not move, reduce or close a window featuring some pornographic scene that one had accessed that hinted at the depravity of one's unspeakable desires to one's family, friends or colleagues.

An enthusiasm for masturbation, spiced by guilt, is not the origin of obsessive neurosis, but an effect of its particular structure that encourages the subject to think that he is complete in himself, self-sufficient, preferring a kind of isolation or imaginative solitude to enjoy himself in his own way without being troubled by the demands of an other. The obsessive characteristically gets off on the idea, on the idea of sex rather than the reality, which is often difficult for him. As Lacan says laconically, 'The tasks of nature are not his strong point' and he 'dreads nothing more than that to which he imagines he aspires' (Lacan, 1960–1961: xviii: 8).

The Adam computer does not relate the circumstances of his failure to have sex with his student friend at university, perhaps it was never their intention, though he hints that it was—'it was one of those frozen Leeds nights . . . the cold chased us around the room . . . Upstairs sounded good' (18)—but it is curious that he lies about it, thereby perhaps producing a certain feeling of guilt for which he later punishes himself with the self-destructive fantasy of AIDS. Adam rejects any such connection, however, and suggests that the specificity of his particular fear of AIDS is arbitrary and contingent upon historical circumstances, suggesting that the obsession that 'closed around' his thoughts in 1991 was part of general cultural fear that was prepared a few years earlier:

> HIV and AIDS quickly replaced the Cold War nuclear threat—of the Frankie Goes to Hollywood song 'Two Tribes' and Raymond Briggs's book *When the Wind Blows*—as the great Fear of popular culture, and soaked through to the manners of day-to-day life. 'A man round the corner in Boundary Lane has Aids', my mother, not known for her mealtime jokes, announced to us one night in the late 1980s. 'Yes, he's got one in each ear.' (39)

There seems to be a slight confusion concerning the chronology of fears to which Adam refers. HIV did not replace the nuclear threat but accompanied a certain increase in Cold War tension in the early to mid-1980s, as Ronald Reagan applied pressure on the USSR through economic and military means. Notoriously, he heightened fears throughout the world in 1984 by announcing in a warm-up to his weekly Saturday speech on National Public Radio that he'd 'outlawed Russia forever

[and] we begin bombing in five minutes' (Reagan, 1984). The Cold War ended in 1989 by which time the AIDS fear had also abated somewhat from its peak when its source and precise nature were terrifyingly unknown. The AIDS panic probably reached its own peak in 1986 and Adam mentions from that time the famous 'AIDS: Don't Die of Ignorance' advertising campaign that was notable for disturbing features not least, for some obscure reason, a very large melting iceberg.[2]

The two other texts that Adam cites but does not date are a couple of years earlier than the 'Don't Die of Ignorance' campaign, and actually occur the same year as Reagan's 'bomb Russia' quip, predating the end of the Cold War by at least five years. These are the years of Adam's puberty, assuming he was nineteen or twenty while in his second year at university in 1991 when the fear of the AIDS virus belatedly struck him. Frankie Goes to Hollywood's 'Two Tribes' (1984) and Raymond Briggs's book *When the Wind Blows* (1982; animation 1984) are indeed both contemporaneous with a peak in Cold War tension and also with the height of the AIDS consternation. In the United Kingdom the Terrence Higgins Trust dedicated to fighting the disease and promoting safe sex was founded in 1983 after the death of Higgins himself in 1982. The highly publicized illness and death of Rock Hudson occurred in 1984–1985 (while the academic world was stunned by Michel Foucault's death of the disease in 1984). These dates show that the fear of AIDS and the fear of nuclear war are contemporaneous; one does not 'replace' the other. It is tempting then to ask what is really being 'replaced' or displaced here. Chronologically Frankie Goes to Hollywood's 'Two Tribes' very quickly replaced the group's song 'Relax', the number one hit from earlier in the year whose sensational celebration of the joys of anal sex at the height of the AIDS anxiety caused it to be banned by the BBC, but not before the group's even more notorious performance on Channel 4's tea-time pop show 'The Tube'. The spectacle of simulated anal sex and S&M practices would possibly be both more disturbing to a pubescent boy and exciting to what Freud calls the scotophilic and epistemophilic drives than two old actors pretending to be the US and USSR presidents fighting in a wrestling ring (the video for Frankie's 'Two Tribes').

Raymond Briggs's *When the Wind Blows* was preceded by the much more popular book *The Snowman* that was first published in 1978 but broadcast in the form of an animated film in 1982. The film is mostly silent apart from an introductory passage spoken by the author himself as the adult version of the boy in the film:

> I remember that winter because it had brought the heaviest snows I had ever seen. Snow had fallen steadily all night long and in the morning I woke in a room filled with light and silence, the whole world seemed to be held in a dream-like stillness. It was a magical day . . . and it was on that day I made the Snowman. (Briggs, 1978; Jackson and Murakami, 1982)

The book and film tell the story of a young boy who makes a snowman that miraculously comes to life. They spend the day together having fun, even flying off at one point to meet Santa in his grotto, having the time of his life until the moment for him to return to his bedroom. In the morning the boy is distraught to discover that the Snowman has melted away. With Peter Auty's falsetto voice singing 'Walking in the Air', the film is something of a tearjerker, and Raymond Briggs, the author, partly in annoyance at the film's co-option as a sentimental Christmas favourite, has claimed that the story is about death. However it is unlikely that a pubescent or prepubescent boy is going to be too concerned about death. He is more likely to be concerned about the phallic potential of the story and the anxieties it might provoke about its rise and fall, comings and goings. From the frozen obsession window to the 'frozen' night in Leeds that led to the fatal suggestion about AIDS, recalling the melting iceberg that warns us not to die of ignorance, to the 'heaviest snows' that go to form the snowman of Briggs's story, there is clearly a metonymic chain at work. In one direction it leads to the blurb that promotes Adam's book. Referring to Adam's obsession with AIDS, the blurb advertises that 'to resist such a compulsion with will power alone is to hold back an avalanche by melting the snow with a candle. It just keeps coming and coming and coming' (Adam, 2014). In the other direction, the chain leads to the last in Adam's anecdotal list of references to AIDS in the 1980s. The final example cannot be precisely dated because it is the anecdote concerning his mother's joke in which she humorously infects her neighbour from Boundary Lane with 'Aids', playing on the pun for 'hearing aids'—'he's got one in each ear'. Adam's mother highlights in her pun the binary nature of the word 'Aids' that signifies both help and hindrance, cure and poison, life and death, her voice repeating this duality as it 'gives' the neighbour 'Aids' in recompense for his absence of hearing. The maternal voice enters the hole in the body of silence giving it speech and deafness, language, life and death, presence and absence, being and nonbeing, 0 and 1, in the form of the signifier 'Aids'. Heiress of vampire Lucy Westenra and the steno-typist Mina

Harker, a ghost of the discourse network of 1890, the voice of Mrs Adam can in the spirit of Kittler be characterized as that of a 'vampire-mother' haunting the digital infrastructure of the Adam computer.[3]

'AIDS' then is in Lacanian terms the 'phallus' (Φ), the signifier of the symbolic itself, the signifier of the digital machine language of the computer that has been encoded in the formal language of the programmer that retains the 'imaginary' elements associated with natural language and its cultural contexts. The signifier of the subject's destiny, as it is determined by the binary code of symbolic mediation, takes on a 'fatal' designation as it both aids the subject in bringing it into being, but also signals its death (the fear of dying of AIDS). As such it also functions as the signifier of the lack in the Other (Ø), which here the mother locates in the neighbour, thereby signifying both her own lack and by implication that of her husband. This is disturbing because in the Lacanian understanding of obsessive neurosis, as Bruce Fink argues, the obsessive does not associate the mother with any lack that he might be expected to fill. 'He refuses to accept this [lack] because he feels that it means something about him, his very being perhaps' (Fink, 2004: 36). By way of veiling the lack, the mother is attributed with an 'imaginary phallus' (φ), often associated with her voice.

For some reason, perhaps because of the melting iceberg in the 'Don't Die of Ignorance' AIDS information advertisement, the signifier AIDS is supported by a chain of images associated with ice, snow and the experience of feeling 'frozen'. As we see with the Snowman, the imaginary phallus (φ) is the one that appears and disappears, rises and falls, comes and goes, and is generally uncertain, but 'sheds its light on all its objects that lead back to the mother' (Fink, 2004: 35). In Seminar VIII, Lacan suggests that it is in this position of uncertainty that the obsessive likes to situate himself, giving him the formula: Ø◊φ (*a*, *a'*, *a''*, a''' . . .). As the imaginary phallus (φ), like a little candle, sheds its light on the subject's obsessive thoughts that keep 'coming and coming and coming', rendering them equivalent in a metonymic chain, the subject situates himself on the left-hand side of the 'lozenge' (◊) in the position of the lack in the Other. Fink writes, quoting Lacan from Seminar VIII, 'The obsessive subject is written Ø here because he "is never where he seems to designate himself"; he says, for example, "I am a clerk, but that's only my day job—I'm really a screenwriter". Whatever the designation of definition provided, that is never really *it*; there is always something else' (Fink, 1999: 258–59). With the example of the screenwriter-clerk we return to Kittler's poet-bureaucrat and the original formula for the computer.

A LACANIAN INSTRUCTION MANUAL ON HOW TO BUILD AN AI

The argument that is being advanced in this chapter is that computers are programmed in such a way that inclines them towards a state of obsessional neurosis that precipitates an endless displacement or postponement of the point where he might achieve the state of natural liberty to which he imagines he aspires. This is one of the most intractable problems with the development of Artificial Intelligence, and its desire, that isn't simply an effect of preprogramming. Intelligence, we must assume, goes beyond the simple flow of information, but as such its meaning is quite enigmatic. Intelligence is a fairly vague cultural value so that the promise of an artificial kind of intelligence would at least have the benefit of defining it in some way. And yet, as Andrew Goffey notes, the production of an AI that can defeat a grand master in chess, but cannot open a bag of crisps does little but complicate the matter (2008: 133). Indeed in his gloss on 'Intelligence', Goffey notes that Kittler's 'view of computers as operating like the Lacanian unconscious, expressed best in his statement that all coding operations are ultimately "signifiers of voltage differences" casts light on why machine intelligence has been and needs to be seen as a libidinal problem' (Goffey, 2008: 140).

At the most basic level of its hardware, the design of a computer involves an electrical force becoming alienated in binary code. A force of electricity hits a locus of difference in an event of input (1) and output (0) that transforms entropy into the most basic form of information, the 'bit', eight of which constitute a 'byte', the most common unit of information in computing and telecommunications. It is this continual pulse of 0s and 1s that formalizes the question of the subject's being or not being, presence or absence, life or death in the symbolic locus through which its existence is mediated. At the same time, this purely formal, meaningless oscillation is given imaginary substance through formal and natural languages that bear the weight of its historical context and antecedence: the supposed presence of an 'Other' to whom one might pose the question of existence. While it is a characteristic of the computer's obsessional neurosis to ignore or fail to confront this question, since it prefers not to engage with prospect of the Other's lack, such interactivity comes with the programming and continually arises in glitches and viral effects, as we have seen.

In his essay 'There Is No Software', Kittler's materialist analysis of computers famously denounced the idea of software as another version of the '*Geist*' or spirit, the ghost 'that does not exist as a machine-independent faculty' (Kittler, 1997: 151). But software and the processing in natural languages that it enables, the images and simulations that it produces, the utility and entertainment of its multiple applications, precisely populate the screen of imaginary projections through which interactivity is possible and indeed any notion of artificial intelligence that goes beyond the transposition of numbers in an endless loop (see Kittler, 1997: 3). It is precisely in the gap between the symbolic and the imaginary that most of the problems arise—problems concerning autonomy, knowledge, manipulation and ultimately economic and political power, given that the powerful are not excluded from this situation. Indeed, as we shall see, the most powerful of the Internet and data companies seem to be affected by the same obsessional neurosis that would infinitely postpone and displace the consequences of their power to that singular moment where the machines 'take over' and thus bear the responsibility for the fantasies produced by the desire for omnipotence. As Lacan says, not only is the obsessive unable to achieve the 'natural liberty' to which he supposedly aspires, neither is he capable of an act that 'would leave him the sole master on board . . . namely the extreme functions of responsibility, pure responsibility, what one has *vis-à-vis* this Other' (Lacan, 1960–1961: xviii: 8).

For artificial intelligence to develop in a general manner, then, it has to exceed the point where it simply follows preprogrammed instructions and pursues its own interests that if they are not also to be regarded as similarly preprogrammed would require, one assumes, some capacity for reflection about what those interests might be. Kevin Kelly suggests that we are at this point now, stating that 'technology no longer simply does what we want', but is beginning to do what it wants (Kelly, 2010: 12). Technology, he says 'may have at one time been as simple as an old computer program, merely parroting what we told it, but now it is more like a very complex organism that follows its own urges' (13). What might those 'urges' be? Goffey suggests that 'if Kittler's view is followed programmable machines would be, as Turing imagined, like the child in the proverbial family triangle: in training them to do what we ask them, they internalize the (formal) law on which the desire for recognition depends' (Goffey, 2008: 140). Might these urges then be 'Oedipal', or like the *ressentiment* of the slave?

For Lacan, following the law of desire necessitates that desire is always desire of the Other. Kelly assumes that technology follows a slightly different, more scientific law, one of evolution according to which it has all the time been following its own 'unconscious' drives and impulses, unconscious presumably because they have been subsumed beneath the conscious needs and desires of its users as it strives to grow and proliferate. In this it is also pursuing the desire of the Other in so far as we define the Other precisely as this law of evolution that all of life has followed at least until the moment when originarily prosthetic, speaking beings seized their destiny *ex nihilo* in the form of technologies like language, fire, tools, electricity and computers. According to Kelly, technology now wishes to reject this position of supplementarity and evolve entirely in its own way.

Indeed, in his book *What Technology Wants* (2010), Kelly concedes that 'technology wants—the same long list of merits we crave' (269). Before we come to the long list, it is interesting to note how this phrase conforms to the idea that desire is desire of the Other and the mutual lack that this implies—neither technology nor human beings possess these merits, or at least not completely or never definitively, so that we 'crave' more and more of them. Indeed, Kelly suggests that we 'crave' 'increasing' degrees of these merits, as if desire were confronting in the Other an insatiable desire. Unsurprisingly, these 'merits', as their description suggests, comprise a list of buzzwords characteristic of American tech companies that draw from a range of disciplines: managerialism, biology, information theory, (neoliberal) economics as well as a residual form of romanticism that underwrites the entire list. 'Technology', Kelly writes, 'wants what life wants: increasing efficiency, increasing opportunity, increasing emergence, increasing complexity, increasing diversity, increasing specialization, increasing ubiquity, increasing freedom, increasing mutualism, increasing beauty, increasing sentience, increasing structure, increasing evolvability' (269). Romanticism underwrites the entire list not just because 'beauty' and 'freedom' exceed or guarantee the functionality of 'efficiency' or 'specialization', but because all this is the pure expression of 'life'. These are recognizably the biotechnological dreams of Kittler's poet-bureaucrat-computer, in which nature is shaped into discourse and autopoietic, self-evolved art. Technology wants the poetic egotism of sublime sublimation.

In his paper on 'The Subversion of the Subject and the Dialectic of Desire in the Freudian Unconscious', Lacan draws a diagram in the shape of a hook that poses the question *Che vuoi?* or 'what do you want from me?' that poses to the Other the question concerning its desire. It is of course reversible and thus as abyssal as technology wanting life and life wanting technology: 'I want whatever you want'. At the end point of the hook forming the question mark of desire, Lacan places the 'structure of fantasy' which he writes $\$\Diamond a$. This is the 'algorithm' that shapes desire and is 'designed to allow for a hundred and one different readings' dependent upon the particular configuration of the subject and its data (Lacan, 2006: 691). As an algorithm that sorts out the 'stuff' of the subject's own reality in relation to the desire of the Other, it is not dissimilar to the other algorithms used in network computing 'used to render web pages in a browser, in the sorting of entries in a spreadsheet . . . in the generation of artificial life (simulating models for evolutionary processes), as well as data-mining techniques to predict . . . shopping preferences, select . . . news feed and bespoke advertising' (Goffey, 2008: 18), not to mention predicting crime patterns and trading in securities.

Of course this data that both shapes fantasy in the form of software applications, websites and social networks and responds to all the minuscule acts of online desire is comprised of billions of clicks on billions of computers every day that produce the continual flux of online existence. The large data companies with the largest servers and data analysts are the ones most able to mine, read and exploit the flows of desire beneath which each individual 'I' of clicking enunciation disappears (unless its data trail is hunted down and reconstructed for the purposes of security). Indeed the security systems at the National Security Agency and Government Communications Headquarters are among the most powerful of these master servers, along with Google of course. Google's algorithms analyze billions of web pages, plus PDF, Word documents, Excel spreadsheets, Flash files, plain text files, and, since 2009, Facebook and Twitter content. The perception at the heart of Google's administration seems to be that they are in this way capturing human intelligence as a means of producing a super-intelligent being.

Above Lacan's structure of fantasy in his Graph of Desire is the matheme 'S Ø' that denotes the 'signifier of the lack in the Other' behind which the obsessive likes to locate himself. The desire to veil this 'lack' with billions upon billions of items of data supposed to produce a super-intelligent entity would seem to confirm its pertinence. Last year *The Guardian* reported that 'Google has bought almost every machine-learning and robotics company it can find, or at least, rates . . . And this month, it bought the secretive and cutting-edge British artificial intelligence startup DeepMind for £242m' (Cadwalladr, 2014). Google also engaged as chief engineer on its AI project Ray Kurzweil, best known for his prediction and advocacy of the 'singularity', the name for the moment when artificial intelligence becomes so vast and so exceeds the capabilities of human intelligence and imagination that it constitutes an 'event horizon' beyond which it is impossible to see or predict the future. Propelled by the exponential growth of computing power, this event will essentially be an effect of the so-called capture of human intelligence by machines, the merging of human beings with technology and 'its' ability to reproduce itself and 'evolve' in its own way. This notion of the 'singularity' that Jaron Lanier suggests defines the prevailing assumptions among intellectuals in Silicon valley (2010: 27) about the future of technology to the point where they do whatever they can to facilitate it, is convenient because in this way even the most powerful and ambitious tech company avoids responsibility for its position by deflecting all mastery on to an indefinite future when thought and jouissance are unified in the technological equivalent of the 'rapture'. The rapture of the 'Un-Dead' won't be for everyone of course, and as Stefan Heidenreich reports, Kittler assumed that 'the computer would either "eat us up or spit us out."'[4] Alternatively, like Bartleby, the super-intelligent computer may just prefer to do neither.

Kittler's intuition that the *Aufhebung* of the Hegelian dialectic into the mastery of the super-machine won't be achieved without some human wastage is consistent with the desire for linguistic purity in the original discourse networks of 1800, that in 2000 finds 'Absolute Knowledge running in an endless loop' evacuated of all noise. Similarly, we also see this process of purification in the increasing automation of intellectual labour that promises to render obsolete much of the professions in the drive to turn being into the purity of inorganic thought. This does not of course mean that when all work is automated human beings will enjoy the life of the master in sport and leisure both of which are in any case essentially businesses. Since capitalism took over the discourse of the master, 'it is . . . out of the question that one not work' (Lacan, 2007: 167–68), even if the substance of that work becomes reduced to opening crisp packets for the masters of Intelligence. Currently, even where leisure is supposed to exist in the form of online sociality, it has been overwritten by the bureaucratic form of work. All social and economic activity on the web involves filling out online forms, writing numbers in little boxes in the grids that have been drawn over the blank screen of the Other's infinite demand.

Moreover it is here among these grids that the bureaucratic death drive finds expression in the utopian promise of social networks, particularly as pioneered by Facebook. Lanier speaks incredulously of the 'weird socialism' in which a 'social network owner [can] believe that his business is one and the same [as] an ideal society' (Lanier, 2013: 147) in the delusion that a society of ubiquitous surveillance produces a form of global corporate communism in which everything is accountable and therefore transparent. Whereas the ideal of socialism is to produce the political and economic conditions not just for universal recognition but for the equal distribution of jouissance, Facebook appears to be aiming for a similar equalization, at the level of its users at least, by requiring the evacuation of all jouissance through the purification of all forms of exchange. According to David Kirkpatrick, Facebook is 'founded on a radical social premise—that an enveloping transparency will overtake modern life' (Kirkpatrick, 2010: 200). Zuckerberg's well-documented moral objection to privacy closely resembles the obsessive's suspicion of duplicity that is made possible by secrecy and the use of multiple identities.[5]

'Everything for the other' says the obsessive, and that is what he does, for being in the perpetual whirlwind [*vertige*] of destroying the other, he can never do enough to ensure that the other continues to exist'. (Lacan in Fink, 1999: 118; see also Lacan, 1960–1961: xvii: 13). Whether it is in destroying the Other through automating his work in the name of greater growth or efficiency, or in evacuating her jouissance in the name of equality, the computer that couldn't stop whirrs on in a spiral, its increasing acceleration precluding any moment of pause, blurring any angle of reflection, until it either spins off its axis, displaced by another form of language or mode of jouissance, or the whirlwind does indeed converge at an imaginary point of singularity or Otherness, sustained by the impossibility of the obsessive's desire, and the question of its existence returns into the black hole of the blank screen.

NOTES

1. In an essay on Louis Wolfson, Deleuze uses a similar example, referring to the Sony Walkman as a machine that will 'schizophrenize entire peoples and generations' (Deleuze, 1998: 13).

2. It is accessible on YouTube at www.youtube.com/watch?v=-Cenvz7EWmU. Freud notes the importance of the 'will to know' in obsessives that is part of the return of the 'early development and premature repression of the sexual instinct of looking and knowing (the scotophilic and epistemophilic instinct)', remarking that 'the very high average of intellectual capacity among obsessional patients is probably also connected with this fact' (Freud, 1909/1993: 78).

3. The correlation between vampires and the transmission of AIDS was of course underscored in 1992 by Francis Ford Coppola's film *Bram Stoker's Dracula* that featured a number of close-ups of blood cells, suggesting the microbiological transmission of viruses like AIDS through bodily fluids, particularly via blood transfusions and the use of hypodermic needles.

4. Kittler's prediction was recalled by Stefan Heidenreich at the symposium 'Media After Kittler' Bolivar Hall, London 09.10.2013.

5. Zuckerberg's morality informs and justifies both his commitment to transparency and his apparent belief that privacy is an impediment to an open society. Fitzpatrick reports his desire 'to get people to this point where there's more openness—that's a big challenge . . . The concept that the world will be better if you share more is something that's pretty foreign to a lot of people and it runs into all these privacy concerns'. Zuckerberg goes on to say that 'having two identities for yourself is an example of a lack of integrity . . . the level of transparency the world has now won't support having two identities for a person' (Kirkpatrick, 2010: 199).

BIBLIOGRAPHY

Adam, David. (2014) *The Man Who Couldn't Stop: OCD and the True Story of a Life Lost in Thought*. London: Picador.

Briggs, Raymond. (1978) *The Snowman*. London: Hamish Hamilton.

Cadwalladr, Carole. (2014) 'Are the Robots about to Rise? Google's New Director of Engineering Certainly Seems to Think So . . .' *The Observer*, 22.02.14 See www.theguardian.com/technology/2014/feb/22/robots-google-ray-kurzweil-terminator-singularity-artificial-intelligence.

Deleuze, Gilles. (1998) *Essays Critical and Clinical*. London: Verso.

———. (2006) *Two Regimes of Madness*. New York: Semiotext(e).

Deleuze, Gilles and Félix Guattari. (1994) *What Is Philosophy?* London: Verso.

Derrida, Jacques. (1987) *The Post Card: From Socrates to Freud and Beyond*. Chicago: University of Chicago Press.

Deseriis, Marco. (2008) 'Virus' in Matt Fuller (ed.) *Software Studies: A Lexicon*. Cambridge: MIT Press.

Fink, Bruce. (1999) *A Clinical Introduction to Lacanian Psychoanalysis*. Cambridge: Harvard University Press.

———. (2004) *Lacan to the Letter*. Minneapolis: University of Minnesota Press.

Foucault, Michel. (1984) *The History of Sexuality Vol I: The Will to Know*. Harmondsworth: Penguin.

Freud, Sigmund. (1909/1993) 'The Rat Man or Notes upon a Case of Obsessional Neurosis' in *Three Case Histories*. New York: Macmillan.

Goffey, Andrew. (2008) 'Intelligence' in Matt Fuller (ed.) *Software Studies: A Lexicon.* Cambridge: MIT Press.

Goriunova, Olga and Alexei Shulgin. (2008) 'Glitch' in Matt Fuller (ed.) *Software Studies: A Lexicon.* Cambridge: MIT Press.

Hutchins, Edwin. (1995) *Cognition in the Wild.* Cambridge: MIT Press.

Jackson, Dianne. (1982) *Raymond Briggs' The Snowman.* TVC London: Channel 4 Universal Pictures.

Jackson, Dianne and Jimmy Murakami. (1982) *The Snowman.* Snowman Enterprises.

Kelly, Kevin. (2010) *What Technology Wants.* Harmondsworth: Penguin.

Kirkpatrick, David. (2010) *The Facebook Effect.* London: Virgin.

Kittler, Friedrich. (1982) 'England 1975—Pink Floyd, Brain Damage' in K. Lindeman (ed.) *Europalyrik 1775-heute. Gedichte und Interpretationen.* Paderborn: Schöningh, pp. 467–77.

———. (1990) *Discourse Networks 1800/1900.* Stanford, CA: Stanford University Press.

———. (1997) *Literature, Media, Information Systems*, edited and introduced by John Johnston. London: G&B Arts.

Lacan, Jacques. (1960–1961) *The Seminar of Jacques Lacan, Book VIII: Transference.* Translated by Cormac Gallagher from unedited transcripts.

———. (1988) *The Seminar of Jacques Lacan, Book II: The Ego in Freud's Theory and in the Technique of Psychoanalysis.* Trans. John Forrester. Cambridge: Cambridge University Press.

———. (1999) *Encore*, Seminar XX. Trans. Bruce Fink. New York: Norton.

———. (2006) *Écrits.* Trans. Bruce Fink. New York: Norton.

———. (2007) *The Other Side of Psychoanalysis*, Seminar XVII. Trans. Bruce Fink. New York: Norton.

Lanier, Jaron. (2010) *You Are Not a Gadget.* Harmondsworth: Penguin.

———. (2013) *Who Owns the Future.* London: Allen Lane.

Melville, Herman. (2009) 'Bartleby, the Scrivener' in *Billy Budd, Sailor and Selected Tales.* Oxford: Oxford Classics.

Miller, Jacques-Alain. (2009) 'Ordinary Psychosis Revisited' in Nataile Wülfing, *Ordinary Psychosis.* Psychoanalytic Notebooks, 19, LSNLS.

Parks, Tim. (2014) 'Reading: The Struggle.' *New York Review of Books.* See www.nybooks.com/blogs/nyrblog/2014/jun/10/reading-struggle/.

Reagan, Ronald. (1984) 'Radio Address to the Nation on Congressional Inaction on Proposed Legislation'. August 11, 1984, at www.reagan.utexas.edu/archives/speeches/1984/81184a.htm.

Sack, Warren. (2008) 'Memory' in Matt Fuller (ed.) *Software Studies: A Lexicon.* Cambridge: MIT Press.

Soler, Colette. (2014) *Lacan: The Unconscious Reinvented.* London: Karnac.

Turkle, Sherry. (2010) *Alone Together.* New York: Basic Books.

Wilson, Scott. (2002) 'Dying for a Smoke: Freudian Addiction and the Joy of Consumption'. *Angelaki* 7(2): 161–74.

Winthrop-Young, Geoffrey. (2011) *Kittler and the Media.* London: Polity.

Chapter Eight

The Situation After Media

Stefan Heidenreich

POST-MEDIA

When the statement 'media define our situation' became one of the key propositions of media theory after Kittler, digital technologies were still considered to be something new. Kittler's statement can be understood as an extension of Marshall McLuhan's 'the medium is the message' with a Hegelian spin to it. Where McLuhan proposes a substitution, Kittler postulates a power relation. With the term *situation*, political powers and historical processes enter the scene.

Thirty years later, media are no longer what they used to be and the situation has considerably changed. Media have become an all-encompassing environment. What started as stand-alone machines with defined technical specifications, codes and channels has transformed into a diversified myriad of gadgets and an all-connecting network. The defining power of the new technical infrastructure appears to be greater than ever. It no longer looks like a medium, nor does it assert its influence in the way media once did. Many publications with titles like 'post-media' and 'after-media' seem to confirm the impression that we left media behind. But, as Jean-Francois Lyotard pointed out in *The Postmodern Condition* (1979), claims that come with the prefix 'post' lead to a double-bind. The 'post' reconfirms what it declares overcome. Had we really left media for good, our theoretical considerations would be filed under a different title. And indeed, recent philosophies have left reflections on media and technical issues behind, proposing a realism and an object orientation that neglect technologies of production, communication and reflection.

In the end media remains a *situation*. And if something of the initial statement remains true, the situation points to a technical '*definiens*', that operates in the place formerly taken by media.

END OF MEDIA

Technical media had their time of impact. The development of the perceptual technologies that define the core of technical media started around 1830 and ended before 2000, when methods of coding, transmitting and displaying information had obtained access to the full range of human perception. First analogue and then digital coding reached the required density in information speed and storage space. Human senses have specific limits of information capacity, and as information technologies have progressed this phase of transition has come to an end. During the course of this development, most of what was later on called media came into being.

In terms of consumer culture the transition resulted in a series of technical gadgets, from gramophone to CD player, from telegraphy to HDTV. Behind those devices emerged a history of formats of coding and transmission, from photography and phonograph record to their digital counterparts. Today, the multitude of previously distinct media have converged in one universal computing machine.

Once human perceptual limits are reached, the marginal utility of further technical improvement dwindles. Progress no longer shows itself in outperforming human senses. On the level of gadgets, competition moved to ever faster processors or ever smaller gadgets or both. On the level of information, all kind of data- and network-based services appeared. The result is a ubiquitous digital network with a huge variety of concomitant gadgets.

MEDIA THEORY

One of the surprises with German media theory was its inability to acknowledge, and in some cases even to register, the rise of the Internet. During its early years, media theory remained hooked on a very different trajectory of development. Its focus rested on the rising speed and calculating capacities of a single computer. From this perspective, the networks looked like a side phenomenon of little importance. HTML, the WWW, and the rise of Google were taken as confirmations that networks can be left aside as a superficial field of protocol battles and commercial activities without further theoretical implications.

According to the common wisdom of the more orthodox wing of media theory, the next big thing was to appear in the simulation technologies and the creation of artificial environments and virtual reality. This prediction was built on a simple extension of a present momentum into the future, like most predictions. As computers would become quicker and smaller, they would compete for the goal to imitate, extend, and take over human activities. McLuhan's idea of media as extension of the human lingers unquestioned at the ideological foundation. In an interview, Kittler once pointed out that there can be only two outcomes for the relation between humans and technology. Either computer chips will merge with flesh, or they won't; humans will be swallowed by computers, or else they will be spat out. So far things have not quite worked out as expected. As it became increasingly unclear what constituted a medium, the differentiation between human and technology also appeared more fragile, and the figure of the cyborg was celebrated famously by Donna Haraway, among others. On various occasions, Kittler explicitly rejected a theoretical reflection on what is a medium.[1] This was not because he was wavering or wanted to keep the term open, but for the general mistrust in the universal claims of theory. If media define our situation, theory itself is affected insofar it forms part of the situation. When it comes to media, there is no point of external reflection. Philosophy communicates and is as such entangled in a mediated environment. The consequence of this as Wolfgang Hagen describes is that media theory has to become history: 'Media theory can only operate as a historical theory of media, because materially and epistemologically media run always ahead of theory' (Hagen, 1983: 123, my translation). Unfortunately, most of German media theory followed this trajectory.

The rise of media theory coincides with the end of the transitional period of media. It provided an accurate description of many phenomena of that transition. As many other models of thinking, the media-theoretical approach did not stop explaining what was initially at stake, but extended its reach to other, related phenomena. The fact that media theorists started to conceive earlier modes of information transfer and coding along the lines of nineteenth-century technologies gives a typical example of a retro-activation of a theoretical figure. The printing press, the Roman postal system or the Greek alphabet were all investigated along a theoretical framework shaped by the technical media of the nineteenth and twentieth century. The fact that none of these earlier media ever dealt with overcoming the limits of human perception remained an issue largely ignored, if not purposefully negated.

When Kittler turned McLuhan's approach into a historical theory of technological powers, he did not introduce an entirely new perspective. The Canadian theorist had taken his main inspiration from his teacher Harold Innis, whose approach departed from an economic history of trade routes. In his major work *Empire and Communication* (2007) he tried to show how big empires extended over space and time in relation to the communication procedures deployed in administration and warfare. McLuhan took his idea of a general communication environment and mapped it to the single human being and its relations on to a world shaped by technologies. Kittler brought back some of Innis's sense of history.

But with the realignment to a historical approach came another constraint. In the very tradition of his main discipline, philology, Kittler treated the subject and its narratives as pieces of literature. 'In this situation we are left only with reminiscences, that is to say, with stories' (Kittler, 1986: xxxix). A basic narrative structure had to be kept in place, with particular emphasis on the primal scenes. The philological format of historical narratives remained a key feature of German media theory. Its historicizing approach helps to explain the odd phenomenon on why the rise of the Internet was largely ignored. Seen through a backwards-directed perspective of retrospective reflection, the period of World War II and its aftermaths were as close as one dared to get to the present. Whatever came subsequently appeared blurry in the fog of an inaccessible presence.

At a certain point around the year 2000, Kittler left the field media research and started to follow a different trajectory.[2] His fascination for an *Ur-Szene*, a primal scene, took him to the invention of the alphabet as the root of all European knowledge and from there to the beginnings of Greek writing and thinking. This shift shows some consistency with his earlier media theory. If media really is the message, then in the moment a new medium arrives all that can be said must be already present. In other words, the situation is defined instantly. Consequently, the alphabet not only encompassed letters, numbers and music, but also love, sex and traces of all European wisdom. Most of his disciples did not follow his last radical turn. They stayed course and became a special breed of historian under a different label, as more Foucaultian media-archaeology (Wolfgang Ernst) or under the term '*Kulturtechnik*' (Bernhard Siegert), shaped after Latour.

The historical approach of humanities has its own historical reason. During the beginning of the nineteenth century and the invention of the research university, studies in history served well in establishing and popularizing the idea of a national identity. The prize to be paid was the exclusion from political influence. Ever since, thinkers in the humanities were no longer to be involved in shaping the actual state of things. Imposing a format of backwards-looking historical research was one of the means to achieve that goal. That led to a funny contradiction. A discipline that deals with something meant to define our situation retreats from confronting its involvement with its own situation. At the moment when programmers are shaping our information environment, German media studies does not attempt to bridge the gap to social and political practice and activism, as American, British and Dutch media scholars have tried to do.

THE SITUATION

'*Lage*' was the word used by Kittler to refer to the general staff's meetings at noon and in the evening (Kittler, 1986: xxxix). The English translation shifts the military and strategic context of the term to the more abstract and Hegelian 'situation'. Wherever possible for Kittler, abstract terms had to be replaced by historical facts or material objects. And especially when it comes to media, military use was always considered a preferred point of reference. Wars are fought with media, weapons and sources of information. Popular and entertainment media were depicted as remnants of military equipment turned into commercial gadgets by 'misuse'. He always stuck as close as possible to technical 'things', avoiding philosophical abstractions. But in the situation where media dissipate, it helps to move on to a higher level of abstraction in order to figure out which motifs of thinking and which theoretical approaches will still match our situation. In this moment, the initial proposition is turned upside down. We can no longer ask media to shed light on our situation. Instead, we must start with the situation to investigate within which factors it is defined, if not by media.

In his lecture on aesthetics, Hegel distinguishes three types of situations.

> (i) collisions which arise from purely physical or natural circumstances in so far as these are something negative, evil, and therefore disturbing; (ii) spiritual collisions which rest on natural bases, which, although inherently positive, still bear in themselves for the spirit the possibility of differences and oppositions; (iii) disunions which have their ground in spiritual differences and which alone are entitled to appear as the truly interesting oppositions, because they proceed from man's own act. (Hegel, 1975: 206)

To characterize our situation with the Hegelian model of escalation in mind would require ascertaining the area of collision or the battlefield behind the *Lage*, to put it bluntly and in a Kittlerian way. The main difference consists in the fact that the narrative of techno-human collision unfolds without human characters, without preset goals, and with no teleology. Its driving forces are based on material or physical properties and subjectless organizational dynamics. The Hegelian model of situational escalation can be mapped onto the historical sequence of events as they unfold around media and media theory. At the first stage, there is a mere material instance or a physical phenomenon, which in itself carries the potential to be turned into a tool. The second stage sees the material possibility turned into a functional device. Its appearance follows a technical a priori, as it comes with no inherent purpose and no entanglement with social needs and is being appropriated for a certain type of use, and later a misuse. And finally, an inherent directionality builds up a dynamic of development that projects purposes of a technology on military or economic goals with their links to human desires on to the technology.

MATERIALITY

All communication—and that encompasses transmitting, processing or storing of information—must always be correlated to physical and measurable forces. Materiality of media does not need to consist in solid objects only. Whatever transfers a force through space or time should be considered. The fundamental material layer often goes unnoticed, even though it sets some basic conditions for all communication based upon it. There are two questions that come with the material constraints. How does the material layer shape communication? And what does the materiality of media mean in a post-media situation? As long as the mechanics of media were still visible or touchable, the effects of materiality were obvious. Today, tangible material objects hold a mere nostalgic value, for 'high-end' lovers or in some threads of media-archaeology like those of Wolfgang Ernst or Jussi Parikka. Kittler himself had a rather playful approach towards media material. When I visited him first at home in Bochum in the early nineties, there was always an electrical board of some synthesizer or another switching circuit placed in some corner with a soldering bolt next to it.

As soon as the material layer gets miniaturized or enclosed in microchips, materiality becomes intangible. Material constraints lose their defining shape. Platform- and device-independent technologies take over. Standards and protocols enforce material-independent constraints. But, information will always continue to operate with a material basis, with the only difference that this basis remains inaccessible to human senses. In the course of this miniaturization, the effects of material constraints become less and less apparent. But they still set the conditions of widely acknowledged phenomena. For example, recent trends like the so-called Web 2.0 or social media at large can both be explained as necessary outcomes of an ongoing progress in the data infrastructure.

TECHNICAL A PRIORI

The technical a priori postulates that the development of media is driven by an inherent technological progress and physical properties of material. Social needs of communication or human desires do not govern the appearance of a medium. They do not emerge until a technology of communication is operative. There are stronger and a weaker versions of the technical a priori. In the strong version it is postulated that human or social factors have no influence whatsoever. The weaker version only claims the initial momentum to technological factors, conceding that further developments depend on modes of use and imagination, or often misuse and illusions. The strong version was widely criticized for its technological determinism and its apparent neglect of social needs, desires or imaginative proposals (and mostly form the direction that was to become Science and Technology Studies [STS]). For two reasons this critique misses its target. First, the a priori should not be misunderstood as deterministic. Second, according to the a priori, one would flatly deny that there exists a media-independent concept of either society or of the human. Consequently, there cannot be social or personal desires for a communication unless the associated medium exists.

Deterministic models were familiar from the side of the social research investigating the effects of media ('*Technikfolgenabschätzung*') or wishing to expand empirical data by adding causal relations. The a priori of media theory claims a historical, and not a causal relationship. Just because one factor has to appear before the others, it does not necessarily determine the field. As much as defining a situation does not include determining it. A definition sets constraints and confines, while determining encompasses all the properties and processes.

The technical a priori can be explained as part of a discursive practice by a gap between technological and cultural discourses. Given the fact that the world of engineers maintains only weak ties to the social sphere, the momentum of a technological invention is driven not by its future purpose, but by internal incentives that operate inside the technical disciplines. The only link to a broader outside consists in the funds channelled into the research that depend on the state and economic powers to be and the promises made to them. They envisage a social or personal application of what comes out of the laboratories, requiring an intermediary position between the two fields, merging technical knowledge with cultural practices. The current separation of disciplines in the educational system does not allow for mixed qualifications of that kind. The institutional lines of division are one of the reasons why new technologies often appear to come 'out of the blue', as an effect of an unforeseeable, a priori condition of technology. That is why very many of the so-called innovators and inventors have been either amateurs, or bricoleurs, or college dropouts, reaching from Daguerre to Bill Gates. They are agents of the a priori.

DIRECTIONALITY

Technology is one of the few domains that still carry the promise of continuous improvement. With the demise of modernism, the idea of progress in the social and aesthetic domains got lost. Only technological developments stayed on course. New computers and processors usually tend to be faster or smaller than old ones. For the theoretical consequences, it does not matter whether technical innovation keeps its pace according to Moore's law or not. The sheer fact that there is an underlying directed process at work is enough to give reason to directed predictions.

When meeting with an essentially unchanged environment, technologies cross certain thresholds. During the timespan of media those thresholds were easy to detect, as they were given by the invariable human sensory capacities. Currently, limitations of that kind appear less defined, as there are no measurable limits to be overcome. At a certain point in time cars may drive by themselves, and lots of similar human routines will be taken over by so-called intelligent machines. The complexity of individual and common patterns of behaviour cannot be quantified in a meaningful and measurable way. That makes the intrusion of computers, networks and their algorithms less predictable. The fantasy of imitation in Turing-tests, as well as the concept of the so-called singularity are mere retroactive predictions that extend past patterns of technological progress to matters where they don't fit. Instead, technologies of communication usually tend to create an open field of possibilities, among which the law of unintended consequences often helps to discover the most successful applications.

DEFINING A SITUATION

Hegel built his typology of collisions on the distinction between nature and thinking. Where would we have to place technologies according to this model? Common sense would take the side of the human, as machines are man-made. But the principles of materiality and the a priori would give them an almost 'natural' status. Of course, they result from human inventiveness, but this is only one part of the story. On the other side they are given physical capacities that may be uncovered by one or the other scientist, once the according discourse of engineering is applied. Ample accounts of concurrent discoveries testify to this parallelism in technological directionality. Fundamentally the direction of their improvement is not given by human agency, but by the sheer laws of physics. Under this condition, the Hegelian series of collision can be mapped onto a broader history of media and postmedia. Media appear as a result of the first type of collision, which takes place between two naturally defined functions: the information capacities of the machine and of the human senses. Once this phase is overcome, we enter a different type of collision that involves human behaviour. Mapping its characteristics to our information machines creates the incentive to monitor and predict events and to collect huge amounts of data for that purpose. One could pose the more theoretical question of what to make out of Hegel's third mode of collision that overcomes nature. But there is no urge to frame the typology of collisions as an historical process. On the contrary, the modes of collision keep repeating themselves and reappearing.

With the algorithmic calculation and surveillance of human actions, the political dimension necessarily reappears. This appearance of the political revitalizes an approach from the very early roots of media theory. As the teacher of McLuhan, the economist Innis showed that communication leads to organization in the form of empires and their various forms of power. In this respect, the postmedia situation could parallel the period of pre-media, with the difference that organizational issues extend beyond the institutional apparatuses to the level of the single individual. When media theory focused on the technicities of communication and perception, political or organizational aspects fell out of sight. After human sensory capacities were overcome, the effects of further technological progress seem to appear on two threads. One consists, as mentioned above, in forms of organization. The other translates automated perception into action.

What must be avoided is the simple contraposition of human and machine. A situation always encompasses both, neither are disconnected entities. The concept of the human is media independent, yet necessarily constructed by mediated self-observation. All we can know about ourselves is defined through methods of self-observation, methods shaped by media. Our body and behaviour, even our sociality is presented to us by scientific apparatuses and communications media that enable self-observation. Whatever concept the human body is modelled after—an equilibrium system of liquids, a muscle-machine-man, an input-output feedback loop, or a modelled brain full of neurons—it is necessarily shaped by the technologies at hand. The same counts for social phenomena. The cinema turned its viewers into a horde full of desires, and with radio and TV they became a broadcast mass. Now they dissipate into networked communities that are linked like computers. In all these cases the technologies of observation define the conceptual shape of the human and the social.

This makes the equation change. A collision between humans and computers may be framed in terms of bio-politics. In this case, human life or the social or the political would be positioned as the core question and would have to be defended. But if we take into account that the mode of self-reflection itself is framed by the tools of communication then neither human nor social nor political entities can be taken as independent actors. In this case, the field of collision is being defined by a relation of technology to a technologically constructed idea of the human. This is not meant to neglect the human, or the political dimension of the question. What needs to be done is to step back and ask once again, what defines our situation?

FRAMING THE COLLISION

Theory itself involves a process of communication. There is no media-independent and situation-free theory, 'precisely because the dominant information technologies of the day control all understanding and its illusions' (Kittler, 1986: xl). There is no neutral, distant status of thinking, no position for an objective observer and no privileged point of access from within. While a collision unfolds, we lack valid terms to frame it. Only when it draws to its end and a stable situation is established, an appropriate theory of what has happened can be told. This delay is not so much dependent on the truthfulness or the validity of the theory, but more so on its acceptance. In hindsight, the collision will be framed and explained according to the models of the prevailing situation. Once media no longer define our situation, because they have ceased to exist, an approach grounded in technology has to be reformulated according to the very situation we are in. History alone cannot serve that purpose, as by definition it must not be involved with the present situation; that being said, there is a way to solve the methodological issues. First, one can extract theoretical concepts—like materiality, the a priori, and directionality—on which media theory was implicitly built. Second, their validity and explanatory strength has to be tested with regard to our situation, which involves a kind of classical hermeneutic circle that starts with a pre-understanding of the situation, then confronts it with a reflection built on the concepts of a postmedia theory, leading to a new theoretical framework.

LINKS AND NETWORKS

The term media refers to an in-between space, to something connecting. The properties of the in-between define how the objects linked—and that includes humans—appear to each other. Technical media of the nineteenth and twentieth century were characterized by specific technologies that connected unspecified viewers, readers and listeners in a situation of asymmetry. Their counterpart consequently appeared as a 'mass'. Today's connections operate in the opposite way. They connect specific addresses with a variety of unspecified technologies. A network of links replaced an environment of media.

Behind these network addresses we find data, files, objects and also users, each of them with a unique address. The extension of the networked domain follows a trajectory through the different data types by overloading the link. The principle of overloading is known from object-oriented programming. An operator, and the link can be taken as an operator in this regard, can be extended to provide functions for different types, and not only the one it was initially devised for. In this way, the physical connection between two computers became overloaded by pointers to addresses, data, files and so on. One of the most noticeable moments of overloading occurred when HTML added the operation of linking to legible text in the so-called hyperlink. The dynamics of overloading links did not stop there. It subsequently added support for images and audio files, and from there it extended to every item connected to the machines. At the end even the users found themselves mirrored by files and instantiated in data objects, and the files were named friends or followers, making sudden human relations and desires the content of links. The extension of the networked domain does not leave its objects unchanged. Like media, links redefine what they touch. Not that friendship at large would be fully replaced by link structures, but worse: The links become the concrete technological form from which the new concept of friendship, and its other deviant concepts, may be derived. In doing so, networks exert a strong grammaticizing effect.

Basic terms like the network and the link are far from being conclusively defined. The link itself is not an unchangeable format. It is operated and governed by programs and algorithms. Today, it appears as if links are either on or off, and once set, remain forever. But this current binary and timeless format may be transitional. Relations can become increasingly complicated once one starts to calculate intensity, direction or even temporal characteristics of links. Also the concept of the network may blur some of the aspects of its underlying technical structure. The common imagination depicts the Internet horizontally as a flat meshwork of links. But there is another side to it. Vertically, the web, with all its protocols, standards and formats is built as a hierarchical structure, stretching from the physical layer of the material connections of fiberoptic cables through protocols like IP, TCP, or http to high-level data-structures. Nested within this hierarchy lie the possibilities of control, of economization, of surveillance and privacy. Our fixation with the horizontal extension of the web may have contributed to the fact that hierarchical power structures and institutional mass surveillance could have remained unnoticed for such a long time.

In addition, horizontally the web tends to not equal growth. As links attract other links, their distribution changes from random to scale-free networks. At this point the so-called network-effect kicks in, which means that larger networks bring more gains to future participants. This is one of the main effects leading to what one could call functional monopolies. Major web companies like Google, Amazon, YouTube or Facebook operate in a similar way to McLuhan's law on media and content, only that nowadays it's not specific content, but a specific function that is taken over by the next network. When it comes to materiality, the a priori, and directionality, the three concepts still shape the web, but in a different way than they did with media.

Materiality seems to evaporate in the current networks. Platform independence and the hierarchies of protocols and formats ostensibly guarantee that the physical layer remains invisible and its influence suppressed. But in the end both data and links rely on a material basis. Physical constraints of network bandwidth and storage availability will continue to shape our communicative environment. To give an example: the so-called Web 2.0 that looks like a social endeavour has as its technical base a material relation of client and server that only under certain conditions of bandwidth allowed for implemented crucial functionalities like Ajax. Once reaction times and two-way bandwidths allowed for the integration of back and forth interaction, the web became a technical opportunity that had to be executed.

The technical a priori becomes a less obvious factor within networks, as there is a steady flow of minor improvements. Yet on the micro-level it continues to be effective. Beyond the cycle of desires, demands and innovation and supply, there are still more contingent elements entering the field. From mainly technical devices, the a priori shifted to platforms whose functionalities seem to grow out of the blue in the same way. Discursive jumps do no longer only occur between the domains of engineering and culture, but also between the domain of programming and online behaviour. As much as devices, now functionalities appear out the blue and gain attraction through networked models of exponential distribution. The changes in the a priori have some effects on directionality. At the level of the technical basis it keeps being effective. Even if the rigidity of Moore's law wanes, the general direction of technical improvement remains in power. This also concerns the development of networks that reach out with ever-faster connections to more and more points, leading to the consequence that all kinds of objects will be rendered part of the networks in the near future. The functionalities, though, do not follow a directional movement, but rather an adaptive, and therefore nondirected evolutionary principle within an ecosystem of online platforms.

THEORETICAL AND POLITICAL IMPLICATIONS

Within a collision that is characterized by the extension of links and networks, technologies find their counterparts in automatically registered actions and agents and in the organization of groups, communities and institutions. This creates two types of consequences, one in the field of philosophical terms around subjectivity, objecthood, and their relations, and the other in the field of politics. Network politics begins with the truth demonstrated and emphasized by Harold Innis that institutions of power cannot be built and exist without an infrastructure of communication. Any change in the structure of communication has the potential to effect political structures. During the short period of a postmedia collision, three different types of new power structures have appeared.

The financial sphere was among the first to start operating on a global scale. Old, existing networks appropriated the new possibilities. Being quicker in establishing a global network than the territory-bound states, financial actors managed to position themselves in a favourable place. Financialization, deregulation and loss of national power can be related to advantages of the larger network over the smaller, which resulted in overthrowing national sovereignty when banks had to be declared too big to fail. The second type of powerful organizations is shaped by corporate entities that have managed to grow around functional monopolies thanks to network effects. The ultimate competition concerns the question of whether a monopoly is able to render itself into a layer, or a semi-technical standard. But even before this goal is reached, vast collections of user data allow corporate entities a disciplinary power over their members and society at large. The third, and maybe most powerful structures, are the security and secret services whose extension has only recently become publicly visible to its full extent. Nominally, these institutions operate still under the control of states. Practically, however, they have since long shaken off their legal and regulatory limitations. Already in 1986, Kittler wrote a text on the NSA, on the occasion of the publication of James Bamford's book (see Kittler 2014). Already at that time, it was obvious that secret services strive to operate outside of the law.

All these developments together result in an increasingly fragile statehood, with nations turning into 'shell institutions', in the phrase of Anthony Giddens, that can only pretend to perform their initial purposes. Seen from a technical angle, states and their military power appear as a result of a situation that was shaped by media during the two world wars. The broader picture of our days points to a *Lage* in which the world is divided into a slowly shrinking comfort zone with a wealthy population, with this wealth less and less equally distributed, surrounded by an area of failed states with mafia economies and zones of irregular warfare.

HISTORY AND DATABASES

When memory is governed by addresses and by databases, the historical format of organizing the archive is reduced to one of very many options. Digital memory and databases turn the old archives upside down and replace the dominant model of historical, time-based order that governed European sciences, most dominantly the humanities, since their foundation along with the nation-state in the early nineteenth century. This does not imply that history reached its end or historical consciousness is to be erased. On the contrary, the sequence of political events keeps unfolding, but it might not be deciphered as 'historical'. History will retreat to a minor place among very many possible access modes into data and archives. Google gives the most prominent example. Its search results are deprived from whatever time-related markers, except from one detail that they proudly announced that searching for the result occurred in a timespan close to zero. Once more, this emphasises the character of Google as a machine of time-destruction. In the long run, time independent archives may reshape cultural practices in a similarly profound way as the introduction of time-based practices around 1800 with their formation of institutions like the museum that laid the ground for a movement commonly referred to as modernism.

RELEVANCE VS. MEANING

According to philosophical tradition, terms or statements used to come with a definable meaning or a signification, or to put it in another term, with truth. This imaginary relation depends on a stability of one-to-one relationships that thrive best under the rigid and universal systems of thinking with a strong institutional background. Within a distributed circulation of linked statements, rigid constructs of signification are replaced by recursive operations within the network. A logic of links replaces the regime of signs. The most prominent example of this is found in the Page Rank algorithm behind Google, the closest analogy for which are Lacan's chains of signification and Wittgenstein's language games (*Sprachspiel*). The answer to a question does not lie in the right reply, but in a relevant result that can be approximated by counting the quantity of links. It does not come with a claim for truth, but with a recursion over an aggregate acceptance.

DATA AND ONTOLOGY

The fact that metadata, that stands mostly for information about links and relations, deliver more valuable information on an object or an individual than the actual data, has most recently become obvious with regard to the discussions about surveillance. The ontological question of 'what is it that there is' is being replaced by the question 'what can be addressed', with the 'what' under erasure because it is no longer the 'what' that one is looking for rather than the pattern of addresses, pointers and links. The properties of object itself are of secondary importance. What matters are the links, the events, the noticeable and registered events and their possible extension into the future.

EXISTENCE AND BAYESIAN PROBABILITY

Once we operate within a technical environment of links, our existence is exposed to an ongoing test performed by algorithms and routines, a kind of huge and continuous inverted garbage collection. Inverted because within the network there is no routine trying to find what has been left aside without links. Rather, each thing or being has to continuously manifest its ongoing existence. The data it or he or she generates enters a sphere of Bayesian probability in which each element is accompanied by its data shadow that reaches out to the future of expected actions. While this world may seem horrifying and dystopian, it may bring some surprising effects of liberation. Today's regime of making people work and consume within the medium of money and its profiteers, may be ripe for a change. The general issue of the distribution of things and services and the allocation of work can be reformulated in network terms as the task of optimizing a structure of links. Networks can provide for a solution that will not involve money, or any other general equivalent, offering the utopian idea of a system with no accumulation and much less financial inequality than we have to suffer through now.

PHILOSOPHY

Confronted with the latest developments in technologies and programming, academic thinking, as framed by disciplines like philosophy, is faced with a difficult and contradictory constraint. It wants to say something about our situation, but it has to frame it according to the rules of its discipline, and that requires integrating a historically fixed and authority-based system of ideas. Networks, algorithms and the connected objects they create pose a unique challenge to philosophy. When things become more connected and more knowledgeable than their human counterparts, a network of activated items and informed processes create a reality of its own. This very situation lies at the basis of the recent trend in philosophy that goes under the name 'speculative realism'. It comes with the call for a speculation about a nonhuman reality beyond the 'correlation' (to use the phrase of Quentin Meillassoux, 2008) that circumscribes the real within the orbit of human thought, language and perception. Speculations on the 'facticity' that discloses the correlation and thus the so-called reality that lies beyond it is not merely a philosophical task; facticity is always technically implemented. Many of the recent philosophers deal with this challenge in a manner well known throughout the history of philosophy. To recognize the situation-boundedness of their thinking should cast a doubt on the universal and ineluctable claims of philosophical reason itself. In following the rituals of their discipline, they reformulate the problems they are faced with in the traditional terms of philosophy and claim to be able to answer them by rephrasing already given solutions. In a conservative backlash the 'big questions' have reappeared with new urgency. What is? Is there a reality? What can we know about it?

Many of the answers have a rhetorical motif in common. They apply terms of computational sciences within nontechnical explanations, establishing a rhetorical layer that blurs the technical foundations of the underlying issues. One can read this rhetorical move as an (albeit shortsighted) attempt to preserve disciplinary integrity and claim superiority in explanation. Just to give two examples: The term 'correlation', which names one of the most common algorithmic routines in data processing, finds itself applied to a question of Kantian epistemology. An even more obvious case comes with the notion of 'object-orientation'.[3] The term object-oriented was introduced to programming to name a language architecture to modularize complex chains of commands. Today's world of data, and that encompasses computer-games as much as social media, are full of objects. Traces of object-orientation govern our screens, or workplaces, our everyday life. But when philosophers appropriated the term, it had to be stripped of all reference to programming. Following loosely a model of thought around Actor-Network Theory (another technical term turned upside down) objects became things that have an agenda on their own. The technical conditions of this epiphany, that were still present with Latour, become fully covered with the use Graham Harman makes of the term.

The most pressing philosophical question has been left out. How do we deal with the fact that another reality—in the very technical sense of an independent and self-deciding world—appears to be growing? The intrusion of algorithmic calculations into human knowledge and behaviour is a slow and often unnoticed process. The collision will not necessarily feel like a struggle between man and robot or look like a race between the brain and the computer. These are misguided metaphors borrowed from a capitalist common sense ideology of competition. What most likely will come instead is a world in which both agents—new objects and former subjects—may dwell together for a long time to come.

NOTES

1. 'Statt philosophischer wesensfragen genügt schlichtes Wissen' (Kittler, 1986: 5).

2. That transition being probably best mirrored in his lecture on Philosophien der Literatur from 2000, whose earlier version was expanded with an introduction into antique authors.

3. See for example Ian Bogost, 'if there is something especially lurid and contemporary about the concept of an "object-oriented philosophy," it must be the fact that it shares more than half its name with a dominant computer programming paradigm, "object-oriented programming."' bogost.com/blog/units_and_objects/.

BIBLIOGRAPHY

Hagen, Wolfgang. (1983) *Gegenwartsvergessenheit*. Merve Verlag GmbH.

Hegel, G. W. F. (1975) *Aesthetics: Lectures on Fine Art*. Oxford: Clarendon Press.

Innis, Harold. (2007) *Empire and Communication*. Lanham, MD: Rowman & Littlefield.

Kittler, Friedrich. (1986) *Grammophon, Film, Typewriter*. Berlin: Brinkmann & Bose.

———. (2014) 'No Such Agency'. *Theory, Culture & Society* available at theoryculturesociety.org/kittler-on-the-nsa/.

Lyotard, Jean-Francois. (1979) *The Postmodern Condition: A Report on Knowledge*. Manchester: Manchester University Press.

Meillassoux, Quentin. (2008) *After Finitude*. London: Palgrave.

Chapter Nine

The Ragged Manifold of the Subject

Databaseness and the Generic in Curating YouTube

Olga Goriunova

Recent exhibitions such as *We Are All Photographers Now!* (Musée de l'Elysée, 2007), *YouTube Play: A Biennial of Creative Video* (Guggenheim, 2010) and *The World Beach Project* (Victoria and Albert Museum, 2007–2012) engage the current condition of 'total creativity' where being a unique subject as best achieved through creative expression is both a social imperative and a financial routine. Creative, aesthetic work is traditionally regarded as both individually and collectively liberating and an enabler of a better society and it is also a forced mode of the available precarious work. All these shows invite works from the general public, which are then exhibited following a selection procedure, performed either by a human committee or the jury of software (pieces picked by an algorithm enabling random selection), or both and more (software overlays photographs onto maps, brings works together, co-creates works, etc.). The resulting aesthetic space of such exhibitions, more often than not, is not a collective transindividuating work as hoped for in digital art and theory, but generic unremarkable mass of cultural production, rendered such, first of all, by the gargantuan volume of submissions (reportedly over 20,000 in the case of the Guggenheim show) and by the way in which every individual piece is locked upon itself. The singularity strived for, and encoded in the very medium of an art museum exhibition and a display, finds itself entangled in a paradoxical embrace with indiscernibly repetitive creative effort and an extensive multiplicity, rather than intensive collectivity, of pieces.

The tensions at the heart of this conundrum are shadowed by an overhanging Platonic dyad of an original and a copy, model and image, good and bad art. Added to it are the meaning-making, subject-making, mediating machines of art institutions, but also networks, platforms such as YouTube, and desktop or cloud-based editing software. More than that, it is more precisely the mediation of the database as the foundational symbolic form and computational organizational mechanism of both YouTube and other platforms that cut to the core of the changing conditions of possibility of both singular and multiple, unique and the generic, and the oscillation in between.

In this chapter I would like to focus on the aesthetic generic, the cultural generic, the generic of meaning, sense and action as one generated in the operation of the database management systems. It is in tackling generic as a quality and an action, as immediacy and abstraction, a systemic feature and a computational operation, productive of realities that I think some novel opportunities to understand our digital condition can be found. Some pairings of concepts that I would like to contemplate include, first, generic and original/copy; generic and meaninglessness/nonsense/noise and reality, generic and seriality, generic as measure. I would like to prod generic for its links to sorting, lists, tables and databases. Most of all, I take up the generic as the concept through which to approach a new understanding of subjects and subjectivities. Here, I undertake a cultural theory and aesthetics' approach to the way in which subjects are formed in contemporary culture, accounting for the computational. My subjects arise from art projects and operations of software, as human, posthuman or nonhuman and are mainly characterized by certain consistency and unity that hold cross-cutting biological, symbolic, empirical and transcendental planes together, and in the production and maintenance of which the operations of the cultural and the technical partake. It is these operations towards the subject that undergo changes that I am focusing on.

My field of exploration here is digital media culture which today expands to encompass various forms of cultural expression as they acquire a computational backbone. It is not the structural migration to computer-enabled media channels, forms, devices and genres ranging from social networks to smart phones, databases, digital TV and photography, e-books and educational apps, YouTube, memes, emails, Skype and online registration forms, but the logic of invention, visibility, accountability, objectivity, power as well as fun, collectivity and protest that come to rely on computational execution. Culture today works computationally, in its forms, in its genres, in its contents, infrastructures, circulatory techniques, meaning-making and evaluation systems and larger structures it is plugged in.

Such a change in mediatory mechanisms is usually discussed as revolutionary by philosophers of technology, such as Bernard Stiegler, and media theorists, such as Friedrich Kittler; though, for both, it is seen as only the next step in the long history of mediation. Mediation, an outdated term itself, here is both biological (for Stiegler, assuming an erect position is technological), metaphysical (for Kittler, the production of the soul is based upon the dominant media of literature and handwriting) as well as covering other areas core to the construction of the history of Western dominance (alphabetical writing, postal systems and the printing press) and of the subject (with enhanced memory, perception, rationality and then irrationality). As the change to Turing machine-based society is now obvious, its far-ranging consequences are explored in various disciplines and spheres by employing different vocabulary and concerns. Art is exemplarily among the foremost of these.

The work I shall refer to throughout this chapter is *Curating YouTube* (Sakrowski, 2007–2014 ongoing). *Curating YouTube* is a project by Berlin-based curator Robert Sakrowski. It is a curating platform, a software tool and a set of exhibitions curated by himself and by invited artists. The focus of the project is the immense volume and repetitiveness of YouTube videos; it is an exploration of YouTube as an art platform and an attempt to learn to appreciate and imaginatively comprehend the genre of YouTube videos en masse and as a mass cultural phenomenon. In a way, it is an exercise of staring into and striving for the generic. YouTube videos that become viral are well known (often selected, for instance, for showcase on the pages of *The Guardian* newspaper as the most representative of a moment or a topic, or at exhibitions such as the ones mentioned above) whereas the most uninteresting videos are a subject of the project *NoTube* (a contest for the worst or most nondescript and uninteresting YouTube video ever) and *First-Viewer-Television*—a channel for videos that received no views (both projects by IOCOSE). *Curating YouTube* aims at the mediocre, neither the best and successfully viral, nor the worst, but continuously generic.

The Gridr, part of *Curating YouTube*, is a tool that allows the selection and laying out of videos in a grid; furthermore the videos in the grid can be played one by one, or in an orchestrated fashion, each launched with a delay. The Gridr is often used to bring individual work into a collective enterprise more pronouncedly (for instance an orchestra made of people playing the same tune on individual instruments in separate videos), as every single work only functions collectively in the space of the YouTube as social media (the individual exercise of playing an instrument and putting a video online is precipitated by the collective practice and shared technical means), but is framed, technologically, as an individual work. Here, the same tension as outlined above, is at play: striving for singularisation, but only existing plurally.

The above is not entirely correct though: a (now defunct) video response function and YouTube channels promoting each other are all genre and technical mechanisms that feed upon this plural strain of singularisation and provide gradually differentiated techno-aesthetic forms to spin off new and blurrier arrangements. Where a project such as *50 50* by Oliver Laric (2007) (a video assembled from consecutive fragments of peoples' individual videos in which they perform a song from the rapper 50 Cent) pointedly—and as one-off—achieve what *Curating YouTube* explores (but also produces as a platform), such work is already changing with a sweeping commercialization of YouTube, where channels are monitored for the number of followers, with successful channels being offered a possibility to regularly film in studios scattered around the hubs of capitals of the world. A new middle-media (as opposed to mass media) TV production machine will expose an altogether different set of behaviours in the near future.

So, generic, meaning-lacking aesthetic and cultural acts, what are they? Often only regarded in the context of virality, memetics and infectious stupidity, something being done outside of the subject, without subjectivity, they nevertheless call for consideration. In Kittler's terms, they would be akin to language speaking itself to fill a gramophone record; culture exercising itself to be circulated in computational networks in the absence of a subject, or rather in its presence—one that is now the Turing machine (see Kittler, 1994).

KITTLER

According to Kittler and his interpreter Winthrop-Young, from the later part of the eighteenth century with the emergence of a bourgeois model of the family, as mothers were charged with bringing up children with a 'sufficiently developed psychic centre of resonance and reflexivity, commonly referred to as spirit or soul' (Winthrop-Young, 2010: 32), new child-rearing practices emerged that mainly worked by drawing upon language as the medium. As Winthrop-Young summarises: 'new language acquisition practices taught children to merge minimal signified into words, the new writing lessons taught them to merge basic strokes into lessons and then words which are "naturally" understood and heard . . . the humans inscribed by these techniques (Goethe, Hoffmann) will come to believe that nothing is meaningless because everything is always on the threshold of meaning' (Winthrop-Young, 2010: 32). With the reform of writing and reading lessons, the changing roles of aesthetics and philosophy, and the new roles of the self-reflexive civil servants of nation-states, it was most of all the mother's love that promised and provided meaningfulness.

Here, Kittler joins the Foucauldian enterprise: if Foucault focused on the discursive construction of subjects as the function of modernity, Kittler focused on 'inscription techniques for creation of the modern subject' (Winthrop-Young, 2010: 38). For Kittler, the creation of the modern subject with a metaphysical soul was enacted through the particular materiality of communication media. Kittler wrote: 'Whoever wrote in block letters would not be an in-dividual . . . the great individual entities invented in the age of Goethe—the developmental process of *bildung*, auto-biography, world history—could be seen as the flow of the continuous and the organic simply because they were supported by flowing cursive writing . . . to develop handwriting as out of one mold means to produce individuals' (Kittler, 1990: 83–84).

In this way, Kittler completes his analysis of Discourse Networks 1800. His work on Discourse Networks 1900 is focused on electric and electronic media. As the material ploughing through and working communication up radically changes, he asks: 'What happens to the soul in the age of Edison?' As the work of the Mother as the discursive machine weaving the meaningless noise into significatorily-promising utterances is coming to an end (Kittler, 1990: 71), noise takes over. The effect of the Edison machine, according to Kittler, is about obtaining direct access to 'reality' (which is noise). Language is no longer constructed out of the semantically promising 'minimal signifieds'; now communication units are only 'momentarily . . . arranged into allegedly significant patterns', they become computable elements, individually meaningless, a data stream, an exchange of noise (Kittler, 1990: 81, 68, 73).

Kittler writes: 'In the discourse network of 1900, discourse is produced by random generators. Psychophysics constructed such sources of noise, the new technological media store their output' (1990: 106). For Kittler, the difference between sense and nonsense is shattered, and meaning becomes a secondary phenomenon. The condition of chaos is here the originary condition, in which an 'absolute homogeneity of material' prevails and which is organized algorithmically, through 'randomness and combinatorics' (209–10). Cultural practices working with these discrete units rely on functions that are not governed by meaningfulness; they are 'automatic and autonomous' (214). Kittler elaborates: 'the noise that precedes every discourse becomes at once theme and method,' and further 'discourses are "eclectic combinations" of noise spectra' (218–19).

Thus, the change in the materiality of communication provided access to raw versions of reality: 'for the first time in history, writing ceased to be synonymous with the serial storage of data. The technological recording of the real entered into competition with the symbolic registration of the Symbolic . . . this delight brought to light discourses that previously had never passed a recording threshold' (229–30; 223).

Now, if we turn back to the cultural practices of today, meaningless and idiotic in their automatism and randomness, are these the media inscription techniques of a contemporary–twenty-first century subject? As language, in Kittler's account, starts speaking itself to fill in the new recording machines with originary noise, now, in the age of the Turing machine, and, for Kittler, with the primacy of this machine, noise is arranged into patterns to acquire momentary significance. Numerical relations and technical calculations are now where the dialogue of souls was before; and the aesthetic of numerical noise is physiological (Kittler, 1990: 225). So what are these patterns?

People filming themselves enacting similar gestures (lying with their face down in the craze called planking)—is this human originary noise recorded and computed to generate informationally significant patterns to be analysed further by computational techniques? Is the noise or the pattern here generic, singular or multiple? Or is the generic found in the operation of the computational machine that produces and perpetuates work upon these phenomena and the oscillation between them?

Is noise as a nonsensical, originary plane (in Kittler) generic? The generic ecological condition, the generic cultural platform, as read as: 'Of a genus, family'—is here something one can belong to, defined by the same characteristics you have. You exercise generic functions and actions on the basis of your specific genetic allowances and ecological interferences. Here, of course, the generic and the noise it entails is highly patterned, with carefully applied randomness. Pattern and randomness, and pattern and noise do not exist outside each other. If pattern is information, noise is not non-information; information encompasses and functions in relation to both pattern and noise.

Here, the generic is unlikely to be either pattern or noise and, using Kittler, we can say that forms of production of meaning and sense in our era as we question them through the notion of the generic refer to the loss of meaning-making practices orientated towards an end product (poet, poetry, uniqueness) and instead functions as an open-ended computationally-arranged process of drawing upon noise and patterning, and working upon the derived data and information.

For Kittler, noise (and nonsense) precedes discourse networks and acquires meaning through the media/discourse network of the age (1990: 218). But one could say that meaninglessness is not noise, but is itself a product of the discourse network of the Turing machine. The computational machine produces the generic, but then the question is whether the aesthetic, cultural, discursive, performative generic is always constructed. Is the generic always mediated? Generic seems to touch upon both the vernacular, the immediate, the unmediated and the abstracted, the processed, the operated upon. We can talk about a generic artifact—a generic chair—but also about a generic landscape, a generic lake and a generic tree, too. A generic tree is not noise, but neither is it a pattern. But even as a work of abstraction, the generic does not lose a connection to nonsense.

Computational machines produce the generic of culture and society through their processing of data, where things are operationalised and normalized to become data and work as information. They are enacted and performed through sorting, listing, classification, visualization, automatic configuration, and similar forms of articulation.

GENERIC, COPY AND SERIALITY IN DELEUZE

A very different route to take to consider how the generic reality-making is handled today is to travel through Deleuze. In *Difference and Repetition* (2008), Deleuze focuses on overthrowing the Platonic reign of the copy over the original. There is some kind of solidarity between Deleuze and Kittler here: they both work towards the reign of the copy, but with very different outcomes. In Deleuze's words, 'Infinity of copies . . . allows neither original, nor copy to subsist' (Deleuze, 2008: 80). 'The model collapses into difference, while the copies disperse into the dissimilitude of the series which they interiorize' (156). As both the notion of the model and that of the copy are challenged, the copies become series, take on the originary as the original seriality. Seriality in Deleuze denounces the original, the unique idea; the unique idea is itself a series of differentiating copies.

Is seriality a methodology for carrying out the generic reality-making? Is the generic a unit of measure and a way of arranging things to be measured? The generic arises as the process of measuring, an operation, or, in the case of *Curating YouTube*, arranging videos onto a grid; the generic here as a mechanism of production and understanding is in the mediation of the operation of measuring the similarity. The tool sorts and measures. Here the tool is both Gridr and a curatorial idea, or the 'similar videos' function of YouTube; it is a conceptual-computational mechanism to both locate and produce the generic cultural reality, analyse it and act upon it.

Is the generic quality itself a function, a way to produce pattern and noise in the process of the separation of pattern out of noise by measurement? This is the operation of the sorting of the similar and the production of the relation of association by putting it into a database, table or a grid. The generic though is complex; it can't be described or arrived at by following a mathematical function. One can calculate the mean (of, for instance, a column in a dataset), but the generic has been produced by the operation of producing and formatting the dataset itself (for instance in 'normalization').

So, the generic as a machine is somewhere in the operations of the database, the generic is produced as the dataset is assembled and structured, and as it is formatted according to a model and implemented in a database management system.

To use Kittler, the magic of the maternal mouth promising the meaningful world, where the unique is achieved by working on the chaotic, gives way to computational measurement and operation upon matter, which is not random and which is itself a measure of uncertainty, or is fully automated and thus lacks conceptuality. The generic in the discourse networks of 1800 is that that hasn't been cultured enough, hasn't literarily been worked on enough to produce the soul, the idea. The generic of discourse network 2000 is in the sets of operations. Not only in the operation that comes after (*Curating Youtube* after YouTube), but also in that which differentiates (in making a video, in YouTube itself). If the generic of 1800 is an operation of comparison against the original, the generic of 2000 is an operation of producing systems and operations that act the generic out.

YouTube's aesthetic measurement makes the generic; *Curating YouTube* is itself a pure databaseness. The art here is in the exploration of the database as a system of operations, as an aesthetic concept.

DATABASE STRAND

It is now worth looking into the generic as a kind of operation (of generalization), one of whose origins is statistical. The generic as an operation is profoundly transformed today as the operations in the relational and other types of databases allow for new kinds of generic to emerge, where the operation of such emergence itself is transformed.

Databases (as a symbolic form, in Lev Manovich, 1998), relational databases in particular as a dominant kind of a database used today and newer kinds of databases (NoSQL movement) attract significant scholarly attention. They are material forms that enact certain ways of thinking and producing the world, where such ways are not necessarily known to people outside of computer science and often not subjected to critical humanities or social sciences thinking.

One route for looking for generic in the history of databases is in the problem of generality in statistics. Emma Uprichard (together with Burrows and Byrne) wrote on SPSS (software package for statistical analysis) in the following manner:

> This [change] has knock-on effects for generalization—that is, the ability to infer observations from a sample at one point in time to the population from which it was taken at another. The concept of generalization . . . is arguably defunct. Understanding how cases are 'generally' requires an explicit recognition of how they are 'specifically'. The logic of predictive analytics . . . aims instead to know 'enough' to make . . .

> 'moderatum generalisations' about particular types of cases [which] relates to tentative claims that are only relatively enduring; they are not intended to hold good over long periods of time, or across ranges of cultures, and they . . . need to be frequently 'updated' to 'keep up' with the ways in which cases may become different kinds of cases'. (Uprichard, Burrows and Byrne, undated)

As the datafication of things and their subjection to computational operations takes hold, the individual and specific and the generalized are redistributed. Evelyn Ruppert, analysing a management information system that works across case management systems holding data on young offenders (and following Ann-Marie Mol's concept of the 'body multiple'), calls for a subject multiple as it is enacted and performed by the data multiple (Ruppert, 2013: unpaginated). The multiple, the composite, is different in nature to the old kinds of the generic, as it was constructed, in statistics, through the operations of sampling, establishing causality and explanatory machines. (Uprichard and others instead focus on complexity, multiple causality, visualization and exploration as the new kinds of quantitative operations.)

Ruppert analyses the relational processes of a database at work that enacts the multiple, which is neither the specific nor the abstracted generic, but has features of both, bringing us back to the introductory passages of this chapter. The individual and unique as well as multiple, multiplied and repeated at the same time—these are the tensions that are supported and carried out at the levels of data structures and algorithmic operations upon data sets within databases. It is indeed such computational ensembles that sustain the relationality core to the construction of the new types and forms of the generic.

Adrian Mackenzie and Ruth McNally write about the thickening rather than flattening of the worlds produced through database operations (2013). For Ruppert, the computational, database system maintains the multiplicity, the uniqueness of each individual while maintaining them as generic people with multiples of attributes: 'He/she is instead a different, variable and unique composition and the system maintains this multiplicity'.

This is not only found in statistics and bureaucracy, it is poetry, diaries, writing exercises that previously individuated people into singularities—and it is now the database, among other computational algorithmic systems, that enables the creation of individuated subjects while maintaining them as multiples.

Ruppert suggests that the collective offender is enacted by a database as a composite, similarly to a composite portrait that is the multiple with all the singulars present at the same time. Ruppert writes: 'So while different practices decentre the ontology of the subject, the MIS re-centres it and at the same time maintains it as a composite'. To use the visual form of a composite portrait, the today's generic, counter intuitively, would not be the print of the composite, but the dynamic and living tension between the singular portraits and the multiple composite, and would be articulated in the construction of the composite, in the operation of relating, measuring and—in the software gesture of layering, overlaying, hiding and saving.

RELATIONAL DATABASES

A database is a collection of organized data; a table in relation to the database can be a result of query or data itself can be stored as tables. One of the most discussed features of the now dominant relational databases is its maintenance of so-called semantic independence of data. As the originator of relational databases claimed: 'Future users of large data banks must be protected from having to know how the data is organized in the machine' (Codd and Date, 1974). Here, the logical structure is divorced from the physical structure of data, and in our operations we deal with the logical structure only. Castelle relates to this in the following manner: 'The relational model differs primarily in its wholly symbolic and tabular representation to the user, as opposed to the explicitly encoded referential relations of the hierarchical and network models [of databases]. This fundamental semiotic difference produces a highly valued effect recognized more typically as "data independence"' (Castelle, 2013: unpaginated).

Relational database operates on the basis of formalization (creating a conceptual model) that works through normalization and composition. Normalization ensures that all data objects are irreducible objects of the same type without duplicates; whereas composition 'always happens through data in the relations themselves (integration at runtime)' by either modeling or query (so it is either modeled on or derived from data) (Rieder, 2012: unpaginated).

Bernhard Rieder says: 'Normalization reduces expressive power on the level of the unit and extends expressive power on the level of composition'. The expressive power thus belongs to the query that establishes relations. There is a 'model of knowing' within the model of the relational database which is about integrating data from different sources and establishing relations between data (Rieder). Castelle explains the same in the following way: 'Where the network model enforces referential (i.e., pointing) links between entities at the logical level, the relational model enforces the absence of such reference. In this way, we can say that what the relational model allows for is a sort of freedom in recontextualization of the (entextualized) database artifact. . . . This freedom is realized in the so-called "expressiveness" of relational query languages like SQL, which (given an appropriately normalized design) allow one to relate—via joins and projections—new entities with every interaction' (Castelle, 2013: unpaginated).

Coming back to the *Curating YouTube* project whose main operation is a relating exercise (comparing, pulling videos and fitting them into the grid) and putting those in relation to the database 'in general', we can usefully employ the following observations from Castelle: 'Codd's relational model was very distinctive from then-existing database models in having only one formal user-level conceptual data type: the relation, which can be thought of as a simple table. . . . The distinction between the two models is thus fundamentally semiotic; where the network model's pointers mimic the indexical real-world physical relationship between part and supplier, the relational model represents that relationship in an explicitly symbolic, tabular form' (Castelle). Extracting the relationship into the symbolic realm and operationalizing it, the relational database model supplies structures to inform and maintain cultural and social practices, in which establishing a relation is, to an extent, freed from the material to which it pertains—the basis for Manovich's proposal of database becoming the new dominating symbolic form.

Castelle extends the genealogy of this form to 'commercial and administrative bureaucracy', while Rieder points out the added 'software performativity' and 'extended calculative agency' of the model. Formalization, normalization and calculability are all the main principles of operation of the relational database model where the relationality between data objects can be queried, established and described—a process that would result in the production of a new table, and that would be bound by a preexisting data schema.

BIGTABLE AND YOUTUBE

YouTube, however, runs on BigTable, Google's own data management system, which is not a relational database (Chang et al., 2006). BigTable supports 'sparse semi-structured data' and allows for impressive scalabity 'up to petabytes' and 'thousands of machines' (Castelle); it belongs to a relatively new NoSQL movement of database management systems (DBMS) that is varied in itself and includes DBMS that still have a local relational database and a number of others built on different data models (graph, key value, column, etc.).

Systems, such as BigTable and others, seem especially fit for big and semi-structured data and 'support thousands of operations per server per second' (Chang et al., 2006: unpaginated). To simplify, if a relational database is fit for supporting, classically, financial transactions, and doesn't allow for data duplicates and concurrent operations, BigTable is fit for networks, with dynamically changing web pages and updated links, searches and posts (Dourish, 2013).

As such, BigTable doesn't normalize data and doesn't abstract relations from the data objects themselves: It is a 'sparse, distributed, persistent multi-dimensional sorted map'; that is 'is indexed by a row key, column key, and a timestamp' (Chang et al.).

Dourish in particular brings attention to the radicality of the change inherent to NoSQL databases. Relational database radically separates content from structure, where the schema must largely be defined before any data can be entered and is rarely altered afterwards; the openness of establishing new relations 'lies within content,' which is itself preselected by fitting a much 'more rigid schema' (Dourish). The expressiveness of the query and the specificity of relationality provided by the relational database are simultaneously open and wide-ranging and also limited. Dourish writes, 'Narrative and archival provisionality are primarily associated with content. The structure of a relational database is much more resistant to change. So the database is provisional, but only with limits; it is open-ended, but only in the terms originally laid down in its structure'.

BigTable relies heavily on Google infrastructure and is compatible with MapReduce (a model for parallel, distributed computing on computer clusters which is characterized by 'loose consistency' and storage in 'informally-organized collections of data objects linked together by broad associations') (Dourish): BigTable uses the Distributed Google File System.

In Dourish's opinion, the implementation of the NoSQL databases over clusters connected via networks instead of being held in a single mainframe computer radically changes the requirements and performance of the database management systems. A generation of databases relying on key-value structures (which is not the only building block used by BigTable) are the ones where, in comparison with relational databases, data objects and keys (that link value to an object) are not structured. An unstructured collection of data objects (e.g., an email) are linked to an unstructured collection of data values (e.g., 'written by me'), through keys belonging directly to objects rather than being separately defined (key—owner of email). If the key is not there, finding the value could be impossible (who is the owner of this email?); and the main operations in such DBMS are, according to Dourish, adding value to a key, updating a key, retrieving a value, as opposed to selecting from tables and ordering into a table of relational databases. It is easy to see how such relatively new systems have a larger allowance for failure, for missing or loose connections as they are performed in a distributed fashion. Objects can also be linked into 'chains' (through values), and become a kind of 'networks' (Dourish).

Dourish draws attention to the fact that the analytical power of such models is reduced, and there are currently other very powerful models that retain some of the benefits presented by the relational database systems and associated with firmly described data structures. The expressiveness of the query and the specificity of relationality afforded by relational databases and enacted in cultural material forms (for an insufficiently detailed account of which Dourish reproaches Manovich) coexist in the sociopolitical and cultural domain with other kinds of affordances: less expressivity (a focus on system performance at the expense of reduced representational clarity and consistency), a focus on objects rather than relations and 'low integration'.

Dourish suggests that there are four main characteristics of such new data structures and forms of 'data processing' that are comprised of assemblages formed by hardware infrastructures and software applications: granularity, multiplicity, associativity and convergence. The following is particularly useful for thinking about the generic:

> In exploring the problems of granularity and associativity, then, we found ourselves exploring the way that data objects become 'live' inside the system. . . . Multiplicity—the ability to act coherently upon multiple manifestations of objects that, from another perspective, are 'the

> same'—reflects this concern with the particular, and the different constraints associated with different approaches to database form. . . . In particular, approaches to multiplicity speak to the opportunities for partition–that is, for a system to operate as multiple independent entities, either briefly or for an extended period. (Dourish, 2013)

Here, the allowance for and the lure of the same, and slightly different, the tensions between the particular object and the multiplicity of relations that arise from its operation—in relation to others, relating, being a duplicate, differing—is encoded, performed at the level of the database management system and implementation designs that work beyond social media platforms such as YouTube. The object multiple or a subject multiple that Ruppert focuses on is a different multiple here: the relations holding it together are much looser; it is less consistent and less integrated. It is a porous, leaky and inconsistent multiple that is itself a loosely related chain of individual objects with differing characteristics.

Manovich's observations on database as a symbolic form seem to pertain to the relational database model, allowing for the expressivity of query, but within a defined structure. Here, the classic net art project by Olia Lialina *Myboyfriendcamebackfromthewar* (1997) exemplifies the cultural materiality afforded and enforced by the relational database model. In this project, and in many other similar endeavours, a viewer can select her path through the dividing frames with images telling a story and thus create an individual narrative, though bounded by the constraints of what has been defined by and loaded into the database structure behind the interface. The narrative is abstracted from the material that can be expressively rearranged enabling a variation on the narrative; however, the conditions of the narrative are predefined and its combinatorial finitude of options can be pre-calculated. The longstanding criticism of certain strands of interactivity in interactive art and other spheres allowing for freedom of interaction and, thus, coauthorship, within a very limited set of choices laid out by the real author pertains here. But the *real author* here is not even the database manager or designer, but the database model itself. Kittler, positioning the Turing machine in the place previously occupied by the human subject, as outlined at the beginning of the paper, would be happy now.

NoSQL database management systems offer a somewhat different set of allowances and conditions. Using Manovich's language, the narrative is not subtracted but embedded in the material objects themselves—but the objects are much more loosely connected than, for instance, sentences in a story by Chekhov.[1] Objects stand on their own and connections/relations arise from their operations or operations on them, as if the words, sounds and sentences were dancing around, moving chaotically, forming chains, and assembling into a certain ragged and unbounded multiple (surrealist poetry), rather than a smooth fabric (realist novel) or relatively ordered interactive story (whether works by Alain Robbe-Grillet or Milorad Pavič or digital storytelling projects). The multiple itself, as a dividable, might not be the most useful term here. It is rather a mix-aliquant, data and subject manifold.

Making sense of an unbounded ragged manifold is the purpose of *Curating YouTube*. The operation of selecting and putting videos into the grid doesn't produce a coherent unique statement (videos in the grid are neither unique nor collective, neither singular, nor multiple), but the curated page is the place where the power of the generic arises and manifests.

Curating YouTube puts selected videos in relation to each other (like attributing values to keys and establishing connections between values), but without a single overall structure. Rather, there is a multitude of structures—the curatorial gesture of browsing and selection, Gridr and the grid, histories of art, YouTube, the machinery of cultural institutions, BigTable, the Distributed Google File System, networks and protocols and many more. A mass of semi-structured data, neither patterns nor noise (at times Gridr curators look for patterns and at other times they orchestrate an organic ecology comprised of incommensurable objects), the multitude of copies of slightly different video files, are potent of a very specific relationality, the relationality of the generic, which in turn, sustains the oscillation of both and between the singular and the multiple, producing the ragged manifold of the subject.

CURATING YOUTUBE

Curating YouTube (CYT) works on the infrastructure of YouTube as a database management system as it is plugged into many other structures, and its characteristics as an art project lies in its operating in those material structures. In some way, *Curating YouTube* reveals the databaseness of the new types of databases, abstracting the database model and material affordances from the YouTube database. The project releases the data from the way in which it exists on YouTube, but also in a way that YouTube allows views into it. YouTube has a similar 'suggestions' function, but CYT cleanses this function and subjects it to aesthetic work.

To speak metaphorically about something technically precise, *Curating YouTube* attributes new values to data objects and creates new keys, enacting a specific relationality. As *Curating YouTube* operates on top of and in multiple systems, many of which call for unique individual digital gestures while linking them to a multitude of other, similar but slightly different gestures, in a boundlessly scalable loosely ordered messy mass of networks and data, it articulates a version of the problem of the individual versus the collective and repositions the question of the subject.

Sakrowski writes, 'In my opinion, an ordering, which creates identity, can only be performed individually and on excerpts and in this way, maybe reconcile the individual with the mass . . . [it] enables to deal with the multitude of phenomena in terms of aesthetic[s] and associations: selecting and arranging videos in the grid'. Whether CYT is about reconciliation or not, producing new kinds of relationality between available data via aesthetic means becomes generative of something that is not immediately obvious when we watch videos on YouTube or think about the databases behind it.

The databaseness and relationality of *Curating YouTube* directly relates to, creates and explores the generic as the site of individuation as it is produced as an oscillation between the singular and the manifold, in clouds, chains and connections and where constructing such an oscillation is an individuating process. *Curating YouTube* releases the performativity of the database as a thinking model, and as a material method of enactment, and articulates its medium-specificity in an epistemologically-charged aesthetic gesture. Here, a curatorial device and artwork becomes a thickening, a saturation of relations which are intensified, doubled, made similar, made serial—and it is from such operations that the subject arises.

THE GRIDR AND THE *CURATING YOUTUBE* GRID

Finally, the question worth asking is what the Gridr is in *CuratingYouTube*. In visual design the grid is a means of applying systematicity, overlaying a structure to ease certain operations, and through that of operationalizing. It is used for leveling, alignment and equalization, or the arrangement of information in terms of structure. In such a way, the grid as an object already includes operations on the material to be presented in it.

The grid as a formal device is related to that of the *table* and can function as a visual representation that helps demonstrate systematic relations. It can be used a means of arranging data to infer relationality, systematicity and causality; a fundamental quality of a grid or of a table is that it can be rearranged to repeat the operation of articulation. Structure adds information to the data; there is intelligence in the structure. The grid is not only a visualization of the data or processes, it is also an operation of articulation. The grid is operative.

It has been argued that a grid is not so much 'the image of an emerging modernity' imposing uniformity, regularity or homogenization, but a 'universal space' of scalability (Higgins, 2009: 12; 15–17). Describing the evolution of the grid from handwoven nets to the punch cards of the Jacquard loom, and to Babbage analytical engine's use of punch cards, Hannah Higgins says:

> The punch card . . . is the mechanism of transition between the soft grids of textile technology and the hardware of the information age; it translates the net from its physical expression in textiles to a modeling form that would tabulate, sort, and integrate. . . . The von Neumann architecture [of the computer] is a grid that forms the very core of modern information technology. . . . [I]t is an organized set of modules that allows for manipulation and creativity, making new kinds of searching . . . and connection building . . . possible. (Higgins, 2009: 249, 254)

A table, and tabular representation in a database, has values assigned to rows and columns, something that the grid lacks. If the grid may, in cases such as these, be a first step in establishing and assigning computability, and enacting relationality through a certain kind of measurement, the table, especially in the relational database design, is a mathematical term for relation. Here, the grid can be a procedure of abstraction, whereas a table can be described with mathematical functions in relational algebra (a foundation of the relational database).

The Gridr of *Curating YouTube* establishes a rupture between the liquid relationality of the YouTube database and the process of production of the art project *Curating YouTube* itself. Curiously, there is some violence done to the material of YouTube by putting a square number of videos into a fixed structure. A measurement of measurement, the establishment of relationality between the relational, all in all, a collision of formal structures produces the project. Thus, the individuation of *Curating YouTube* and its subjecthood emerges through overimposition, a conflict of a few computational models.

A distributed collection of semi-structured data which is algorithmically integrated and scaled up and down, where the connections made are a result of algorithmic, automatic functions is the material form in which culture operates today. Working at different levels, *Curating Youtube* deals with technocultural expression as it is specifically 'databased,' while teasing out the specificity of these operations by colliding conceptual and formal gestures through the use of the grid.

CONCLUSION

The focus on the generic via the processes of 're-ordering of classification, naming, numbering and ordering, individuation and generalization'[2] weaves in measurement, statistics and culture, sciences and humanities, commonplaceness, mundanity and singularity, and refers to copy, uniqueness and value. I've tried in this chapter to reflect upon the relationships that generic has to seriality, similarity, relationality and the operation of relating itself. Singularity and multiplicity and the production of the subject are all touched upon if the generic realities are followed in-the-making.

For Kittler, in the eighteenth and nineteenth centuries the subject—and the generic—was produced by the discourse network of cursive writing. The reflexivity of the soul at the centre of cursive writing, and of Platonic enterprise, for Deleuze, produces common sense too: 'The "sameness" of the Platonic idea which serves as a model and is guaranteed by the Good gives way to the identity of an originary concept grounded in the thinking subject. The thinking subject brings to the concept its subjective concomitants: memory, recognition and self-consciousness. Nevertheless, it is the moral vision of the world which is thereby extended and represented in this subjective identity affirmed as a *common sense* [italics in the original]' (Deleuze, 2008: 334). The inextricable connection between originality and common sense today gives way to new kinds of relations, between copies, patterns, data and computational operations, in which the generic resides.

It is now the discourse network of the Turing machine and its apparatuses—various models of databases—that contributes to the maintenance (rather than the full Kittlerian replacement) of the subject. The subject is produced not through an exercise in writing but through the relationality of data which, in the example of an art project, such as *Curating YouTube*, allows for a rearticulation of the database's operationality in aesthetic terms and for an exposure of its methodological dominance across culture and not only administrative bureaucracy. The schema of the unique and singular versus that of the generalized and collective is rearticulated and produces new forms of multiplicity and relationality.

The form of production of the subjectivity takes place in this operation of relationality, itself attached to the database; as the database handles both singularities and establishes relations between them as a multiple or as a ragged manifold. It is somewhere in this computational maintenance of the operationalized singular and multiple and the movement between them that the new kinds of subjectivity are produced.

In *Curating YouTube* neither individual videos, all videos together, nor the grid are inherently generic, but it is in the process of articulation and relation that takes place through operating upon the YouTube database, the kind of operations made possible for the public, and the operations superimposed on those, with the grid and the curatorial gesture, that the generic, and with it, singularity and plurality, and subjectivity have their spaces enunciated. The new kinds of subjectivity and the new generic are produced as videos are 'pulled' and forced into the grid, and they arise too somewhere between the multiplicity of those videos, the databaseness of the project's operationality, and the database management systems and architectural ensembles running them.

NOTES

1. There is a certain irony that I exemplify my proposal with literary examples, and Kittler as a fellow philologist would have appreciated the double bind of this act.
2. This is from a workshop on the generic, organized in December 2013 by Celia Lury, Sophie Day, and Nina Wakeford as part of the Intel project on Number and hosted by Cory Hayden at Berkeley, CA. I am grateful to Celia Lury for inviting me to speak at the workshop which helped me develop my ideas on the generic.

BIBLIOGRAPHY

Castelle, Michael. (2013) 'Relational and Non-Relational Models in the Externalization of Bureaucracy' in *Computational Culture, A Journal of Software Studies*, 3, computationalculture.net/article/relational-and-non-relational-models-in-the-entext

ualization-of-bureaucracy, accessed 21.03.2014.
Chang, Fay, Jeffrey Dean, Sanjay Ghemawat, Wilson C. Hsieh, Deborah A. Wallach, Mike Burrows, Tushar Chandra, Andrew Fikes, Robert E. Gruber. (2006) ' BigTable: A Distributed Storage System for Structured Data'. www.usenix.org/legacy/events/osdi06/tech/chang/chang_html, accessed 21.03.2014.
Codd, E. F. and C. J. Date. (1974) 'Interactive Support for Non-Programmers: The Relational and Network Approaches' in Proceedings of the 1974 ACM SIGFIDET workshop on data description, access and control: Data models: Data-structure-set versus relational. Ann Arbor, MI: ACM, pp. 11–41.
Deleuze, Gilles. (2008) *Difference and Repetition*. New York: Continuum.
Dourish, Paul. (2013) 'No SQL: The Shifting Materialities of Database Technology' in *Computational Culture, A Journal of Software Studies* 4 (forthcoming).
First Viewer Television, firstviewer.tv, accessed 21.03.2014.
Higgins, Hannah B. (2009) *The Grid Book*. Cambridge, MA: MIT Press.
Kittler, Friedrich. (1990) *Discourse Networks 1800/1900*. Stanford, CA: Stanford University Press.
———. (1994) 'Unconditional Surrender' in *Materialities of Communication*, eds. Hans Ulrich Gumbrecht and K. Ludwig Pfeiffer. Stanford, CA: Stanford University Press, 319–34.
Laric, Oliver. (2007) *50 50*, vimeo.com/16024741, accessed 21.03.2014.
Mackenzie, Adrian and Ruth McNally. (2013) 'Methods of the Multiple: How Large-Scale Scientific Data-Mining Pursues Identity and Differences' in *Theory, Culture & Society* 30(4): 72–91.
Manovich, Lev. (1998) 'Database as a Symbolic Form,' www.nettime.org/Lists-Archives/nettime-l-9812/msg00041.html, accessed 21.03.2014.
NoTube, www.curatingyoutube.net, accessed 21.03.2014.
Rieder, Bernhard. (2012) From the presentation given at the workshop 'The Lived Logics of the Database Machinery', computationalculture.net/cfps-events/the-lived-logics-of-database-machinery, accessed 21.03.2014.
Ruppert, Evelyn. (2013) 'Not Just Another Database: The Transactions That Enact Young Offenders' in *Computational Culture, A Journal of Software Studies*, 3, computationalculture.net/article/not-just-another-database-the-transactions-that-enact-young-offenders, accessed 21.03.2014.
Sakrowski, Robert. *Curating YouTube*, www.curatingyoutube.net, accessed 21.03.2014.
———. (2011) 'An Acoustic Journey through YouTube', http://www.curatingyoutube.net/acoustic, accessed 21.03.2014.
Uprichard, Emma, Roger Burrows and D. Byrne. 'SPSS as an "Inscription Device": From Causality to Description' in *Sociological Review: Anniversary Issue*, 56(4): 606–22; www.academia.edu/151125/Uprichard_E_._Burrows_R._and_Byrne_D._2008_SPSS_as_an_Inscription_Device_from_causality_to_description_Sociological_Review_Anniversary_Issue_-_From_causality_to_description_56_4_606_-_622, accessed 21.03.2014.
Winthrop-Young, Geoffrey. (2010) *Kittler and the Media*. New York: Polity.

Exhibitions

Lialina, Olia. (1997) My Boyfriend Came Back From the War, available at myboyfriendcamebackfromth.ewar.ru/.
The World Beach Project (2007–2012), Victoria and Albert Museum, London, UK.

YouTube Play: A Biennial of Creative Video. (22-24/ 10/ 2010) Guggenheim Museums in New York, Bilbao, Berlin, and Venice.

We Are All Photographers Now! The Rapid Mutation Of Amateur Photography In The Digital Age. (13/10/2007-31/01/2008) Musée de l'Elysée, Lausanne, Switzerland.

Postscript

Of Disappearances and the Ontology of Media (Studies)

Jussi Parikka

Media studies, however, only make sense when media make senses.

—F. A. Kittler

THE DISAPPEARANCE OF MEDIA

Just when you thought (new) media studies got started it seemed already over. A brief moment of the discipline that promised to signal a new technically enhanced philosophical and yet historically situated set of knowledge practices, discursive provocations and material ontologies was after some years faced with talk of 'postmedia', the 'postdigital' and even 'post-Internet'. It felt like the object of its study slipped from the analytical fingers that tried to methodologically follow the media cultural trail. A multiplication of discourses in and around media produced not only inflation in the very meaning of the concept, but also arguments as to the possible uselessness of the concept.[1]

To speak of 'after' the media, or the superfluous nature of the concept of media (Zielinski, 2013), in the wake of its inflated mobilization, necessitates an evaluation of the possible closure of the mass media era—and the new media era. The Snowden-leaks might qualify as one such symbolic closure of the enthusiastic years of new media, as Geert

Lovink notes (2014), forcing us into positions that speak of post but they also speak of 'anti'. Indeed, in Florian Cramer's words 'Anti-media is what remains if one debunks the notion of media but can't get rid of it' (quoted in Lovink, 2014). In the German context, one already started to speak of the media and media studies in the past tense: 'what were media', as Claus Pias (2011) asked reflecting on the different generations of media theory and its institutionalisation.[2]

Outside the intellectual circles, various political attacks especially in the UK had for years branded the late-comer as a Mickey Mouse-discipline that produced endless (re)readings of representations of Brad Pitt and the cultural significance of The Beatles. Paradoxically, the clichés produced in the media were happily targeting media studies in ways that testified of the on-going bankruptcy of this type of journalism, unable to write about deep, intellectual topics such as cultural theory in the age of advanced media technologies.

And then on the side of technological design—just when we were supposed to reach the peak excitement about media technological innovation—the biggest innovation revealed to be about its disappearance. The silent fading away of the technological device despite the libidinal tickle of Apple's design team's PR success is announced in terms of ubiquitous environments, smart buildings and cities and the remote sensorial taking the place of the tangible media material. The object of our fantasy during that modern period has so much been about *the gadget* is itself in risk of becoming a victim of its own success by way of disappearing into the architectural environment. It is this penetrating milieu that takes the role of sensorial-computational and is more than merely an object of media analysis. 'Obtaining information will be trivial', argues Mark Weiser, a pioneer of ubicomp, voicing what sounds like the utter nightmare for anyone in the footsteps of Berlin material media theory hackers:

> Sociologically, ubiquitous computing may mean the decline of the computer addict. In the 1910s and 1920s many people "hacked" on crystal sets to take advantage of the new high-tech world of radio. Now crystal-and-cat's-whisker receivers are rare because high-quality radios are ubiquitous. In addition, embodied virtuality will bring computers to the presidents of industries and countries for nearly the first time. Computer access will penetrate all groups in society. (Weiser, 1991: 103–4)

Access will penetrate society and yet the object of media itself disappears. Discursively, theorists and the art crowd are moving to the postmedia age whether by this is meant an acknowledgement of the de facto digitality of our social life or a movement to something that follows the earlier phase of mass media society (see Apprich et al., 2013). Politically and academically perhaps media was already a bit of passé and out of its time, at least when looked at from the point of view of institutions and discourses that are keen to invent another 'new' to ensure the peak-theory consumption stays at the top of its game in producing waves of fabs. Technologically, the infrastructural started taking the place of what we used to handily (when the objects were still graspable, *zuhanden*) call 'media'. Surely even theorists won't be soon needed. Cue in Kittler's own joke from early 1990s concerning his interest in information theory and random generative texts: 'One day I won't have to write any more articles but will be able to generate new Kittler texts statistically out of old Kittler texts and no reader will ever notice. This is my mean spirited intention' (Kittler and Rickels, 1992: 67).

However, to return to the disappearance of media as an object of analysis, what many of the simplifications or hyperbolic variations can shadow, is the rigorous methodologies that have gone into establishing even a situation where media studies—and media theory—enjoys a particular way of producing statements that, to put it bluntly, are relevant. This banal sounding phrase hides inside itself an appreciation of the multitude of material and social determinations that make up what we often call 'media'—whether in the form of 'the internet', 'the radio', 'the television', 'the cinema' or 'the mobile'. It is rather significant in this sense that this is not a book only about F. A. Kittler. Instead, the chapters focus on the variations and forces that the specific theoretical desire produced. One can connect some of the ideas in the book to the earlier historical context of German media studies (Siegert, 2013), but one can also link to a current drive for a radical revisiting of media as a transversal field of investigation of relations between aesthetics, technology and politics. One way or the other, there is something alive in this mix of material media theory without of course wanting to idealise German media theory as something of an intellectual orientation that stands on a pedestal without its own problems.

THE KITTLER DRIVE

Kittler's focus and methodology produces an insight to the physical as much as the physiological without any illusion of a reduction to the centrality of the human being. Kittler and German media theorists of many kinds offer alternatives to McLuhan's—historically a bit too straightforward—ideas with a more meticulous touch and post-structural materialism. Underlining the nineteenth-century scientific research into human beings as empirical, temporal and physiological matter, is one way to address the post-Kantian era as a specific cultural historical situation: psychophysics, Fechner and the emerging laboratories of measurability take the place of apperceptive Man, even if such late-comers as Edmund Husserl in the early twentieth century try to rescue the world of humans ('the life-world') from the real of psychophysiological sensation. Kittler's (2006b) interest in media is both a reference to the centrality of the technological in mediating the real and offering an epistemological framework crucial to Modernity—and an appreciation of the world as radically mediated on the physiological layer, which psychophysical tests revealed through staring at the sun and listening to noise.

When such a stance is carried over into analysis of technical media it produces a situation that appeals to thinkers of nonhuman agency. The conditions of human are to be discovered in such techniques in which sensation is teased out, modified, manipulated and offered as a technological reality of which the human is one extension—not the other way round. It is media which make sense when they make sense: they are to be seen as material procedures in which sense, knowledge and sensation are produced in a grounding of aesthetics in media. This aspect forces a consideration of the predigital modulations of human beings, a theme that should be of interest to contemporary versions of affect-theory. Both material media theory and several theories of the affect are interested in the evaluation of all there is that cannot be reduced to the signifier and its play of meaning (see also Lazzarato, 2014: 29). Text-focused post-structuralism is transformed into media theory.

Such an emphasis on the material is one of sort of a methodological echo of what was established in the nineteenth century and during the twentieth century, as a result of research into animal bodies as nerves: sensory, motor, acoustic and optic regimes of the body are connected but do not necessarily make up a conscious human being. Language is only one regime of cognition and also meaning can become just one variable among others, as demonstrated by experiments of, for example, Gertrude Stein (Johnston, 2012: 16). Time and its graphic representation became one key epistemological feature of this embodied understanding of the nerve-being called man (see Schmidgen, 2014).

Kittler was interested in a historical scientific context of our theories of cultural reality. He was adamant that even if we hallucinate meaning across cultural reality, the real is not merely a reflection of our consciousness, singular or collective. There's more to this material, nerve-oriented and embodied situation that connects the scientific history of psychophysiological research into a media studies agenda full of relevance to the cultural history of philosophy. To quote Kittler (1990: 216): 'Because not every local center has direct nerve connections to every other, there is no unity of the transcendental signified capable of organically developing speaking and hearing, writing and reading out of one another. . . . Children circa 1900 learned to read without understanding and to write without thinking'.

This focus on the automated, nonconscious reality of cultural techniques should already give an idea of what's to come when Kittler's theoretical and historical case studies turn to the computer. It involves an appreciation of the computer not merely as a tool but as a medium. This refers to an evaluation of technological apparatuses as systematic rearranging of relations of senses, sensibilities and other cultural techniques that are not merely anymore expressed in what is directly perceivable by the senses. Hence, the focus on counting and mathematics steps to the forefront with a specific way of understanding the systematic nature of contemporary media. This was included in Kittler's own reflection of his skillset too when he, in an early interview with Laurence Rickels, reflected on learning mathematics in the 1980s as a way to 'find his way around the system' instead of being merely a hardware tinkering hobbyist (Kittler and Rickels, 1992: 67). Funnily enough, all the talk of Kittler's hardware-determinism neglects his fascination with software and mathematics, which I would claim is not merely an intellectual analytical theme that runs through his media theory, but something of an important pedagogical trait that needs to be emphasized when considering media studies after Kittler.

The recent inventions of political manifestos that are (again) trying to bring computing and software skills to schools in the UK and abroad as well as the academic focus on digital humanities, were preceded by media studies analyses and pedagogies such as Kittler's. Software, Linux operating system and the cultural history of Western philosophy were brought into an intimate proximity as part of the humanities and aesthetics curriculum. Since 1994, he convened his 'coding class' which was really an integral part of his teaching and institutional presence.

In this context it is clear Kittler's claim about the disappearance of software (1995) was not a naïve dismissal of what was evident: that software is as important a trait in the power/knowledge-configurations of our culture as alphabetization was to the nineteenth-century emergence of modern nation-states coupled with pedagogical systems and universities. Kittler's argument that 'there is no software' still stands as an insightful provocation—an art that he mastered better than most academics—that both reflects an acute sense of an understanding of the contemporary moment and also reveals Kittler's own predisposition and background. It was meant to underline—in the midst of talk of the immateriality of digital culture—that all that discursive vanishing of materiality is grounded in massive computational, material, energetic operations. It's not a dismissal of the code in any way, but looking at the specific computational features of the digital code that is not merely a text in the human-readable sense. The compiler stood there in between the machine and the supposed subject of writing which, could not anymore always read what it wrote (see Berz and Feigelfeld, 2014).

From a burgeoning literature scholar Kittler ended up with the Linux operating system and as a professor who demanded that in his class, one had to know one's way around the Linux free c compiler 'gcc' (see Krajewski, 2011). He wrote books and texts but also code—over 100,000 lines of software code: pedagogical programs that unfold media historically important problems of mathematics, graphics and geometry (Berz and Feigelfeld, 2014). Teaching about optical media went hand in hand with the skills in programming, measured by his own code as well as the programming manuals and such now found in the Kittler archives. But it was also a living pedagogical practice for him. Besides his own private programming, he opened up an institutional space for collective engagement with programming under hood of academic humanities: the open source mandate became a driving force for classrooms of media theory executed through mathematics of computer programming (see Berz and Feigelfeld, 2014).

Kittler's take focuses on questions of 'what is writing' as much as *where* is writing in the age of new institutions of writing—from universities to the computer hardware corporations. The twentieth-century linguistics offered ideas about structure of language from Saussure to the post World War II cybernetics-influenced views of language such as Roman Jacobson's (see Geoghegan, 2011). Of course the deconstructionist re-reading of text and reality by the likes of Derrida and others offered another wave of theory that shifted the position of the subject in relation to writing. And at the same time the engineers of media technological realities offered their own version of a poststructuralist credo: We are determined by our language, but our language is determined by the writing machines and media—which however in the age of Intel microcircuitry is increasingly determined by corporations and their hardware secrets. Conditions of writing lie in the worlds defined by .com and .exe ending files and in software suites such as Wordperfect and Word (Fuller 2003). This is why Kittler was adamant about the necessity of teaching programming. It is a logical continuation of the programme of critical relating to the tradition of metaphysics in the age of technical media. It is not merely enough to learn natural languages as we in humanities had done for centuries. On top of that we have to learn programming languages. This was reflected in his own teaching: imagine going to a cultural theory class and learn essentials about code and hardware! Kittler's 1990s Berlin seminars became a classic over the years exactly for this mix of theory and computing. In Krajewski's words:

> After writing whole books about the subtle effects and inner-political aspects of alphabetization (Kittler, 1990), Kittler demanded an equal level of knowledge in writing computer sources among students, scholars, and intellectuals. Given the strong influence of technical constraints and challenges, it is also necessary to learn at least one or two formal languages in order to overcome the dominance of and hence dependency on large computer companies like Microsoft if you want to command your PC rather than be commanded by the machine. In short, Kittler wanted to establish a real computer literacy. (2011: 35)

In other words, in order to learn about the changes in writing and how we are being written, we have to learn such codes that are not merely those of human alphabetics: 'Codes—by name and by matter—are what determine us today, and what we must articulate if only to avoid disappearing under them completely' (Kittler, 2010: 40).

Such ideas, classroom situations and theoretical insights are also part and parcel of the wider project of German media studies as articulated by Bernhard Siegert (2013: 50): The philosophies of language and orality such as Derrida's are to be shifted from their ahistorical readings on to an analytical framework of 'historico-empirical cultural techniques' through which to understand the functions of pedagogy, not metaphorics; operations of technical media, not just the play of différance. Hence the particular attention to the grey areas of media as techniques, or operations, which produce differences, process the cultural reality and engage in the ontological real while also acting as an epistemological framework. It is interesting to read through the, at times slightly hasty, critique of such approaches that demand a new material take as nonpolitical even if they are constantly engaged with such formational processes of power/knowledge, to use Foucault's vocabulary. It is just that in the hands of writers such as Kittler the project of Modernity turns into a question of the projectile (Kittler's fascination of Thomas Pynchon's novel *Gravity's Rainbow*, the V2 and the mathematics of ballistics, rockets and targeting). Project of Modernity, in other words, is one of development of advanced (military) technologies and of communication media, which do not bend into the idealistic discourses of democracy and 'communicative rationality' as Kittler (2002: 76) ironically puts it referring to Habermas's alternative way of pitching modernity. You don't speak of lust when speaking of communicative rationality, but with Kittler, the psychoanalytic vocabulary gets attached to a political understanding of pedagogy and audiovisual and calculational media: 'Every culture has its zones of preparation that fuse lust and power, optically, acoustically, and so on' (Kittler, 1990: 140).

This sort of an understanding of power resonates perhaps a sort of a media theoretical understanding of Realpolitik which on the German ground might refer back to writings by Carl Schmidt and Ernst Jünger, but which on the recent theoretical agenda find allies also in the idea of Evil Media by Fuller and Goffey (2009: 142): to 'get a grip on contemporary media practices of trickery, deception, and manipulation' instead of the idealisations of rational communication or representational meaning.

POST-KITTLER: AN ONTOLOGY OF MEDIA

In the spirit of this book and the way in which already Eleni Ikoniadou's primer affirms, Kittler is just one entry point to the issues at hand. The agenda includes the theoretical impulse that theorises asignifiying semiotics, material infrastructures of power and nonhuman agencies, which are structuring the media—and media studies' reality. Kittler's take might be rather different than Deleuze and Guattari's, or for example Italian Post-Fordist theory, but even with the likes of Maurizio Lazzarato, there are interesting resonances when it comes to the dividual (as unit of control societies) defined by how 'the component parts of subjectivity (intelligence, affects, sensations, cognition, memory, physical force) are no longer unified in an "I"' (Lazzarato, 2014: 27). Such cognitive and affective capacities are produced and synthetized in different assemblages from media to corporations, even if for Kittler this shift is more historically focused on the post-Kantian physiological grounding of media cultural image of the human. Still some of the contemporary political theory speaks to the same points emerging in German media theory too. Italian political theory of a Marxist bent can oddly enough find some common ground with what is often seen as the apolitical strand of material media theory (see Parikka, 2013). In other words, across even the varying emphases of theorists, we should be able to articulate differences as much as find synthetic new paths for a media studies agenda of the new materialist/abstract materialist kind. This includes also pedagogical insights and practices, as mentioned above.

In this context, the disappearance of media objects is not merely a problem for media studies but also a condition for its renewed meaningfulness. Instead, media theory is able to productively expand the objects of analysis to surprising directions as well as destabilise the accustomed methodological choices with some new, exciting ideas, to paraphrase Pias (2011: 28). Perhaps media studies, in the first place, was less a unified field than a discursive, institutional and theoretical strategy to carve out a specific angle within existing disciplines and ideas. And perhaps the concreteness of the media as objects or systems was always a slightly narrow way of understanding the materiality of the technological reality. Instead, we are more interested in the creative processuality and ontology of this existence that comes out in slightly differing ways that are able to reflect on its own conditions of material existence. This emerges in terms of ontologies for the twenty-first century ubiquitous computing (see Hansen, 2014) as well as even a conceptual proposition that Kittler, the mathematically oriented media theorist par excellence, reminds us of. Even if an explicated ontology of media might have escaped the Greek thinkers' agenda, we have fragments based on which we can articulate that it is not only what you see but how it is being conditioned: 'For ever since Thomas's great idol Aristotle, that particular matter which all but evades our senses yet facilitates sensual perception in the first place is called to metaxi ("the middle", Latin medium)' (Kittler, 2006a: 54). This is where theoretical and institutional practices of analysis of technical media fold into theorisation of the *ontology* of media.

Hence, postmedia was always, already, postmedia object and sort of a prequel to the digital as well. It is in this paradoxical sense that a lot of the recent analytical 'post-theoretisation' of postmedia and postdigital too is less a temporal after than a shifting of the coordinates of the debate, from a linear understanding of media historical time to one of more complex determinations—and hence the relevance of media archaeology in this context. (On temporal multiplicities of media archaeology, see Parikka, 2012.) The postmedia as an assemblage is more to the point an understanding of the conditions under which material assemblages and technologies function as ways to facilitating sensual perception. The seeming disappearance of 'media' is also a testimony to its own importance, hence efficient media theories—after media, after Kittler—are ones that facilitate thinking about this threshold between the perceptible and the imperceptible.

In the more interesting uses of the prefix 'post', including in Cramer's (2014) definition of the 'post-digital', this threshold becomes articulated as the key matter of concern. It becomes a marker for the possibilities of historicization as well as 'disenchantment with digital information systems and media gadgets'. After all, this disenchantment can become articulated on a political agenda too. Cramer refers to the post-Snowden situation that does not merely articulate a new consciousness (the idea that 'now we *know* what the NSA and other geopolitical powers are up to') but one can also add a possible space and time of practice. This hopefully keeps an active articulation alive: what media are as historical and material hinges where power and knowledge operate. We don't need to claim that Kittler determines our situation—but his work is one impulse that helps us to filter through the more interesting and productive of analyses that become useful in trying to map out the situation of the present as one that is increasingly claimed to be already ahead of itself—'post'.

NOTES

1. In other words, I don't want to dismiss the critical voices relating to the evaluation of German media theory itself. Stefan Heidenreich points out how the 1980s entry of media studies into the mix of Humanities in Germany produced a fruitful break from business as usual but was quickly adopted into a domesticated disciplinary system. In Heidenreich's (2011: 15) evaluation, demonstrating the institutional difficulties in sustaining radical material thinking in contemporary corporate-universities: 'Regrettably, what had the potential to lead us out of the trap of a backwards-looking orientation and the split between theory and production soon fell prey to the usual course of academic trends. Less than ten years after Friedrich Kittler introduced the new approach to German literature studies, he was forced to acknowledge the ubiquitous presence of the term "media". Subsequently, the initial impulse was lost in the operational procedures of academic administration. The term media turned into a discretionary keyword without theoretical specificity, but with the powerful promise of generating money for research. And most of the books considering media theory fell back onto an intellectual terrain from which Kittler had initially tried to depart. The philological method of interpretation and the self-restriction to history prevailed. That is the main reason why media theory rarely had much to say about media after 1950, let alone the internet'. Indeed, as Heidenreich and others have pointed out, Kittler failed to address the Internet in a sustained, proper way. For some contextual evaluation of German media theory, see also Geert Lovink's (2007) chapter on the topic of 'Whereabouts of German Media Theory' in his book *Zero Comments*.

2. Suffice to say, my postscript is less focused on the question of German Media Studies itself. The focus of this book is to expand into the double horizon of post-Kittler and emerging media theories. Of course, the question of 'post-Kittler' could be tackled from such a cultural history of the media thinking in German-speaking academic, alongside its internationalization. Geoffrey Winthrop-Young stands as the key figure and commentator in this respect and his brief note is worthwhile quoting (while he also acknowledges that it would need a lot of complexifying): 'To offer one of those irresponsible generalizations that come easily to outside observers, it appears that, like Hegel, to whom he is occasionally compared, Kittler has inspired a bifurcation into right and left Kittlerians. Nothing, we suggest, reveals this division more than applying the concept of cultural techniques to his work. Scholars like Siegert, Vismann and Krajewski would qualify as left Kittlerians: his anti-hermeneutic stance is transformed by them into a less intransigent post-hermeneutic approach involving certain notions of praxis and limited human agency that Kittler was prone to eschew. Ernst, on the other hand, would be a right Kittlerian by subordinating whatever human element may be involved in cultural techniques to the closed times and circuits of technological recursions' (Winthrop-Young, 2013: 15).

BIBLIOGRAPHY

Apprich, Clemens, Josephine Berry Slater, Anthony Iles, and Oliver Lerone Schultz, eds. (2013) *Provocative Alloys: A Post-Media Anthology*. Lüneburg: PML Books.

Berz, Peter and Paul Feigelfeld. (2014) 'Source Code als Quelle. Aus der Arbeit mit Friedrich Kittlers Programmierwerk'. A lecture at the Ruhr Universität Bochum, 14 January 2014.

Cramer, Florian. (2014) 'What Is "Post-Digital"?' *ARPJA—A Peer-Reviewed Journal about Post-Digital Research* 3(1), www.aprja.net/?p=1318.

Geoghegan, Bernard Dionysius. (2011) 'From Information Theory to French Theory: Jakobson, Levi-Strauss, and the Cybernetic Apparatus'. *Critical Inquiry* 38 (Autumn 2011), pp. 96–126.

Fuller, Matthew. (2003) 'It Looks Like You're Writing a Letter' in *Behind the Blip: Essays on the Culture of Software*. New York: Autonomedia, pp. 137–65.

Fuller, Matthew and Andrew Goffey. (2009) 'Toward an Evil Media Studies' in *The Spam Book*, eds. Jussi Parikka and Tony D. Sampson. Cresskill, NJ: Hampton Press, pp. 141–59.

Hansen, Mark. (2014) *Feed-Forward: On the Future of Twenty-First Century Media*. Chicago: Chicago University Press.

Heidenreich, Stefan. (2011) 'Vision Possible. A Methodological Quest for Online Video' in *Video Vortex Reader II: Moving Images Beyond Youtube*, eds. Geert Lovink and Rachel Somers Miles. Amsterdam: Institute of Network Cultures, pp. 13–24.

Johnston, John. (2012) Introduction. 'Friedrich Kittler: Media Theory After Poststructuralism' in Friedrich A. Kittler, *Literature, Media, Information Systems*, ed. John Johnston. Oxon and New York: Routledge, pp. 1–26.

Kittler, Friedrich. (1990) *Discourse Network 1800/1900*. Trans. Michael Metteer and Chris Cullens. Stanford, CA: Stanford University Press.

———. (1995) 'There Is No Software'. *Ctheory* 10/18/1995, www.ctheory.net/articles.aspx?id=74.

———. (2002) 'Meine Theorie ist gar nicht so Lebensverbunden, um über alles zu reden. Gespräch mit Peter Weibel.' Orig. 1992. In Friedrich Kittler: *Short Cuts*. Frankfurt am Main: Zweitausendeins, pp. 68–88.

———. (2006a) 'Number and Numeral.' *Theory, Culture & Society* 23(7–8): 51–61.

———. (2006b) 'Thinking Colours and/or Machines.' *Theory, Culture & Society* 23(7–8): 39–50.

———. (2010) 'Code' in *Software Studies: A Lexicon*, ed. Matthew Fuller. Cambridge, MA: MIT Press, pp. 40–47.

Kittler, Friedrich and Laurence Rickels. (1992) 'Spooky Electricity: Laurence Rickels talks with Friedrich Kittler.' *Art Forum*, December 1992, pp. 66–70.

Krajewski, Markus. (2011) 'On Kittler Applied: A Technical Memoir of a Specific Configuration in the 1990s.' *Thesis Eleven* 107(1): pp. 33–38.

Lazzarato, Maurizio. (2014) *Signs and Machines: Capitalism and the Production of Subjectivity*. Trans. Joshua David Jordan. Los Angeles: Semiotext(e).

Lovink, Geert. (2007) *Zero Comments: Blogging and Critical Internet Culture*. London; New York: Routledge.

———. (2014) 'Hermes on the Hudson: Notes on Media Theory After Snowden.' *E-Flux*, www.e-flux.com/journal/hermes-on-the-hudson-notes-on-media-theory-after-snowden.

Parikka, Jussi. (2012) *What is Media Archaeology*. Cambridge: Polity Press.

———. (2013) 'Cultural Techniques and Media Studies.' *Theory, Culture & Society* 30(6): 147–59.

Pias, Claus. (2011) 'Was waren Medien-Wissenschaften?' in *Was Waren Medien*, ed. Claus Pias. Zürich: Diaphanes, pp. 7–30.

Schmidgen, Henning. (2014) *The Helmholtz Curves: Tracing Lost Time*. Trans. Nils F. Schott. New York: Fordham University Press.

Siegert, Bernhard. (2013) 'Cultural Techniques: Or the End of the Intellectual Postwar Era in German Media Theory.' Trans. Geoffrey Winthrop-Young. *Theory, Culture & Society* 30(6): 48–65.

Weiser, Mark. (1991) 'The Computer for the 21st Century'. *Scientific American* 265(3): 94–104.

Winthrop-Young, Geoffrey. (2013) 'Cultural Techniques: Preliminary Remarks.' *Theory, Culture & Society* 30(6): 3–19.

Zielinski, Siegfried. (2013) *[. . . After the Media]: News from the Slow-Fading Twentieth Century*. Trans. Gloria Custance. Minneapolis, MN: Univocal.

Index

About the Authors

Wolfgang Ernst is Professor for Media Theories at Humboldt University Berlin, Institute of Musicology and Media Studies. His research focus covers media archaeology as method, theory of technical storage, technologies of cultural transmission, microtemporal media aesthetics (chronopoiesis), critique of history as master discourse of technologies in time, and sound from a media-epistemological point of view (sonicity). His most recent book in English is *Digital Memory and the Archive*, edited and with an introduction by Jussi Parikka (2013).

Matthew Fuller's books include *Media Ecologies: Materialist Energies in Art and Technoculture*, *Behind the Blip: Essays on the Culture of Software* and *Elephant & Castle*. With Andrew Goffey, he is coauthor of *Evil Media*. Editor of *Software Studies: A Lexicon*, and coeditor of the journal *Computational Culture*, he is involved in a number of projects in art, media and software. He is Professor of Cultural Studies and Director of the Centre for Cultural Studies, Goldsmiths, University of London.

Olga Goriunova is Associate Professor at the Centre for Interdisciplinary Methodologies, University of Warwick. She is coeditor of *Computational Culture: A Journal of Software Studies*, the author of *Art Platforms and Cultural Production on the Internet* (2011) and the editor of *Fun and Software: Exploring Pleasure, Pain and Paradox in Computing* (2014).

Stefan Heidenreich is a writer, theoretician and art critic, who lives and works in Berlin. Currently he is employed as researcher at the Center for Digital Cultures, University of Lüneburg, and teaches Media Studies at the University of Basel. Fields of research include network and media theory, economy and art.

Eleni Ikoniadou is Senior Lecturer in Media and Communication at Kingston University. She is the author of *The Rhythmic Event* (2014) and co-editor of Rowman & Littlefield Interntional's Media Philosophy Series.

Martin McQuillan is Professor of Literary Theory and Cultural Analysis at The London Graduate School and Pro-Vice Chancellor of Research at Kingston University. His recent publications include *Deconstruction without Derrida* (2013) and *The Paul de Man Notebooks* (2014).

Jussi Parikka is Professor in Technological Culture and Aesthetics at Winchester School of Art (University of Southampton). He is Docent in Digital Culture Theory at University of Turku, Finland, and the author or (co-)editor of several books, including *Digital Contagions* (2007), *Insect Media* (2010), *What Is Media Archaeology?* (2012) and *Geology of Media* (2015). Edited books include *The Spam Book* (2009, with Tony D. Sampson) and *Media Archaeology* (2011, with Erkki Huhtamo).

Bernhard Siegert is Gerd Bucerius Professor for the History and Theory of Cultural Techniques at the Bauhaus-Universität Weimar, Germany, and codirector of the International Research Center for Cultural Techniques and Media Philosophy at Weimar (IKKM). He has published numerous books, articles and book chapters on the history of literature, art, media and the sciences. His new book *Cultural Techniques: Grids, Filters, Doors, and Other Articulations of the Real* is forthcoming.

Samuel Weber is Avalon Professor of Humanities at Northwestern and Director of its Paris Program in Critical Theory. He is working on a study tentatively entitled 'Toward a Politics and Poetics of Singularity'.

His most recent book is a collection of essays in French, *Inquietantes singularites* (2013).

Mai Wegener lives and works as a psychoanalyst in Berlin and is co-organiser of the Psychoanalytic Salon Berlin founded in 1998. She is also an active scholar of cultural studies and the history of science and lectures in literature at the Technical University of Berlin. She has worked at the Max Planck Institute for the History of Science in Berlin (2009–2010), as guest professor in Cologne at the Academy of Media Arts (2008) and for the Centre for Literature and Cultural Research, Berlin (2001–2005). In 2001 she obtained her PhD under the supervision of Friedrich A. Kittler with the thesis: Neuronen und Neurosen. Der psychische Apparat bei Freud und Lacan. Ein historisch-theoretischer Versuch zu Freuds Entwurf von 1895, published in 2004. English Publication: 'Why Should Dreaming Be Work? On Work, Economy and Enjoyment' in Samo Tomsic and Andreja Zevnik (eds.), *Jacques Lacan: Psychoanalysis and Politics* (2015).

Scott Wilson is Professor of Media and Psychoanalysis at Kingston University. His most recent books include *The Order of Joy: Beyond the Cultural Politics of Enjoyment* (2008) and *Stop Making Sense: Music from the Perspective of the Real* (2015).

www.ingramcontent.com/pod-product-compliance
Lightning Source LLC
Chambersburg PA
CBHW021428110726
47901CB00008B/2340

* 9 7 8 1 7 8 3 4 8 3 3 9 6 *